STUDIES IN GERMAN LITERATURE,
LINGUISTICS, AND CULTURE

VOL. 13, PART I

STUDIES IN GERMAN LITERATURE, LINGUISTICS, AND CULTURE
Vol. 13, PART I

CAMDEN HOUSE
Columbia, South Carolina

Wilhelm Lehmann

VOLUME I

WILHELM LEHMANN, 1906

Wilhelm Lehmann
A Critical Biography

Volume I
The Years of Trial
(1880-1918)

David Scrase

CAMDEN HOUSE

Set in Garamond type
and printed on acid-free paper.

Contents

Illustrations

Acknowledgments

AS IS PARTICULARLY the case with a biography, many institutions and individuals have helped in different ways and in varying degrees in the preparation of this book.

I am especially grateful to Professor Dr. Bernhard Zeller, the Director of the Deutsches Literaturarchiv in Marbach am Neckar, to Dr. Werner Volke, head of its Manuscript Department, and to Dr. Hans Dieter Schäfer, Lehmann's literary executor, for permission to consult and quote from materials housed there, and for all their assistance and encouragement. Indeed, I am greatly indebted to the whole staff of the Deutsches Literaturarchiv, especially to Reinhard Tgahrt, whose help over many years has been immense, to Ute Doster, whose ability to seek out obscure documents was remarkable, and to Ursula Fahrländer and Winfried Feifel, who were both of inestimable value to me in deciphering the handwriting of the numerous manuscript materials. I should like to thank Walter Scheffler of the Archives' *Bild-Abteilung* for permission to use the portraits appearing as Illustrations 5, 6, 10, 20, 26-28, 31, and the frontispiece. The staff of the Bailey-Howe Library at the University of Vermont, especially Sandra Pease Gavett, were also most supportive. I am grateful to the Flechsig Verlag for permission to include Illustration 11.

Several organisations have accorded me financial help, for which I am extremely grateful and without which this book simply could not have appeared. The Alexander von Humboldt-Stiftung has been most cooperative and most generous, assisting me greatly over a number of years in my research and travels, and providing a very substantial printing subvention. Their help has been the major factor in the completion of this book, and I am therefore exceedingly grateful to them. I am also indebted to the University of Vermont, whose Committee on Research and Scholarship has been very generous in awarding me both research fellowships and a printing subvention. In addition, the German Academic Exchange Service and The British Academy have furthered my work through research grants. I am also grateful to my college and my department for their encouragement and material support.

Lehmann's two surviving children, Agathe Weigel-Lehmann and Generalmusikdirektor Berthold Lehmann, have kindly granted me numerous interviews, access to letters, pictures, documents, and memorabilia. They have permitted me to use the portraits of Wilhelm Lehmann and other family members reproduced here as Illustrations 1-4, 7-9, 12-15, 18, 19, 22, 23, 29, and 30. Both have been patient, kind, and generous with their time and memories, and have exerted themselves energetically to make my task easier and pleasanter in every way.

Helene Aeschlimann, née Pahl, very kindly provided me with much information covering sixty years of Lehmann's life, and allowed me to use the pictures reproduced as Illustrations 16, 17, 21, 24, and 25. Her memory is remarkable, and her help has been enormous.

Many other relatives, friends, colleagues, and former pupils of Wilhelm Lehmann gave freely of their time and knowledge and responded to my many questions with patience and understanding. They include: Günter Bauer, Dr. Heinz Bruns, Marliese Egge, Ursula Enseleit, the late Professor Dr. Walter Erben, Professor Leonard Forster, Michael Hamburger, Frau Dr. Else Horn, the late Professor Dr. Hans-Windekilde Jannasch, Lisbeth Jessen, Anne-Marie Jung, Dr. Hans Lorenzen, Dr. Uwe Pörksen, Professor Siegbert Prawer, Professor Dr. Ernst Schlee, Professor Guy Stern, and Professor Ulrich Weisstein. Professor August Closs, who first introduced me to Lehmann, and Professor Norbert Fuerst, whose guidance meant so much to me at a crucial time, have also earned my most profound gratitude.

I owe an especial debt of gratitude to my friend and colleague Professor Wolfgang Mieder, who has been a constant source of help and encouragement. My heartfelt thanks also go to the following friends and colleagues who read my manuscript and gave me many valuable hints and insights: Katharina Badenhop, Huguette Herrmann, Professor Mark Pomar, Constance Putnam, Professor Michael Stanton, Professor Henry Sullivan, Professor Pieter Wesseling, and Dr. Helmut Winter. I am also grateful to Cristine Buckett for help with the proofs. Many are the improvements stemming from their suggestions; the errors and shortcomings still remaining are mine.

Finally, I should like to extend my warmest thanks to my wife, Mary Ellen Martin, who was always a sustaining, encouraging, and guiding force throughout many years of trial and labor.

List of Abbreviations

SW = *Sämtliche Werke* of Wilhelm Lehmann (Gütersloh: Sigbert Mohn Verlag, 1962), three volumes.

SZ = *Sichtbare Zeit,* the one book of poems by Wilhelm Lehmann to appear after the *Sämtliche Werke.*

1
Parents and Early Childhood (1880-1900)

WILHELM LEHMANN'S FATHER, Johann Heinrich Friedrich Wilhelm Emil Lehmann, was born in Lübeck in 1851. He came, as his son likes to point out in his autobiographical writings,[1] from a family of musicians and restaurateurs. He was rather short and stocky, and had somewhat wavy, light brown hair and a full beard. He was possessed of a sharp temper on occasions, but was otherwise easy-going and made friends rapidly. He seems to have been interested in natural history, for in 1880 he brought "eine größere Anzahl Süßwasser- und Meerfische, einige Schlangen, Reptilien und Krebse aus Puerto Cabello," as is gratefully recorded in the annual report of the Lübeck Natural History Museum (to which he presented them) for the year 1880. This apparent interest in natural history was to manifest itself later in his children, particularly Wilhelm. Friedrich Lehmann was musically gifted, playing the piano and singing in a pleasant baritone. He was wont to lead a full social life, enjoyed a drink, and fancied himself, with justification, as a lady's man. His love of ease and a propensity for self-indulgence left him with an incorrigible lack of responsibility but high hopes for a financially successful career—the two proved incompatible.

Lehmann's mother, Agathe Margarethe Henriette Lehmann née Wichmann, was born in Hamburg in 1855. Her father had worked his way up from "Barbier" to "Wundarzt," while she herself, as a woman in Wilhelmine Germany, was sufficiently capable and forceful to make her way into a profession. She received her teaching diploma from the "Lehrerinnen-Seminar der Unterrichts-Anstalten des Klosters St. Johannis" in Hamburg in 1874 and taught at the same institution for the next two years. Her report cards here, and from her earlier schooldays, were seldom less than excellent. From 1876 to early 1878 she was a governess in England, and on her return she became a teacher at Julie Buck's school in Hamburg until Easter 1881. She practiced her profession with great commitment, diligence, and success, both at this stage of her life and later. In contrast to the easy-going Lehmanns, the Wichmanns were striving, painstaking, and ambitious. Above all, they were desirous of respectability.

JOHANN HEINRICH FRIEDRICH WILHELM LEHMANN (1819-1875)

JOHANNA LEHMANN, NÉE WULF

CHRISTIAN WILHELM HEINRICH CARL WICHMANN (1823-1883)

CAROLINE WILHELMINE JULIANE WICHMANN (1823-1891)

In his autobiographical accounts the poet in Lehmann obtrudes on the biographer, for the details he "remembers" are highly significant ones, fraught with subtle hints and extra meaning. He remembers a young lion in the garden of the Venezuelan villa where he spent the first three years of his life, for instance[2]—and somehow we can picture an Henri Rousseau jungle scene with those quiet but vital beasts peering out of the undergrowth as representatives of the emotional powers which lurk in our subconscious—the "Dunkler Untergrund des Daseins" as Lehmann puts it.[3] How well this fits with the sense of the Dionysian in his paternal forebears—music and intoxication—is not difficult to see. Then, quietly accompanying those clear-headed, diligent, and respectable strivers among his maternal ancestors in Lehmann's remembrance of them are the furnishings of the Wandsbek living-room: the "vier Klassiker," some reliefs of the hours by Thorwaldsen and a bust of Apollo himself, who intrudes as quietly as the Rousseauesque cat—and as significantly. If his father brought those Dionysian attributes of drink and music into the family, then his mother countered with her own form of Apolline *ratio,* a love of the written word, for not only was reading a love which she passed on to, and fostered in all three children, but she also longed to become a famous writer.

But it is not necessary to clothe the contrasts in Nietzschean terms to appreciate that Friedrich Lehmann and Agathe Wichmann were such widely different people as to be ultimately incompatible, although initially, at least, there was the attraction of opposites. The courtship was not easy, mainly because of Agathe's rebuttals. The main problem was her distrust of men in general. She herself alludes to it at regular intervals in the correspondence subsequent to the engagement.[4] Then there was clearly a distrust of Friedrich in particular who, she felt, "mich nie verstehen könnte."[5] The other prime difficulty lay in her independence, which she guarded all the more fiercely for its having been so dearly won. She speaks of this quality on numerous occasions, too, often linking it with her great pride: "Du weißt, ich stehe seit geraumer Zeit auf eigenen Füßen,"[6] and "Dann und wann bäumt sich so ein Rest von Stolz in mir auf und flüstert mir zu, mich doch nicht so gänzlich offen Dir hinzugeben."[7] But having once fallen for Friedrich's undoubted charm, she gave herself to him fully, though not without realizing the sudden volte-face:

> Ich habe mir immer eingebildet, der Himmel habe mir den reichen Erfolg und die große Befriedigung in meinem Berufe gegeben, weil mir das höchste, idealste Glück des Weibes versagt sei; ich hatte mir auf Grund meines Berufes meinen ganzen Lebensplan gezeichnet, bin im Geiste schon Schriftstellerin und bedeutende Pädagogin geworden, sehe mir en idée meine Altjungfernwohnung eingerichtet,— da muß mir die Liebe zu Dir so übermächtig ins Herz ziehen, muß all meine Ideen über den Haufen werfen, und ich werde Deine glückliche Braut.[8]

Friedrich, for his part, having been made to work so hard in the conquest of this proud and independent woman, also surrendered to her completely, and the couple became engaged on 17 August 1880.

AGATHE MARGARETHE HENRIETTE WICHMANN (1855-1918), c. 1881 THE YEAR OF
HER MARRIAGE.

JOHANN HEINRICH FRIEDRICH WILHELM EMIL LEHMANN (1851-1895), 1886

On 21 September 1880 Friedrich left Hamburg on board the *Bavaria* and, after stopping in Le Havre and at St. Thomas, arrived in Puerto Cabello, where he was greeted by many friends, on 20 October. The letters exchanged by the couple from the moment they parted are full of the most fervent avowals of love, as each described to the other the preparations for their future life together: the trousseau (with the painstaking embroidery of monograms), and the acquisition of furniture, including a piano, on which Friedrich played works by composers such as Mendelssohn, Beethoven, and Mozart.

After a few months of separation, however, Friedrich's letters to Agathe began to diminish in both length and number. His fiancée remonstrated, and questioned the depth and steadfastness of Friedrich's love. When she went so far as to suggest that he might be unfaithful to her, his rejoinder was sharp: "Bei Gott, liebe Agathe, Du thust Unrecht. Ich bin nur Dein, auf ewig Dein und lebe nur in Dir."[9] The abruptness of his response and the strong language in which it is couched reveal not so much his quick temper—this is after all a written response—as a guilty conscience.

The considerable German community of Puerto Cabello led a vigorous social life. There were concerts and theatrical evenings, a great number of "Abschiedsessen," which, as Friedrich admitted apologetically, he was *obliged* to attend,[10] and various consular functions from time to time. That Friedrich took part in such functions as well as others of a rather more dubious nature comes out on a later occasion.[11] Meanwhile, back in Hamburg, Agathe lived "wie eine Nonne."[12] But it is not just a difference in life-styles which suggests that this couple was ill-matched. It is rather the characters of the lovers as they emerge from their correspondence. Friedrich suffered from a certain lack of constancy; he was unable to maintain the tone of his letters and was too obviously playing down his social life and playing up his long and busy working days. Agathe, on the other hand, was constancy itself. But, as she herself reveals, she had undergone such a dramatic change in giving in to her love for Friedrich that she had fallen out of character. Her romantic notion of married life in general and of her future life with Friedrich in particular were such that disillusionment would soon, inevitably, set in.

On 5 June 1881 Friedrich Lehmann returned to Europe on the S.S. *Lafayette,* arriving at St. Nazaire less than three weeks later—he had taken the fastest ship running as urged by Agathe. The couple were married in a civil ceremony on 9 July and followed this up with a wedding feast. At the end of the month they set off on the long return journey to Venezuela, first of all stopping in Aachen, where they attended a "Nachmittagskonzert" on the Lousberg. They then proceeded to Paris, where they spent four days in the Hotel Saint-Georges near the Opéra. On 6 August they were in St. Nazaire, and, after staying overnight in the Hotel des Messageries, they embarked for Puerto Cabello.

Settling into their new life together and into their new home left them with little leisure, although the employment of a German cook and, later, a native

Venezuelan nanny who cared for the children, relieved Agathe of a considerable amount of drudgery. Nonetheless there were family evenings arranged by the "Gesang-Verein Sängerlust," concerts, dinner parties such as that given in honor of His Highness Prinz Heinrich von Preussen in November 1883, and the annual party of the "Turn-Verein Gut-Heil," which had been founded in 1881— to all such functions the Lehmanns were invited, and they would usually attend. There were, therefore, undoubtedly happy times together but those early suggestions of probable tension soon became reality. Agathe made no attempt to conceal these tensions from her parents, and a mere five months after their arrival in Venezuela her mother wrote to the young couple offering her own sensible appraisal of the situation, putting forward a rather positive view of it:

> Eure lieben Briefe... brachten mir aufs neue den Beweis: daß Ihr trotz ewigem Zank und Streit, ganz gemütlich miteinander lebt, da sieht man doch, daß selbst Hund und Katze zuweilen ganz gut miteinander hausen können.[13]

By this time Agathe was well into her first pregnancy and, on 4 May, Wilhelm Heinrich Lehmann was born. There were no complications and the general delight was further increased by the fact that the child was a boy. From Germany Frau Wichmann plied the young mother with advice on everything from when and how the child should sleep to breast-feeding. Herr Wichmann, for his part, was concerned only that the young couple would bring up "einen guten, braven und folgsamen Sohn."[14] There was anxiety about the tropical heat and how mother and child would fare. But however it may have affected his mother, it seems to have been just what young Willi wanted. He, and later his brother Walter, "gedeihen wohl prächtig bei der Hitze, und von den Scherereien der Eltern ahnen sie nichts, glückliche Jugend," as their grandmother so matter-of-factly puts it in a later letter.[15]

The reaction to Wilhelm's birth on the part of the Lehmann side of the family in Lübeck was also one of delight. But there was no detailed advice. It was not only that the Wichmann ambitions centred on family improvement to a far greater degree than those of the Lehmanns, but that the latter were more preoccupied with their own problems. The family was in debt, and Friedrich helped out as best he could by sending sums of money to them at various times in 1882. Then, on 11 August, Agathe's father suffered a stroke which severely incapacitated him. Although he regained partial use of his limbs and some degree of speech, he never really recovered and he died on 4 January 1883. The financial sacrifices necessary in order that Friedrich might help both families must certainly have added to the strain on his own marriage.

Meanwhile Agathe was pregnant again, and Walter was born in December 1883. Agathe's hands were full and she complained of fatigue and despondency as she tried to cope with the household and her two children more or less singlehandedly, for her German cook had meanwhile left, and Friedrich was putting in excessively long hours at the hardware store. By early 1884 there was

WILHELM LEHMANN (1882-1968) WITH HIS NANNY.

WILHELM LEHMANN WITH HIS FATHER, PUERTO CABELLO, c. 1884.

talk of a return: "Wenn Ihr hier wäret," wrote her mother,[16] "dann solltest Du Dich nicht so allein abplagen meine Gathe mit den Gören...." Agathe even went so far as to contemplate returning to Germany alone with her children, so unhappy was she with her lot. Clearly the "ewige Zank und Streit" already evident in the early months of the marriage had not vanished with the arrival of the children. And although Friedrich's absence due to his work may have helped lessen the arguments somewhat, Agathe's enforced loneliness gave her more opportunity to brood on her lot and see how bleak her future prospects were. Here she was, cut off from her family and profession, in a foreign environment with no command of Spanish,[17] frustrated in her bourgeois aspirations and plans, with a growing family and with no apparent intimate friends in whom she could confide. Friedrich, despite his long hours, was not tremendously successful: "Aus Deinem letzten Brief an Mile [i.e. Emilie, her sister]," wrote Agathe's mother in July,[18] "erfahre ich, daß alle Mühe und Plaggerei Deines lieben Mannes, so wenig von Erfolg gekrönt ist, denn drüben bei einem Leben voller Entbehrungen nicht mehr zu verdienen, als gebraucht wird, das ist doch trostlos." To this bleak picture she adds a telling comment: "ich habe immer gehofft, daß Dein lieber Mann in einigen Jahren so viel herausschlagen würde, wovon Ihr hier alsdann gemütlich leben könntet...." Her thoughts, we may be sure, were also Agathe's, and the frustration of these ambitious dreams may have been the hardest blow to withstand.

By the end of 1884 the decision to return in the spring of 1885 rather than in 1886 (as had been the original plan when they first left for Venezuela) had been taken. The relief was general—with the exception of Friedrich, whose love of the tropics was deep. A combination of this love, the pressure of work, and personal reasons induced Friedrich not to return immediately but to remain a little longer in Puerto Cabello. Agathe was sufficiently unhappy with her life in Venezuela, and sufficiently strong-willed and independent to undertake the journey even without her husband. By the time Willi's third birthday came round on 4 May 1885, she and the two children were on board ship heading for Europe, and the exotic beginnings of the future poet's life were at an end.

****

The significance of these first three years spent in South America for Wilhelm Lehmann is considerable. The unusual warmth and particularly clear quality of light in which he grew up remained a delight which he only rarely and imperfectly relived in the temperate climate of northern Germany. The poet thrived in great heat and excessive sun, conditions which he constantly sought to recapture in his poems. The love of lush and thriving vegetation, of the vitally pulsing plantlife which so marks his fiction and poetry probably also goes back to the luxuriant profusion of that Venezuelan garden where Lehmann thought he saw a young lion. And his later love of language and languages is certainly linked to his multilingual origins where German, Spanish, English, and French were all frequently heard, as well as to the love of languages shared by both parents. The mature poet reminiscing about his earliest childhood and seizing on, for him, relevant and significant features of his early years alludes to all these aspects. He also remembers an affliction of the eyes which troubled him and his brother as they returned to Europe.[19] There is an irony here. It is almost as if his eyes were objecting to being forcibly removed from the brilliant translucence peculiar to the tropics. It was this quality of light together with the subsequent adjustment to north German conditions at the age of three which led to Wilhelm Lehmann's tremendous capacity for close observation—a capacity to which he himself obliquely alludes,[20] and which so many critics and admirers stress as the mainspring of his best work. And the sensuality which later surfaced in both his work and life and which seems to come to him through his father was perhaps nurtured somewhat in the heat of Venezuela.[21] His exotic beginnings are also the manifestation of his early realization (a realization which was to bother him not a little, incidentally) that he was someone if not exactly special, then certainly somewhat different. All these circumstances, together with those conflicting traits inherited from his father and mother, undoubtedly were of importance in the moulding of Lehmann's complex personality.

Upon arrival in Hamburg, Agathe and her two children settled first in Eimsbüttel, which at the time still preserved much of its rural character, with timbered houses and thatched roofs, and which was accordingly the goal of many a weekend excursion for the people of Hamburg. But the tremendous urbanisation of the *Gründerjahre* was gradually effacing meadows and parks with apartment building complexes, so that between 1880 and 1890 the population increased from 16,229 to 46,154 inhabitants. Here a third child, Frieda (known as Lita in the family) was born, and to here Friedrich himself now returned from Venezuela and settled back into family life for a while. From a letter from Agathe to her mother[22] emerges a rather complete picture of the family at that time. Much of the letter is taken up with the children, clearly the subject of greatest interest to mother and grandmother; but there is much about Friedrich as a father, and a few remarks which describe the family situation. She begins by stating, with some relief, that they are all in the best of health, although "zum herzlichen Frohsein fehlt ja viel." She goes on:

> Und dann unsere Kinderchen! Gar zu süß sind die Görchen; der Willy wird so selbständig, so klug, und Walter ist ja stets sein treuer Kamerad.... Frieda ist aller Welt Liebling.... Wenn Friedrich mittags nach Hause kommt, streckt sie ihm gleich beide Ärmchen entgegen und stammelt, Pa-pa-pa-pa. Der Papa ist natürlich überglücklich mit seinem Töchterchen; hat er die Jungens schon so verzogen, wie wird er es erst mit dem Mädel machen! Nur gut, daß ich strammes Regiment führe, das ist nun einmal nötig, besonders bei den Knaben, denn zu ordentlichen Menschen will ich sie mit Gottes Hülfe doch erziehen. Am Sonntag Morgen liegen der Vater und seine 3 Kinder in schönster Einigkeit zusammen im Bett, während ich mich

anziehe; sputen muß ich mich doch, denn lange dauert es nicht, da beginnt das Trampeln und Treten und Kneifen und Schreien etc. und die Toilette wird eiligst gemacht. . . . Mit Willy muß man sich schon in acht nehmen, er hört und beobachtet alles, ist fürchterlich klug; er hat immer noch das weiche, süße Gesicht mit den treuen Augen und die himmlischen Backen, ist ein lieber, lieber Junge. Ich muß ihn manchmal tüchtig abstrafen, er ist oft ungehorsam und rücksichtslos, aber wie schwer wird mir das und wie weh thut es mir. . . . ich hätte es auch früher nicht gedacht, daß aus mir eine so emsig schaffende Hausfrau und Mutter werden würde, und ich kriege doch alles fertig. Abends sitze ich jetzt mutterseelenallein; mein Friedrich kommt nach Hause, ißt zu Abend und geht dann wieder fort, um einem Geschäftsmann die Bücher zu führen, hier in der Nähe, kommt dann gegen 11 Uhr nach Hause. Es ist gräßlich genug, aber der Verdienst ist immerhin uns etwas werth, und später kann Friedrich sich's auch für 2 oder 3 Abende der Woche einrichten.

Clearly their material circumstances were less than comfortable (although they were able to employ a maid), and this fact undoubtedly added to the strain on the marriage. There is a somewhat smug tone to Agathe's revelations as to how well she herself was managing in a role she had clearly felt to be foreign to her. Friedrich was so spoiling the children that the burden of a strict upbringing fell entirely on her shoulders—and she did want them to grow up to be decent citizens. Willi, it seems, was already extremely bright and observant and was beginning to assert himself in somewhat rebellious fashion. Later in the same letter Agathe complains about the goings-on between her maid and a gentleman lodger next door. Her high moral standards were quite outraged by such laxity, although her fear that they would not be able to afford a new maid prevented her from dismissing the woman.

At this time Friedrich did, at least, have employment, although he was neither pleased with the work itself nor with the salary provided by Blohm und Voss, the well-known shipyard.

Within a year, however, he was unemployed and searching desperately for a position. Once again the family fortunes were on the downgrade and the marriage sorely tested. Such problems, of course, were still of no concern to young Willi. There were long walks with both his mother and the maid. His mother would sketch for him, much to his great delight, and he spent hours trying to copy her drawings. This activity continued right up to early adolescence and further attests to his burning desire to *see* things. In 1892 Willi prepared a little book containing his own drawings of animals as a Christmas present for his aunt Emilie. Under each animal his mother penned the name in German and in Latin. Although there is no sign of any extraordinary artistic genius, the pictures are carefully and skillfully executed.[23] Every day there were stories, and the maid would sing songs for the children. On their walks through the parks and meadows the boys would seek out snails and beetles and play with them, bedding them in the velvety moss and generally living in a world of their own. Back at home they would be drawn to the cockroaches which infested the otherwise spotless kitchen despite all efforts on the part of Agathe to eradicate them and spend hours watching these repulsive creatures.

By the autumn of 1887, when Willi was five years old, the family fortunes were at a low ebb. Friedrich was out of work and there seemed to be no prospect of employment. To his mother and sisters he wrote:

> ... doch fehlte mir bis jetzt der Muth, Euch irgendwelche Mittheilungen zu machen, da verschiedene Aussichten auf Anstellung schwebten und schließlich sämtlich in den Sand verliefen.
>
> Mit dem Muth der Verzweiflung gehe ich nun—und zwar Mittwoch, d. 19ten via St Nazaire nach Vera-Cruz, Mexico u. zwar auf gut Glück, mit den besten Empfehlungen ausgerichtet um dort mir eine Lebensstellung zu erringen.[24]

Agathe and the children remained behind. His fare was paid by his mother-in-law. On 2 December Agathe received a letter reporting his safe arrival in Veracruz, where he was received "an Bord schon von Herrn Düring ... und," as Agathe wrote to her mother and sisters-in-law, "dann *sofort,* denkt nur, engagiert!"[25] But the small salary and Friedrich's optimism were not sufficient to keep him there in the "Lebensstellung" he wanted, and by the autumn of 1889 he was back in Eimsbüttel. Once again there was a desperate search for employment which was not immediately successful. Meanwhile the rent and the school fees had to be paid somehow, so Friedrich again turned to his mother and sisters, having already borrowed money from Doris, his closest sister, in order to buy a winter overcoat.[26] His request was turned down, and he found himself obliged to write again more urgently a mere three days later stressing that there was no-one else he can turn to.

It is typical of Lehmann's father that he should not stop to consider the other side's point of view. Neither Doris nor her mother was rich, and both were probably wondering when Friedrich's requests for money were going to stop. Yet Friedrich had clearly not foreseen the possibility of a negative answer. Meanwhile the children were in the best of health, as indeed was he himself, all things considered. Agathe, on the other hand, was "sehr schmal und angegriffen."[27] Fortunately, by early 1890 he had found a position with the Hammonia metal-work factory in Barmbeck, but his spirits were still rather low: the pay was poor, the hours long, the work hard, and his feet were bothering him. In addition, the factory was so far from Eimsbüttel that he was obliged to find lodgings nearby, and he returned home only for the weekends.

In May the family moved to Wandsbek and occupied part of the so-called "Pächterhof." Agathe's mother moved in with them and occupied two upstairs rooms. She paid half of the moving expenses and a third of the rent. In his correspondence with his sister Doris, Friedrich alluded to her no longer as "Schwiegermama" but as "Mutter Wichmann." The relationship between Friedrich and his mother-in-law was strained. Agathe, for her part, now had an ally in the house, and the gap between Wichmann propriety and Lehmann irresponsibility gradually widened into a definite rift, so that the marriage, too, began to be seriously threatened.

The small town of Wandsbek at this time was connected with Hamburg only by a recently installed horse-drawn tramway, and although it, like Eimsbüttel, was growing rapidly (21,666 inhabitants in 1895), it still preserved a great deal of its rural character and charm—especially in the outlying part where the Curvenstraße and the Pächterhof lay. Lehmann remembered the years spent in Wandsbek with great affection and described them in his autobiographical writings and in his essay "Sprache als Ereignis" accordingly.[28]

The Pächterhof was a long, two-storied building with a red-tiled roof. It was divided up into three adjacent dwellings. Between the street and the house was an extremely narrow front garden, but behind the house was a much larger garden, part of which was cultivated, while the rest was given over to grass and was shaded by cherry trees, elms, and black alders. It was here that the children spent most of their time, and here that Willi was allowed to tend his own small plot, shaping it in the form of a coffin—much to the annoyance of his grandmother, who would rake everything flat only to have her grandson re-shape the soil in the coffin form which he apparently so adamantly wanted. Adjacent to this paradise—the mature Lehmann saw it as a Brozeliande complete with Merlin[29]—were the large park-like grounds of a coal merchant with the somewhat unlikely name of Sauber. The Curvenstraße at this time was connected with the Goethestraße in the residential part of Wandsbek by a path which the children simply called the "Feldweg." Near the Feldweg was a pond, a spot known to the children as the "Froschteich," and much favored by the boys. The garden, the uncultivated field with the pond and the woods just beyond the house provided the children's playground, and nature provided the toys. There were frogs and toads, birds, fish, woodlice, and ladybirds together with domestic pets such as guinea pigs and rabbits. The boys spent hours with these creatures, carefully observing their behavior and transporting themselves into a world of their own set far apart from the grown-ups around them and set apart, even, from their contemporaries.

Just how easily and completely young Willi slipped into this paradise garden with his brother Walter comes out beautifully in his autobiographical writings:

> Das bloße Dasein war ein Rausch. Es verzauberte mich, ich kauerte als sein Geschöpf, als sein ergriffener Schüler. Wurde ich schon gerufen, um die heilige Wildnis der Erde zu bewahren? So muß Makarien zumute gewesen sein. So müssen Erdgötter fühlen. Alles bot mir sein Gesicht, alles war. Ich brauchte es noch nicht zu erzeugen. Mich mühte noch kein Ideal.[30]

The mature man of three-score years and more clearly saw himself set apart even as a child, and there is no denying that young Willi was in many respects a boy of rare sensitivities, a loner who was happier unrolling woodlice than shooting at birds with a catapult. The art historian and writer Walter Erben, who knew

Lehmann well, picked out this solitary preoccupation with nature rather than people as his overriding characteristic.[31]

While the boys were withdrawing to the basement, or the attic, where they kept their fish or birds, their parents were teetering on the brink of matrimonial and economic disaster. Friedrich, always one who enjoyed a drink, was beginning to find it indispensable, and was indulging in liquor to a frightening degree. Under the pretext of singing in a men's choir, he repaired regularly to a local beer cellar where, under the tutelage of a rubicund and bloated Kantor Lampe, he would sing and drink far into the night. Even the Sunday walk with the children would invariably end up at Sonderman's general store where he would buy the children chocolate and himself some beer. In addition to the strain put on the marriage by Friedrich's drinking, there were the usual financial problems. Willi burst into tears on hearing that his mother could not find the small sum of money he needed for a school trip, but his grandmother was able to give it to him. At Christmas 1890 Friedrich was unable to give the children any Christmas presents—although he actively continued his membership of the men's choir. Agathe was mortified and despaired of her husband's ever contributing anything substantial to the marriage, which had so far deteriorated that they were, by now, no longer sharing a single bedroom. It was all far removed from those romantic pictures of conjugal bliss so touchingly described in Agathe's letters to her idealized fiancé.

Friedrich had had ready access to cash, other people's cash, most of his working life. Indeed, he had himself kept the books in Puerto Cabello and did so in some of his subsequent positions. This cash must have been a powerful attraction to someone who spent money as if the fortune he dreamt about were reality. In the spring of 1891, as we know from a remarkable postcard Friedrich sent his sister Doris,[32] he was an active partner in a business which seemed to have had everything necessary for success except capital. The postcard is difficult to decipher. After completing the one side, Friedrich simply turned the postcard through ninety degrees and superimposed a second side of writing over his first. (It was not, by the way, an uncommon practice of Friedrich's, and indicates two aspects of his lifestyle: lack of money and lack of forethought and planning.)[33] He begins with birthday greetings for Doris and then continues:

> Im Geschäft ist Leben; doch fehlt flüssiges Capital. Sonst ist das Geschäft gesund. Wenn mir jemand nur c. 5000 Mk vorstrecken könnte, dann wäre alles gut. Fritz hat seinen Geldbeutel zugeknöpft. Mehr als er eingeschaffen [?], giebt er nicht her. Trotzdem er und alle Leute einsieht, daß wir die größte Zukunft haben. Unsere Februar Bilanz weist einen reinen Gewinn von Mk 2100,- auf. Natürlich steckt alles im Geschäft.

Somehow Friedrich's abilities as a businessman do not stand out convincingly. Small wonder his partner, Fritz Lehmann (an uncle) put his wallet away. Within

"WILLI LEHMANN IN DER 2TEN KLASSE 7 JAHRE ALT. 1. JUNI 1889. MEIN ERSTGEBORENER." INSCRIPTION IN HIS MOTHER'S HAND ON THE REVERSE. LEHMANN IS IN THE FRONT ROW, SECOND FROM THE LEFT.

WILHELM LEHMANN, c. 1894.

a month Friedrich had fled and gone underground, as we learn from a letter
Agathe sent her sister-in-law Elisabeth:

Endlich hat mir Onkel Fritz die bestimmte Zusage gegeben, daß er von einer
gerichtlichen Verfolgung abstehen wolle, "um Ihretwillen", sagte er "sonst wäre es
aber ganz anders gekommen." Am 21. Juni hatte ich eine Karte von Friedrich aus
Hannover, also entweder ist er bei Euch, oder er hat seine Flucht so sinnlos ins Werk
gesetzt, daß er sein mir gegebenes Wort, ein braver Mensch wieder werden zu
wollen, wohl kaum erfüllen kann; ohne Garderobe, ohne Mittel! d.h. Fritz
behauptet, er habe Geld, habe am letzten Nachmittag 200 Mk einkassiert. Magda hat
er Weihnacht um 500 Mk gebeten, 100 Mk hat sie ihm gegeben, Mk 80 hat er zur
selben Zeit in der Fabrik geborgt, dabei nicht für einen Pfennig seinen Kindern zum
Fest geschenkt; meinen Nachbarn, Hrn. Gundlach, hat er um Mk 2000 gebeten, zum
Glück nicht bekommen. Und diese Betrügereien sind nichts gegen seine andere,
größere Schuld, die zu strafen keine Qual dieser Erde ausreichen würde; aber das
sollt ihr nie erfahren. Mich und die armen Kinder nimmt nun vorläufig Mama auf;
Gott wird uns ja beistehen, sie zu ernähren und zu sittlich festen Menschen zu
erziehen. Stellung habe ich schon, die erste, um die ich mich bewarb; so Gott will,
finde ich noch mehr Arbeit und komme redlich durch, verwöhnt bin ich ja nicht.
Eine gerichtliche Scheidung zu beantragen, fehlen mir ja momentan die Mittel; im
Falle seiner Wiederkehr schützt aber vor jeder Roheit eine Anzahl von Herren und
im Hintergrund die Behörde. Es ist erhebend, zu fühlen, wie Wahrheit und
Rechtlichkeit in der schlimmen Welt doch noch den Sieg erringen, zu nett begegnen
mir alle Freunde, alle meine gebildeten, feinen Nachbarn. Gott im Himmel, was
habe ich für den Mann gethan und wie hat er es mir gelohnt! Frag' mal Doris Biethin
[?], die kann schon Geschichten erzählen; schon drüben soll es arg gewesen sein, nur
ich in meiner überschwenglichen Liebe zu ihm sah und hörte nichts, wollte nichts
hören; viel strenger und härter hätte ich sein müssen, aber stets verzeihen, stets
helfen, durch Geld oder durch mein Ansehn, das taugte nichts, das war falsch. Ich,
der jede Unwahrheit so fremd, wie habe ich gelogen um seinetwillen, um ihn rein zu
waschen! Mein Willi kommt Sonnabend als Primus der Sexta nach Hause. Ach,
wenn ich ihn nur in der Schule lassen könnte. Die Kinder fragen selten nach dem
Vater, er hat sich ihnen ja so gründlich verhaßt gemacht; sie werden ihn vergessen
mit der Zeit. Wie ein Aufatmen geht es durch uns alle, obgleich wir in bitterster Not
sind; Frieden und Ruhe und Harmonie, kein rohes Element im Hause. Hätte ich
keine Kinder, ich wäre ohne Frage mit ihm gegangen und hätte treu bis ans Ende
meine Pflicht an ihm gethan, wäre mit ihm verkommen, da er kein Halten zu
denken war; "jetzt aber", sagt der Prediger, "liegt Ihre Pflicht bei den zarten
Kindern, die müßten Sie vor dem bösen Einfluß hüten!" und das will ich, Gott stehe
mir bei! An seinem Segen ist alles gelegen, er gebe mir Verstand und rechte Einsicht
                    Deine
    Agathe

There follows a postscript:

Grüße mir unsere arme Mutter, wie muß sie leiden: wüßte ich, daß meine Söhne
nicht brav werden, begraben wollte ich sie lieber jetzt. Mutter, Mutter, Du wüßtest
es ja nicht, was ich gekämpft und gelitten habe seit 6 Jahren, schon nach Mexico ging

er als Betrüger, und war dort fort, ach, es ist zu schrecklich! Wie kann ein Mann, der eine gute Frau, reizende Kinder und ein nettes Heim hat, dem alle freundlich gesinnt waren, bis er sie enttäuschte, so etwas thun! Mir ist es wie ein Traum, was ich seit 10 Jahren erlebe—

Heut Nachmittag sind Frau Lehmann und Frau Höppner bei mir zum Kaffee gewesen. Mit dem Geschäft steht es schlimm, er kann keinen Compagnon mit Geld bekommen und hat 10-12000 Mk zu zahlen. Er ist wütend auf Friedrich, der ihn in solche Lage gebracht; es war auch unverantwortlich, beide verstanden nichts von der Sache und dann solches Unternehmen.[34]

This letter raises more questions than it answers perhaps, but it does reveal some fascinating information. Friedrich had been looking after the books of the firm of Pumplün & Lehmann, the "Hamburger Fabrik verzinkter Blechwaaren für Haus-, Küchen- und Bau-Bedarf." The Lehmann side of the firm was represented by Fritz Lehmann, Friedrich's uncle. This firm wrote to Agathe in 1894[35] asking her to kindly repay what her husband owed them from 1891. Whatever the form of Friedrich's fraud, legal proceedings could have been taken against him. And this seems to have been not the first time that he had cheated his employers. As far back as 1887, his actions were apparently not entirely aboveboard. Perhaps his continual difficulty in finding a position was because he was persona non grata in mercantile circles, where everybody from Hamburg to Puerto Cabello seems to have known everybody else.

The extent of his bad reputation emerges from a letter written to Agathe by Frau Valeske Kock, a former neighbor in Puerto Cabello, shortly after Friedrich's flight: "...bevor er nach Mexico ging [i.e. prior to October 1887], hatte ein Seemann hier erzählt, daß er in sehr schlechter Gesellschaft verkehre und Ihre Frau Mutter eine Scheidung wünsche weil er Sie schlecht behandele."[36] In the same letter Frau Kock states that Friedrich was generally known to drink more than was good for him even during his earlier Venezuelan sojourn and that "sein Lebenswandel in Valencia so sei, daß seine hiesigen [i.e. Puerto Cabellan] Freunde sich sehr kühl benommen." Even allowing for some scandalized exaggeration, we can see that Friedrich had earned himself a notorious reputation through his behavior. And Frau Kock's mention of his Valencia life-style reminds us of his own bragging early in 1881 of all his "Freundinnen" in that city. Friedrich's vices, then, encompassed fraud, excessive drinking, and a weakness for women.

Agathe, as we have seen, was scandalized by the revelation of his fraud, but, as she said in her letter given above: "diese Betrügereien sind nichts gegen seine andere, größere Schuld, die zu strafen keine Qual dieser Erde ausreichen würde." To ascertain just what this "größere Schuld" was, we have only to look at the somewhat veiled statements of Wilhelm Lehmann in the "factual" account of his "Bildnis der Eltern" and at the equally factual "fiction" of *Der Überläufer*. In the former Lehmann puts it thus: "eines Nachts verirrte er sich in eine fremde Kammer des Mietshauses [i.e. the Pächterhof]."[37] In his novel Lehmann is less discreet: "Daß der Vater, spät nach Haus gekommen, von Ida [i.e. Agathe] aus dem Bette der Magd geholt werden mußte, als unverständlich schrecklich erfuhr es Hanswilli."[38] Just when Friedrich was so dramatically caught in flagrante delicto is impossible to ascertain, but it must have been around this time. At all events, circumstances were now such that Friedrich was obliged to flee. It seems likely that Agathe refused to allow him to stay in the house and that, having no real future in the Hamburg area, he absconded with a considerable sum of money.

Friedrich fled first to his sister Elisabeth in Hannover and then across the Atlantic to New York and down through the United States to Mexico. Between his departure from Bremen on 23 June 1887 on board the *Havel* and his death in 1895 there were a number of letters and postcards to Doris and others in his family. They leave us with only a vague picture of his life in Mexico after his separation from his family, a picture which the poet himself rather faithfully reproduces in *Mühe des Anfangs*. On his way through Texas, Friedrich stopped at the picturesque town of Laredo on the Mexican border, and went to the hardware store of J. Deutz & Son, perhaps to investigate employment possibilities. They had no position available but provided him with some headed notepaper on which he wrote to Doris. In this letter he looks upon his fraudulent actions rather lightly as an "unglückselige Geschichte" and tells his sister that he has found a position in the port of Tampico, Mexico:

> Wenn alles ruhig und in Ordnung ist mit der unglückseligen Geschichte, so wäre es das Beste, den Koffer mit meinen *ganzen* Vermögen direct per Hamburger Dampfer an
>
> C. Holck & Co. Tampico—Mexico
>
> abzusenden. Jedoch mit der größten Vorsicht damit kein Mensch erfährt, wo ich bin.[39]

Soon after his arrival in Tampico, Friedrich fell ill and took to his bed with a high fever. Happily, as he boasts to Doris,[40] he already had many true friends who cared for him and nursed him back to health. This is a distinct contrast to that earlier occasion when he pleaded for money from Doris because he had no other friends to whom he could turn! In the same letter Friedrich viciously attacks Agathe: "O, Gathe, schäm Dich bis in Deine schwarze Seele hinein, Du Ausgeburt der Frauenseele. Xantippe." This is a response to the bitter accusations against Friedrich which Agathe had sent Doris, a copy of which Doris, for her part no doubt somewhat confused by the turn of events, forwarded to Friedrich. Like Agathe, Friedrich was now looking back to see when the nightmare began, and like her he saw the origin to lie right at the beginning of the marriage. Unlike her, however, he was by now convinced that his mistake did not lie in financial and sexual deceit so much as in his decision to marry Agathe in the first place:

> ... kurz nach unserer Abreise von St. Nazaire, hatte ich schon die Überzeugung, daß ich einen Mißgriff gethan, doch es war *zu* spät!

In most of the letters there is a considerable amount of self-pity and self-righteousness. He sees himself spending Christmas alone and miserable—despite the friends who have just seen him through his fever! He feels he has aged so much that he can never pick up the shattered pieces of his life and start anew. "Die Zeit, die alles heilt, wird meine Wunde nie schließen," he writes to Lischen and his mother, "aber so Gott will, werde ich ruhiger und zufriedener mit der Zeit. . . . Ich bin zu tief gebeugt über das Betragen meiner Frau. Und wenn ich gestohlen und *gemordet* hätte, das Weib soll ihren Mann nicht verlassen."[41]

But his old optimism and desire for success, especially financial success, still shine through. By December 1891 he had joined the firm of Juan J. Viña, mercantile agents. By June 1893 he had high hopes of being made "Chef" of this firm, and indeed he was. There are no surviving letters after this point. All we know (from a voluminous correspondence involving the German Consulate in New Orleans, the legal firm of Lexzau & Scharbau, and others) is that Friedrich Lehmann died of "Fieber palustre," or malaria, in the house of Luis Wohlenberg in Tancanhuitz, Mexico. When the news reached Wandsbek, Agathe, who had suppressed all tender feelings for her husband for so long, was greatly touched and she broke down in tears.[42] Despite all the disappointment and all the anguish occasioned by her wastrel husband and their unhappy marriage, the repressed memory of her one and only love welled up again fresh in all its bittersweetness and overcame the tough self-control resulting from her exaggerated sense of propriety. Wilhelm Lehmann records with bland irony that his father left, among other things, Tolstoi's *Kreuzersonate* and a book entitled *Höllenbreughel als Erzieher.*[43] But from the consular correspondence it emerges that Friedrich also left the proceeds of two life insurance policies with the Home Life Insurance Company of New York, which together amounted to 8,000 Dollars. The net proceeds of the policies, by the time various expenses had been deducted, amounted to some Mk 28,533.84. Although the first installment was paid in 1896, the final sum was not remitted until June 1898. The reasons for this delay were many. Friedrich, typically, had entrusted the policies to an Irishman, whose name he never recorded, and which, in his delirium, he could not recall. By the time the consular official, one Freiherr von Meysenbug, had tracked this gentleman down, wrangled with numerous officials over death certificates and birth certificates, located Agathe in Germany and dealt with the lawyers, no less than three years had passed.

Meanwhile Agathe, after the initial shock of the news of her husband's death, set about the upbringing and education of her children with even greater steadfastness of purpose and energy. What she strove for is not in doubt. Her letter of 10 July 1891 (quoted above) spoke of the necessity of bringing up her children "zu sittlich festen Menschen," and expressed a hope that she could keep Willi at school. Nothing had happened to change her resolve. The pastor had exhorted her to keep the children from the "bösen Einfluß," and for Agathe, Friedrich was still, even dead, an evil influence, and she never forgot this.

From the point of view of material comfort in the Lehmann family, little changed after the death of Friedrich. Much of the money from the insurance policies Agathe had used immediately to pay back what Friedrich had owed the Fritz Lehmann firm (the Pumplün affiliation had disappeared by 1897). This she was able to do by 31 August 1897. What remained was immediately put into the bank by the prudent and solicitous Agathe. There was the schooling of her three children as an immediate concern, and Agathe was ambitious enough for her two boys that she put aside sufficient for a university education, too. In addition, there was the compulsory one year of military service. Were the two boys to serve as officers—and Agathe's blind ambition admitted of no other alternative—this would be a costly business. Finally Lita, even if no other expenses on her behalf materialized, would presumably be in need of a dowry before long.

Agathe had been working ever since the departure of Friedrich in 1891. After the death of her mother later in the same year, she took in lodgers in order to supplement her income and found herself able to support her family entirely on her own. Upon Friedrich's death she did apply to a benevolent foundation for financial support for her children's education, but to no avail. Meanwhile, and to a great extent under her direct influence, the children devoured one book after another. In "Bildnis der Eltern" Wilhelm Lehmann describes the books contained in his mother's book-case, as he remembers them: Georg Ebers' *Eine Ägyptische Königstochter,* an "archäologischer Roman" typical of the age that produced a Felix Dahn; Immermann's *Oberhof* (i.e. that part of the *Münchhausen* novel, which, to its detriment, often came out in separate form); various "Klassiker"; Christian Öser's *Briefe an eine Jungfrau über die Hauptgegenstände der Aesthetik*; a classical mythology "doch auch die rotgelben Hefte der *Deutschen Rundschau* mit Erstdrucken C.F. Meyers, Kellers und Storms."[44] The list is a striking example of the subtle way Lehmann is able to insinuate more meaning into a passage than the actual words themselves contain. On the one hand, he is saying, his mother's reading tastes were so conservative that they included the classics and an eighteenth-century blue-stocking tract (Öser). On the other hand, there were also the current authors who figured in a journal such as the *Deutsche Rundschau.* The force of the "doch" is to suggest not only that Agathe is up with current trends, but that Lehmann was introduced at an early age to an influential journal which was later to be of great importance to him. Agathe had always been interested in literature. Her own letters and those of Friedrich to her reveal that reading was a great love, and her father's letters to her shortly after her marriage included, along with his descriptions of Imperial visits to Hamburg, or disastrous floods in that city, an account of the unveiling of the Lessing-Denkmal (in 1881). Others recounted the devastating fire in the Viennese Ringtheater in 1881, which led to the closing of so many theatres in Germany for fear that a similar catastrophe might befall them. There is no doubt that she was, initially at least, a great influence on, and example for, young Wilhelm.

But a combination of over-solicitude and a desire to present a solid front of propriety at all costs gradually began to grate on her adolescent eldest child. Her constant admonitions that he should strive to be a pillar of respectable society and avoid even the slightest hint of his father's weaknesses began to alienate Wilhelm, who soon saw flaws in the more attractive side to his mother, namely her love of literature and music. As Wilhelm began to collect his own library, for example, her jealousy and suspicion of his independent judgment caused her to dismiss everything with the words "Ach, das ist ja alles nur Schöngeistiges."[45] Books and learning, as Wilhelm began to suspect, were for her simply an outward manifestation of respectability, simply something one presented to the aspiring bourgeoisie as one's credentials. From money he had earned by giving private tuition young Wilhelm bought himself Nietzsche's *Zarathustra:* "Bei einem Damenkaffee wurde dieses mein Buch herumgezeigt, und meine Mutter sagte, sie habe es mir gekauft—das war eine Unwahrheit."[46] Small wonder that tension between them grew. True, it was not always Agathe's fault. Wilhelm himself had always tended towards introspection, and he resented the intrusion of other people into his inner world. Even when younger, he had inwardly seethed when he and Walter were obliged to appear before his mother and her city friends and show off their various pets, and they "sahen mit zornigem Argwohn behandschuhte Hände unsere Geliebten täppisch berühren."[47] His choice of the words "Geliebten" and "berühren" is significant.

The same situation pertained with music. Friedrich had not joined the Gesangverein simply as a pretext to drink. He loved music, and Wilhelm remembered his father as possessing an agreeable baritone voice. At the Wandsbek Matthias Claudius Gymnasium Wilhelm was a keen member of the choir, and he enjoyed the piano lessons his mother arranged for him with a friend of her sister's—although his "Klavierspiel kam über den Rausch der Hingerissenheit nicht hinaus."[48] When they attended a Beethoven concert in Hamburg one day, his exhilaration knew no bounds, and as they walked back to Wandsbek through the rain, he attempted to put his enthusiasm into words. His mother dutifully tried to reciprocate in kind, but "ihr Versuch, es mir an Begeisterung gleich zu tun, stieß mich als unwahr ab. Es geschah ein plötzlicher, böser Riß zwischen ihr und mir." Looking back on the occasion, the poet can see the root of the problem: "Kein Zweifel, ich hatte sie überflügelt an Fähigkeit der Empfindung für die Kunst—das wollte ihre ehrgeizige Natur nicht wahrhaben."[49] The same pride, ambition, and independence which caused so much strife in her short-lived marriage now began to separate son from mother.

It was not always as bad as this. As long as Wilhelm had not outstripped his mother in his ability or capacity for appreciation, and as long as her behavior was not obviously dictated by her desire to be looked up to as the epitome of bourgeois respectability, all was well. Wilhelm had begun English in the Obersekunda and, since his mother's command of English was good as a result of her stay in

England as a governess, they had sat down together to read Walter Scott's *Lady of the Lake*.[50] There was no tension or animosity.

Wilhelm had started Gymnasium full of promise, having been, as his mother proudly asserted, "Primus der Sexta." But a similar trend seems to have set in there, too. As soon as he began to see through the sham knowledge and pseudo wisdom of the various teachers, he withdrew into himself or lost interest. Mathematics was always a weakness, and it proved necessary for Wilhelm to take private lessons. He was simply unable to come to terms with the abstraction of this discipline, but needed the visible or imaginable tangibility of concrete reality, the natural sciences and their preoccupation with observable phenomena, or language where one could make the word flesh. But even in subjects which had initially presented no problems, like Latin and Greek, history or geography, Wilhelm gradually subsided into mediocrity. Even German literature, taught by teachers devoid of sensitivity, insight, and knowledge of their subject, lost its charm and attraction. Only the writing of essays kept Wilhelm's interest and provided him with a continual challenge. Not that there were any signs of precocious genius, as in the case of Hugo von Hofmannsthal and many others. Far from it. Unable to give adequate expression to his "drängendes Gefühl,"[51] he would simply throw in a phrase from Stifter or Storm. No one was sufficiently well-read to spot the plagiarized passage, and the only remark was an occasional "verstiegen" scrawled in the margin by someone just able to discern a change in style. Wilhelm was, in fact, trying his hand at poetry by 1898. In this year, impressed by Hofmannsthal's "Reiselied" ("Der lyrische Fluß dieser Verse war für mich berauschend"[52]), he sent some poetic attempts to the Austrian, who was only eight years his senior, and received some kind words of encouragement in answer. But even if Wilhelm Lehmann was not yet writing good poetry, he had reached the stage where linguistic precision was a priority—he was a poet searching for the necessary tools before embarking on his trade.

The only subjects in which Wilhelm excelled were French and English, both taught by Oberstudienrat Till. Till's love of his subject, his ability, and his ironic disposition were such a refreshing change that Wilhelm took to him immediately and soon proved as linguistically gifted as his parents. His ability to pronounce foreign words correctly sometimes got him into trouble. A particularly insensitive pedagogue named Schumann, who taught German, mocked Wilhelm's correct Spanish pronunciation of Puerto Cabello, insisting that it was pronounced the way it was spelled. He was no more encouraging when it came to Wilhelm's well-written and above average essays, branding them "unkindlich."[53]

With so little to gain and hold his interest at school, it is not surprising that Wilhelm often played truant. It was a simple matter. In a fashion worthy of Felix Krull, he would fake a headache or some such affliction and have his mother write a note of excuse. Once she was out of the house and on her way to teach at Lili Meyer's Höhere Töchterschule, Wilhelm would leap out of bed and set off blithely for the woods and fields around Wandsbek and spend the day exactly as he wished: away from his fellow-humans, and carefully observing flora and fauna. But this means of escape was all too soon to be stopped. One day his mother arrived home unexpectedly early and discovered him returning bookless to the house. It was obvious what he had been doing, and it was equally obvious that this was the "böse Einfluß" of Friedrich at work. Agathe said as much, and no doubt gave the dagger of guilt just that extra twist to make her point. Small wonder then, given Wilhelm's character and the quality of the average schoolteacher in Wilhelmine Germany, that he ultimately just scraped through his *Abitur,* thanks only to a superlative essay (in which he avoided any "verstiegene" phrases). Small wonder, too, that Wilhelm Lehmann was to show nothing but eternal contempt for the schoolteacher—although he himself, ironically, was obliged to earn his living as one for the rest of his life. Of his graduating class, incidentally, only two survived World War I.

Wilhelm's only real friend was still his brother. But there were a few schoolmates who figured fairly prominently for a while during and, briefly, after his schooldays. One was someone surnamed Ulrich, poetically sensitive but a total misfit at the school. Then there was Rudolf Franz, the son of the Direktor of the school—one of the few teachers for whom Wilhelm had any respect. Franz and young Lehmann found they were allies in their mockery of the many Philistine teachers and pupils. Later, when Wilhelm was a student in Berlin, Franz turned up again, and they spent a fair amount of time together.

In the Prima, Wilhelm also got to know Heinrich Lehmann. Heinrich, unrelated, was a year older than Wilhelm and, in many ways, his very antithesis. In place of Wilhelm's lack of self-confidence and gaucheness was a "kühn-natürliches Betragen"[54] and instead of Wilhelm's guilt-ridden fear of sexuality induced by his Puritan mother, there was the brash curiosity and penchant for dirty jokes more common in adolescents. Heinrich, like many a Primaner, was already enjoying a certain emancipation from the restraints of parental control. He and others would meet in a bar on the Wandsbeker Chaussee on a Saturday evening, where Wilhelm joined them, laughing at the jokes to cover his embarrassment and discomfiture. He was in dire need of emancipation from Agathe's repressive and nagging solicitude, yet tortured by guilt as he sought this liberation. Heinrich Lehmann was undoubtedly a small but significant help to Wilhelm in precisely this regard. Like Rudolf Franz, he was set apart from the average schoolboy at the Matthias Claudius Gymnasium. He was intelligent and musically inclined, and had an ear for poetry. Wilhelm Lehmann's lifelong adulation of Detlev von Liliencron stemmed to some degree from Heinrich, who quoted to him two lines of Liliencron's poetry which may well have contributed in no small measure to Lehmann's later poetic development:

> Auf allen Gräbern fror das Wort: Gewesen,
> Auf allen Gräbern taute still: Genesen—

It was Heinrich, moreover, who introduced the younger "Lehfuchs," as he called him, to Ibsen, giving him a copy of *Brand.* And when Wilhelm experienced his first teenage "crush," it was to Heinrich that he wrote confiding this significant event. The encouraging answer which came back from Heinrich, who was meanwhile away on manoeuvres while completing his "Einjährigen," is treated in *Mühe des Anfangs* in some detail.[55] The poet clearly remembers the importance to him of the relationship at that time. Wilhelm was gratified to find an older person taking an interest in him, so much so that he for a while attempted to adapt his own handwriting to resemble Heinrich's. But they went their separate ways, and there was no further contact.

The fact was, although Agathe had confidently asserted that the boys would soon forget their father completely,[56] Wilhelm was in great need of a father figure in his life. Heinrich Lehmann, for a while, served this function. There were others, all as shortlived, during his schooldays. One was the person the children referred to as "Onkel" Twarz. He was married to Agathe's friend of long standing Magda and was, therefore, not a true uncle.[57] Wilhelm and Walter used to spend their holidays with Twarz, who had a small farm in the Holstein village of Willinghusen. Here they could ride the horses, help with the milking, and simply enjoy watching men doing men's work and feel themselves equal by association. But Twarz took ill, sold the farm and, after moving into town, died, so that the boys were back where they started. Not altogether surprisingly, Agathe thought that this agreeable substitute father was a drunkard and entirely unworthy of her friend Magda.

But, as Wilhelm grew older, girls began to figure in his thoughts and, to a lesser degree, his life. The fact that he had a sister did not make contact with the opposite sex much easier. Wilhelmine Germany was repressive enough, but a combination of societal repression and Agathe's determination to keep Wilhelm away from the lure of sex was overpowering. She would even go so far as to keep her sons out of sight of Lita's girl-friends when they came visiting, and all contact with the opposite sex came to be secret and, therefore, guilt-ridden. "Das heiße Blut mußte sich selbst befriedigen," as Wilhelm put it.[58] True, there was Lisa Wiemann, the girl next door, and one day Wilhelm, in the desperate belief that he "müsse auch einmal lieben,"[59] tried to kiss her—she ducked and he hit his head against the Pächterhof wall.

The summer before his Abitur, Wilhelm went with the whole family to the Schönberger beach on the Baltic. He and Walter fell in with a group of young people, and Wilhelm soon thought he was in love. The girl's name was Therese Rougement and, after the holiday, they exchanged a few letters. Wilhelm, out of a combination of natural bashfulness and his mother-induced guilt complex, decided that it would be wiser to have Therese send her letters to him poste restante. But, alas, his mother found out and was doubly horrified: firstly at Wilhelm's receiving letters from a girl, and then at the subterfuge involved— honest citizens just did not receive letters poste restante. Meanwhile Therese had hardly fared any better, for Wilhelm had foolishly sent her a volume of poems by that devilish atheist and libertine Shelley, which had unfortunately been intercepted by her mother. This innocent relationship busied Wilhelm right up to his early student years, although they were never to meet again and also soon gave up writing. Lehmann's diary for 1901-02 contains many passages where Therese is the main preoccupation.[60]

It was towards the end of his schooldays that Wilhelm began to take an interest in the theatre, and it was this institution that provided Lehmann with another lady to adore: Ella Heuberger, an actress at the newly inaugurated *Deutsches Schauspielhaus* in Hamburg. Her performances of Thekla in Schiller's *Wallenstein* and Luise in the same author's *Kabale und Liebe* so delighted the teenager that he sent her flowers. Once again he kept this adoration from his mother—successfully this time—and entrusted his thoughts only to his diary. Another performance at the *Deutsches Schauspielhaus* which captivated Wilhelm was that of Hauptmann's *Michael Kramer* in 1901. The play deals with two problems which were of burning interest to Lehmann at this time: the conflict between the artist and the bourgeoisie (especially as dealt with in Act III)[61] and the search for one's artistic self (as depicted through Kramer and his two children). Wilhelm's feeling that he was somehow different from his fellows had been steadily growing through adolescence and was to result in a crisis of sorts in the next few years. By now, too, he was aware of another world beyond the proper gentility and patent Philistinism of the bourgeoisie. He was accordingly not at all surprised, indeed he was smugly amused, to watch a lady walk out at the beginning of the final act of *Michael Kramer* indignantly asserting that she had not paid to see a corpse laid out on the stage.

Wilhelm's theatrical experience at this time was not only passive. Direktor Franz, whose (unfortunately rather dry) book *Der Aufbau der Handlung in den klassischen Dramen* testifies to an interest in the drama, decided to put on Sophocles' *Oedipus*. To Wilhelm, the very epitome of the shy and gawky adolescent, fell the role of Jocaste—Franz felt the lad should come out of his shell. The performance, whatever its shortcomings, received generous applause, and Wilhelm, too, was obliged to take a curtain call. Fearful that he might entangle his robes in the footlights, he raised them so high, that the audience, much to his chagrin, burst into good-natured laughter.

By now Wilhelm had decided to study English and French. The decision was arrived at more by chance than through deliberate reflection. Walking home one day from school, Wilhelm was obliged to wait at a railway crossing and thus fell into conversation with Till, who asked him what he was going to do when he left school. Wilhelm found himself saying that he would probably study modern languages, and he was encouraged to do so by the teacher. The decision, it seemed, had been taken. Once away from school, he could rapidly complete his studies, become a teacher and begin to support the family. In this way he would be able to silence Agathe's continued complaints about the difficulty of keeping the family together, and thereby assuage his guilt in feeling that he, along with the whole male sex, was to blame. He accordingly prepared to leave home, having decided to begin his studies in Tübingen, and looked forward to this new step with great anticipation, hoping first for liberation from his mother and her dominating and protective interference, and second for a new community of like-minded spirits. He was to be disappointed in both regards. Before he left, Agathe went off for a last walk with her first-born and took the opportunity to tearfully warn him about the evils of sex—she, who had been so sorely used in her own relationship with her husband, lost no opportunity to inhibit the free sexual development of her son.

2
Tübingen, Strasbourg, and Berlin (1900-1902). "Triumph. Trotz alledem"

WHEN WILHELM LEHMANN finished his schooling at Easter 1900 and left shortly after to begin his studies in Tübingen, he was fairly well read. At Gymnasium, of course, he read little other than the standard classics of Greek and Latin literature, the German classics, and the German Romantics, who were at this time just being re-discovered. The latter were certainly part of the Primaner's favorite reading. In addition to his school reading there were those books he happened upon as he combed the secondhand bookstores of Wandsbek and Hamburg and began to build up what was soon to become a large collection of German and world literature, books like *Godwi* and Brentano's *Märchen*, works by Eichendorff and Mörike. Other authors he was reading at this time were Storm, Keller, and Fontane, who could be found in the issues of the *Deutsche Rundschau* in his mother's bookcase. Other prominent writers who appeared in this journal in the latter part of the nineteenth century, and whom Wilhelm might have read, included Paul Heyse, Otto Brahm, Georg Brandes, Wilhelm Scherer, and Eduard Hanslick. What this journal, together with the Feuilleton of the *Neue Hamburger Zeitung* and *Die Nation,* undoubtedly gave young Lehmann was a taste for the literary journal, and in 1898 he began to subscribe to the *Neue deutsche Rundschau,* edited at the time by Oscar Bie. As a direct result, Wilhelm became acquainted with such contemporary authors as Hermann Stehr, whose *Schindelmacher* appeared in this journal in 1899, Emil Strauß, Gerhart Hauptmann, and, above all, Moritz Heimann. Then, as we have seen, Lehmann's reading took in Liliencron, Ibsen and Walter Scott. To these names we should add those of Baudelaire, Byron, and Shelley, who belonged to the "underground" literature of those few misfit pupils adventurous enough to defy parents and teachers and acquire such generally suspect authors. Scott, Byron, and Shelley signified the beginnings of a great love of English literature which encouraged and sustained him to the end of his life.

Despite this rather wide reading and his definite interest in literature, Lehmann had no burning desire to study, certainly no aptitude for the structured study necessary to complete his *Staatsexamen* and become a teacher of modern languages. He was, therefore, extremely unlikely, given the German university system, to achieve his immediate goal in the short time envisioned by his mother. In view of this lack of any great commitment to study, the absence of a guiding father-figure noticeable during his school years became more sorely felt during his student years. Had he been able, as he undoubtedly desired, to find those like-minded souls he so eagerly yearned for, all might have been well. But this was not yet to be the case. And instead of being able to escape the Philistine mediocrity he had lived with and suffered from, he found it impinged on his life at the university in just the same fashion as before. His sheltered, repressed existence might have forced a different person to break out, rebel, and live a Bohemian life. But Lehmann, blessed to some extent with the impractical, romantic irresponsibility of his father, had so often heard from his mother where it might lead, that his rebellion, if such it can be called, took place inwardly. He accepted the very same bourgeois respectability he so despised in his mother because the alternatives seemed so fraught with danger. Nonetheless, as if escaping from jail, he left Wandsbek and set off south for a new life in Mörike's Swabia.

At the turn of the century Tübingen was even more of a picturesque relic from a bygone age than it is today. It was a city of about 15,000 inhabitants, charmingly situated on the Neckar, with narrow, winding alley-ways and steep, worn steps. It was possessed of a beautiful Town Hall and, overlooking the whole town, the Schloß Hohentübingen. It was, in fact, just the romantic and medieval setting one might connect with a late Romantic balladeer like Uhland, who was a true son of Tübingen and honored accordingly by his city with a statue by Kietz. At the time, the only memorial to the greatest poet connected with the city, Hölderlin, was the tower overlooking the Neckar in which he ended his days and the simple gravestone in the city cemetery. But at the turn of the century Hölderlin was only just being discovered by critics like Norbert von Hellingrath and Moritz Heimann. The city was, perhaps, best known for its venerable university (founded 1477), which numbered about 1,500 students in Lehmann's time, and just over 100 professors. In addition there was the famous Tübinger Stift, where Kepler, Hegel, Schelling, Hölderlin, Schwab, and Mörike had all studied.

When Wilhelm Lehmann arrived in Tübingen, he came as a widely read, intelligent young man of eighteen with no conception how to direct his energies towards accomplishment. He was in great need of intellectual stimulus and of an opportunity for the exchange of ideas, but he did not possess the personality to attract those whom he so sorely needed and desired. He was gauche in manner and movement and usually ill at ease in company. In spirit he was a poet on the brink of a poetic message, but as yet without the insight to conceive it or the means to express it. It would have to be a remarkable figure who perceived the lad's potential *and* the problems which inhibited it; it would have to be a person with great patience and charity, a person possessed of a generous measure of perspicuity and with a poet's soul. Lehmann, alas, did not find such a person in Tübingen and was obliged to rely primarily on his brother's letters for support and sustaining comfort. His Tübingen semester was, on the whole, a negative experience: what he should have been doing, his philological studies, did not attract him; what he enjoyed doing, botany, could not carry him to his present goal. The romanticized picture of Swabia which Lehmann had formed for himself from his reading of Mörike proved to be different in reality, and his dream of settling down in a peasant's vineyard hut far from the bustle of human kind rapidly faded. Instead, he found an attic room in a house overlooking the Neckar.

If it proved impossible to recapture the Swabia of Mörike in the reality of his Tübingen sojourn, Mörike did at least lead him to the music of Hugo Wolf, and Lehmann spent hours trying to capture the essence of Wolf's Mörike-Lieder on the piano in his lodgings. Lehmann venerated this tragic composer for the rest of his life, captivated by the perfect fusion of poetry and music and finding the gentle melancholy and quiet pathos of his music most congenial.

If anything positive, apart from his newly acquired love of Hugo Wolf, came to him from his Tübingen semester, it was his deepening love of botany. His botanical excursions and laboratory sessions spent determining the various finds served not only to sharpen his already considerable faculty of observation; they brought into focus the deep conflict between the concrete and the abstract. This is how Lehmann described the problem in *Mühe des Anfangs:*

> Warum galt Botanik nicht als reine Gestaltlehre? Als solche vertrug sie sich mit dem Wort und brauchte keine Mathematik. Zu ausschließlich hing ich den Dingen an. Von ihnen sollte ich mich wegdenken—wo sie strebten, sich zu mir hinzudenken? Heute weiß ich, daß Novalis recht hat, wenn er einem dichterischen Menschen Beschäftigung mit Abstraktem, mit Mathematik und umgekehrt rät. Mir diente die Abstraktion nur als Würze, den Traum des Konkreten nicht schal werden zu lassen. Es gab ja Abstraktion genug; aber die Mathematik ist ihre realste Form. Sie fehlte mir; ich empfinde das als einen Mangel. Jedoch, sinnliches Dasein und das Wort als seine Wiedergeburt—dem bohrte ich unklar entgegen, voll Schmerzen, voll Öde, voll glücklichem Leid. Ich irrte durch Wüsteneien; da wollte kein Brunnen springen. Sollte ich von vornherein verzichten, da ich kaum begonnen hatte? Meine achtzehn Jahre konnten sich nicht in die geläufige Ordnung schicken. Vielleicht wäre mir dienlicher gewesen, als Gärtnerlehrling bestimmte Arbeiten zu verrichten, statt vage ins Vage zu schweifen. Wahrscheinlich ist mir gerade das Unnütze nützlich geworden.[1]

To exclude the force of abstraction from one's view of the world was dangerous. It meant leaving poetry and nature in a void where they could be measured against nothing and thereby lost their obvious poetic character. As long as Lehmann denied the realm of the abstract, his poetic aspirations would be thwarted. It was to prove necessary to wait for a while, for a number of key experiences and exposure to a few congenial thinkers and their ideas before he was to resolve the dilemma. The resolution came in the recognition of a necessary dialectic. As long as Lehmann felt that the word could be the thing, he was denying the dialectic. The dilemma was, of course, widespread at the turn of the century. It was occupying, in particular, Hugo von Hofmannsthal, to whom the young Lehmann had sent his first poetic attempts,[2] and it was soon to bring Hofmannsthal to his much cited Chandos letter.

Meanwhile Lehmann continued to read voraciously, although without any real direction, and he continued to buy as many books as he could. Upon his return to Wandsbek in July, his mother was shocked at her son's almost emaciated appearance—he had often gone without food in order to buy books. His plan to change to medicine, which stemmed from his interest in botany, was quickly quashed by Agathe on the grounds that such a course of study would be too long and costly. Lehmann's misery was complete: he was hardly back in the oppressive atmosphere of his home, as lonely as ever, when his one possible chance of entering a congenial field of study was peremptorily dismissed by his mother.

Encouraged by his former schoolmate Wiemer, Lehmann decided to go to Strasbourg for a semester at least—in fact he stayed for two. Situated on the north-south axis provided by the navigable Ill (on which the town lies) and the Rhine, and on the east-west axis of the old trade route which runs north of the Vosges mountains through Nancy to Paris, Strasbourg has always had commercial and strategic importance. As the capital of Alsace-Lorraine, and straddling the language frontier of German and French, it has long been a city caught between those apparently irreconcilable cultures and temperaments: the Teutonic and the Gallic.

After the siege and bombardment of 1870-71, the city became part of the German Reich and, under the somewhat autocratic rule of the commissioner of police, Back, the damaged fortifications were removed and new ones begun farther out. The space thus gained allowed for considerable planned expansion. Near the pentagonal citadel, almost totally destroyed during the bombardment and now further flattened to provide landfill, a new residential area was built, and it was here, in the Schwarzwaldstraße, that Lehmann found lodging. Under Back the damage to the inner city, including the tower of the cathedral, was made good, drainage improved, and a better school system adopted. Not surprisingly, when elections were held in 1885 for the first time since the war, the populace changed from its anti-German stance, and elected Back mayor.

More than many cities, Strasbourg had suffered and profited by turns, both economically and culturally, because of the vicissitudes of history. It had been a center of mysticism in the middle ages (Meister Eckhart and Johannes Tauler); it became a center of humanism in the fifteenth and sixteenth centuries where Sebastian Brant, Thomas Murner, and Jakob Wimpfeling figured prominently. The university was founded in 1566, only to be suppressed during the French Revolution as a stronghold of German sentiment. In 1872 it was re-opened and, by the time Lehmann came as a student in the autumn of 1900 it had re-established itself as a major place of learning and spread out towards the citadel and the Schwarzwaldstraße. But the inner city, with its complex maze of narrow streets and its timbered and gabled houses, preserved its medieval character, despite the new electric tramway which made its appearance around the turn of the century. The cathedral, so important for the young Goethe when he was a student in Strasbourg, remained a splendid centerpiece, before which young Lehmann stood lost in admiration.

Unfortunately he was lost in other ways too, and Strasbourg proved to be no great improvement over Tübingen. The philologists were, for the most part, dull and unattractive. Lehmann made no comment regarding the English Lektor J. G. Robertson, whose courses on the English school and university system and whose class on English translation he took. Robertson was soon to become well known for his standard work *A History of German Literature* (1901), a text which would continue to be staple fare for British and American students of Germanistik right up to the present. Wiemer was often a companion but not a friend, and his dry mathematician's mind was no stimulus to Lehmann. More stimulating was the company of one Josef Ennen, who was also attending French classes; but if anything the fortunes of Ennen, in love with a waitress named Ella who laughingly repulsed all advances, made Wilhelm only too well aware of the gaping void in his own love-life. The opera, at least, was a delight, and here Lehmann had his first taste of Wagner. The Strasbourg opera at this time fortunately enjoyed the services of a Wagnerian singer of great ability and rising fame: Thila Plaichinger. This Viennese soprano possessed a fine, powerful voice and was a particularly dramatic actress.[3] Lehmann's new-found liking for Wagner and his passion for Hugo Wolf clearly indicate that he was firmly behind modernism in music at this stage—all the more so in that Brahms, the epitome of the traditional in music, could find no favor in the young student. But his predilection for modernism was not to keep pace with the trends of the twentieth century.

There were, of course, always books, and the great discoveries for the nineteen-year-old Lehmann were Emily Brontë's *Wuthering Heights,* Büchner's *Leonce und Lena,* and the novels of the Danish writer Steen Steensen Blicher. But, in general, Lehmann was as lost as ever: yearning for love but unable to attain it; in need of direction, but with no goal he believed in and no one to push him; lost in admiration of great writing, yet unable to say why; desirous of writing his own poetry, but all too aware of his severe limitations; needing to direct his energies towards the completion of his studies, but lacking any interest in his discipline. Lehmann recounts an experience which aptly sums up his frame of mind at this time:

Als ich von den Weihnachtsferien ... zurückkehrte und des schweren Koffers wegen eine Droschke zur Schwarzwälderstraße [sic] nahm, antwortete ich auf die Frage des

Kutschers: "Welche Nummer?"—"Ich habe keine Nummer." Diese verdutzte Antwort drückte meinen Zustand aus.[4]

Happily this sorry situation was, in many respects, to change dramatically for the better with Wilhelm's next move.

Berlin had been suggested by friends of his mother as a possible place of study. His mother doubtless felt that the presence of these friends might prove a steadying influence and was consequently in agreement. Lehmann, for different reasons, also saw Berlin as a logical choice—after all, the *Neue Rundschau,* the books and the people who wrote them all came from Berlin. So, by the beginning of October, Lehmann was installed in the third largest city in Europe, still searching, still hoping for some catalyst to help direct all those pent-up yearnings towards their realization, still hoping for success in love, art, and his studies.

In the middle of the nineteenth century Berlin numbered less than half a million inhabitants and was, if we are to believe Henry Adams: "a poor, keen-witted, provincial town, simple, dirty, uncivilized, and in most respects disgusting."[5] By 1885 the population had risen to over a million and, twenty years later, to over two million. It was a city rich in theatre and music and with numerous important museums. In Unter den Linden a grand dual carriageway with a central promenade shaded by four rows of lindens and chestnut trees and with a separate riding-path, it possessed an imposing and elegant thoroughfare stretching from the Royal Palace to the Brandenburg Gate. On this street, the imposing eighteenth and nineteenth century architecture of the state and ministerial buildings, hotels, and large department stores bore eloquent witness to the buoyant growth of the capital.

It was, in fact, a city obsessed with expansion and money. The stock exchange was unquestionably the most important in Germany, the railway systems encompassed fourteen main stations, then there was the suburban railway and the streetcar system. The huge growth in the population came about primarily because of the tremendous influx of people from the east, so that the comfortable Biedermeier Berliner of earlier years became swallowed up in a great metropolitan mix. For amusement the new Berliner had not only the great range of theatrical and musical entertainments right down to the ubiquitous "Gassenhauer," but also several newly laid-out parks in addition to the *Tiergarten*. The *Tiergarten* was initially an enclosed area for deer and wild boar, but then, started by King Frederick I of Prussia and completed by Frederick William III, it was converted into a park laid out with ponds, paths, flower-beds, benches, pavilions, and the "Zelte," a row of refreshment booths. Adjoining the *Tiergarten* were the Zoological Gardens, further out were the wooded parks: the *Friedrichshain,* the *Humboldthain,* and the *Grunewald.*

Moabit, where Lehmann first took lodgings, lay far from central Berlin on the streetcar line. Originally set aside early in the eighteenth century for French Huguenot refugees, it was now primarily an industrial area. As such it was too noisy for Lehmann, and this fact, together with the presence of roaches in his room, soon sent him over to neighboring Charlottenburg, where he found a room in the Dankelmannstraße. Charlottenburg was still a separate town and was a strange mixture of palace and gardens, factories, and residential areas. It was a city of 160,000 inhabitants, but not without some vestiges of rural character.

The University of Berlin (founded in 1809) was at this time at the height of its fame. It had always been able to muster an impressive array of celebrated scholars right from its first rector Fichte through to its current rector, the famous theologian Adolf von Harnack. Hegel, Savigny, Ranke, the Grimms, Droysen, Virchow, Ernst Curtius, Mommsen, Treitschke, Dilthey, Scherer—they had all taught at Berlin. The art historian Wölfflin arrived at the same time as Lehmann, but the student had no contact with him. The two most substantial scholars he did come into contact with were Erich Schmidt, the illustrious discoverer of the *Urfaust,* and Georg Simmel, the philosopher.

Schmidt, who usually sported an artist's cravat and a short velvet smock, was possessed of an engagingly eccentric personality, and was a good conversationalist with ready wit and a sardonic sense of humor. He was the center of attraction at the celebrated "Germanistenkneipe" just off the Potsdamerbrücke. But he was full of self-importance and given to theatricality, and it is no surprise to find that our shy student did not take to him and, unlike scores of other writers and scholars, did not find his way into the "Germanistenkneipe." Moreover, Lehmann found Schmidt's lectures unduly tedious, and he spent the lecture hour translating Shakespeare's sonnets. The most complete translation surviving is that of the 73rd Sonnet, whose poignant and resigned melancholy particularly appealed to young Lehmann in his current frame of mind. The translation is not good, but it does have a felicitous phrase or two and it does demonstrate that the nineteen-year-old student had endeavored to find his way out of certain problems with his own poetic devices rather than with mechanical direct translations of the English. Lehmann was perhaps attracted to Shakespeare and the Sonnets through his contact with the Shakespearean scholar Alois Brandl, who was for many years the editor of the *Shakespeare Jahrbuch* (1898-1919) and whose course on the history of English literature Lehmann took. Certainly Brandl introduced him to Elizabethan literature, which was to become a great love as time went on. His love of nineteenth-century English literature probably was fostered more by the young English Lektor F. Sefton Delmer. Delmer's *English Literature from Beowulf to Bernard Shaw,* a kind of English forerunner to Frenzel's *Daten der deutschen Dichtung,* is well known to every German student of English. Brought out by a German publisher in 1910, it ran into 22 editions and was brought up to date in 1951 by A.S. Harvey. Lehmann's contact with Delmer was a personal one: they planned a Meredith translation as a joint venture, but nothing came of the project.[6]

If Lehmann was not exactly the model student who read what was prescribed and passed examinations in rapid succession, he was a voracious if undisciplined reader. His diary kept during the Berlin period contains long lists of books and authors which he read or intended to read, and these lists showed that his tastes were continually broadening, even if they were not changing. All the German Romantics figure prominently, as does Ricarda Huch's study of the movement. Then there are the Realists, Naturalists, and other contemporaries: Storm, Keller, Stifter, Hebbel, Hauptmann, Conradi, Herman Bang, Stehr, Rosegger, and Strauß. Foreign literatures are also represented, and Lehmann read the English and the French for the most part in the original: Shakespeare, Keats, Shelley, the Brontës, Blake, and Verlaine. Among the Scandinavians—to some extent en vogue in Germany at the turn of the century—were Ibsen, Steen Steensen Blicher, and Jens Peter Jacobsen.

Most of the reading was taken on independently of his lectures, which he generally found dull. Most professors, too, bored him:

> Eine Ausnahme bildete ein junger Privatdozent, knabenhaft mit kurzgeschorenem Kopf, der in einem kleinen Raum über vergleichende Grammatik der indo- germanischen Sprachen las oder vielmehr in unprätentiöser Weise ohne Manuskript sprach. Seine kombinatorische Phantasie interessierte mich.[7]

This young man, ten years older than Lehmann, was Ernst Zupitza, who later moved to Greifswald. Attesting to the value of this course for Lehmann is a series of neat, comprehensive notes on folio sheets, which Lehmann later (in 1904) had bound in stiff, black boards. Lehmann's respect for Zupitza led him to an interest in aspects of his discipline which he had not possessed before. He corresponded with Zupitza on linguistic matters for the next few years, but then lost all contact with him.

Apart from the newly found interest in comparative philology resulting from the encounter with Zupitza, the only other truly positive gain directly accrued from Lehmann's two semesters at the University of Berlin came from Georg Simmel. There were two courses given by Simmel and attended by Lehmann: "Philosophie des 19. Jahrhunderts von Fichte bis Nietzsche" and "Formprobleme der Kunst." The auditorium was invariably packed for this remarkable scholar, who, as a Jew, was barred from full professorship: "Die Energie seiner Sprechweise fesselte. Seine Stirn näßte Schweiß; man sah ihn denken."[8] It so happened that Simmel's thoughts at this time turned on a subject of crucial importance for Lehmann and they probably found expression in at least one of the courses he attended. It was the notion of *leicht-schwer* and the role of this polarity in artistic form. Simmel's view of the binary opposites is contained in a short essay which appeared in the *Berliner Tageblatt* on 10 June 1901. In it, Simmel argues in favor of duality, pointing out the necessity of the "Schwere" (of resistance, of matter) for the exercise of the "Leichte" (of freedom, of spirit, and art). Whether Lehmann ever read this article is uncertain. What *is* certain is that he knew of its existence, noting in his journal on 9 January 1902 "Georg Simmel hat eine 'Aesthetik der Schwere' geschrieben. Ich *muß* sie lesen." The opposition *leicht-schwer* has interested many German mystics and poets from Jakob Böhme through Goethe to Hofmannsthal. It is therefore not at all surprising that Lehmann, too, should find himself fascinated by it. At this stage in his general and poetic development it offered intriguing insights into two questions which greatly concerned him: notably the question of the role of art, and secondly the tragic division of self and nature. Much of his unhappiness and insecurity at that time stemmed precisely from his inability to come to terms with these problems, and also from his dawning sense of his poetic calling and his inability to realize it. The refinement and use of the *leicht-schwer* polarity was to prove a major component of his artistic credo as it developed, and was to provide him with some degree of comfort as he tried to come to terms with an unpleasantly alien existence. The polarity appears already in his poetic attempts of the Berlin period.

In two instances (Zupitza and Simmel), the University of Berlin was able to provide Lehmann with some degree of interest and challenge, together with a modicum of spiritual sustenance. This, Tübingen and Strasbourg had signally failed to do. With regard to friendships with his peers it was, however, the same sorry story. Apart from Rudolf Franz, his comrade from his schooldays in Wandsbek, he had no contact with his fellow students. Even this relationship was neither lasting nor deep, and Lehmann's attitude to Franz was fraught with an ambivalence which almost defies explanation. On the one hand he was able to describe him in his journal as follows:

> Rudolf Franz erscheint mir als ein sehr unbedeutender Mensch, der viel zu viel aus sich selbst macht—wie alle Kleinen thun.[9]

On the other hand he often saw him in a totally positive light:

> R. Franz ist jedenfalls—und das ist am Ende alles oder dàs Bedeutendste—ein *freier Geist.*[10]

He attempts to describe their friendship:

> Unsere Freundschaft ist wie ein Pfauenauge, das auf einer Sommerstaude ruht und das der leiseste Schritt des Wanderers verscheucht—und doch sinke ich so gern in sein Innern[?][11]

The latter passage is followed by two drafts of a poem "An Rudolf Franz," which more or less restates the description of their friendship. The two young men were clearly united more by similar dislikes and similar aspirations than by a mutual sympathy. They both despised the Philistines around them, the heavy-footed bourgeois who disturbed their precarious butterfly friendship.[12] They were both aware of a higher calling as yet unattained—the poem contains the image of their two selves as "zwei hohe Flammen" in a passage whose imagery is poetically striking, but too unbalanced and extreme to be successful:

> Ins Riesengroße treibt die Welt: doch du und ich sind fest zusammen,
> Wenn fest zusammen können sein zwei hohe Flammen.
> Ich grüße dich und fließe selig in dein inneres Leben
> Und fühle hoch mich selbst bis zu den Sternen schweben.

In fact, within a few years both were appearing in print. Franz brought out a Büchner edition and, as a convinced socialist, wrote several books and prepared some editions with a socialist view of literature. The relationship at its best clearly meant a great deal to Lehmann, who saw Franz as soul-mate and a support (as the image in the above lines indicates), but at other times Lehmann felt threatened by the apparent optimism and boisterous self-confidence of Franz. At such times he even felt that the friendship was more a result of his bowing to Franz's attention than his actively seeking a mutually sympathetic relationship: "... es ist hier oder überhaupt nirgends jemand, der mir so hartnäckig nachläuft wie Du."[13] Lehmann's feeling that he was being pursued must have begun to prey on his mind as time went on, for he began to dream of him. In the night of 30 June-1 July 1902 Lehmann dreamed that he

> ... in wilder Flucht über Böden voll Kohlenruß und Heufäden—es muß oben in unserem alten Gymnasium gewesen sein—vor R. Franz gewesen [war]. Zugleich aber war mir Heinrich Lehmann begegnet, er erwarb sich spielend die Gunst eines Mädchens (*Verkäuferin* oder ähnlich)—und ich bewunderte ihn.[14]

From this dream, which came to him two years after he left school and home, we can begin to see not only how he was reacting to the friendship with Franz, but also what a traumatic effect the Wandsbek Matthias Claudius Gymnasium had on him. Furthermore this mixed dream begins to suggest the nature of Lehmann's admiration for Heinrich Lehmann, whom he had neither seen nor heard from for over two years, but who is rather often mentioned in Lehmann's journal at this time. Heinrich was a person possessed of that confidence, especially in matters relating to the opposite sex, which was so lacking in Lehmann himself.

The problematic nature of the adolescent Lehmann's desire for love, or, indeed, mere contact with girls did not change much with his arrival in Berlin. His diary contains many references to Therese Rougement—so many, in fact, that one might imagine that the brief encounter at the seaside had progressed meanwhile despite their separation, and that their relationship was developing into love as they exchanged letters: "Und plötzlich," writes Wilhelm in September 1901, "ist es mir herrlich klar—wie könnte ich je daran zweifeln?— daß sie mich liebt." But alas, even this confident statement, so re-assuring in itself, is followed immediately by the pathetically doubting parenthetical statement "Oder ist es schon jetzt nicht mehr so klar?"[15] In point of fact this entry was made in a mood of excitement and re-kindled interest after Lehmann decided to write to Therese again. She had not written to him for several months and was not to do so for another year. The relationship, for from being a happy one, or even one bitter-sweet in separation, was in essence a non-relationship raised to an artificial life in the searching and inventive mind of the nineteen-year-old youth.

This was not the only "crush" on unattainable women in the young student's life. The memory of Ella Heuberger, the actress whose Luise Miller he had adored in Hamburg and who had been regaled with flowers bought at great sacrifice with his hard-earned pocket money, continued to hold the lad enthralled. As often as not he would simply write her name in his journal. Sometimes he would write a few lines of adulation, and once he wrote a poem "Ella Heuberger tanzt" which, although of little poetic worth, indicates what he saw as the tremendous vivifying effect of her presence on both desperate humanity and nature.

A second actress who was well known at the time and who had just achieved such popularity in Munich that she became known as "die deutsche Duse," was Irene Triesch, who moved to Berlin's *Deutsches Theater* in 1901. Here Lehmann saw her and was immediately enthralled: "Irene Triesch. Wie soll ich meine Gefühle in Worte fassen?" he sighs to his journal on 3 November 1901.

Then there was a mysterious "Eveline," whose name crops up even more often than those of the other ladies admired by Wilhelm. Despite the many diary passages concerning Eveline, it is very difficult to ascertain who she in fact was, if indeed she actually existed. For in all probability she was purely a figment of Lehmann's over-active and fertile imagination; or possibly she was a young lady worshipped from afar but never addressed and therefore probably oblivious to Lehmann's yearning, but self-induced passion.

When he came to Berlin, then, Lehmann led a lonely existence in which he was obliged to live out much of his social life in his rather lively imagination. Unfortunately this surrogate existence was not sufficient in itself, so that he continually sank into the depths of despair. Almost all the possible activities open to the student in Berlin which might have led to some form of much sought-after human contact were left untried. He avoided the cafés and beerhalls where students, artists, writers, and socialites foregathered. The only sources of entertainment he utilized were the theatre, concert-hall, and opera—precisely those forms of entertainment where he was thrown in upon himself and not brought into contact with others. Indeed, he resented the presence of the audience: "Ich thue im Theater, als störte mich das Publikum."[16] Having attended his lectures (sometimes), having spent a few hours in either the Royal Library or the University Library, and having once bidden Rudolf Franz goodbye, he would take the tram back to Charlottenburg, retire to his attic room, light the lamp, and sit brooding before his books and his open journal. This journal is a fascinating jumble of book titles, names, and quoted passages; it contains Lehmann's thoughts, yearnings, his remarks about other people, and a number of pitiful banalities. From it we get the vaguest idea of the events in his outer life but a valuable and rather complete insight into the workings of his inner life.

On the flyleaf of the journal are several quotations and formulations which, by virtue of their prominent position and their content, make an excellent introduction to a study of this young man's personality:

> Wenn der Geist nur nicht zu viel Ekel an sich selbst, zu viel Freude an sich selbst empfände.

and

> Mein Lebenslied, falls es ein Lied ist: nicht einmal so schön wie der miauende, schreiende Bussard ist es. Klein erbärmlich, ohne Liebe, ohne innere Musik, ohne *Alles*.

For the moment only the first part of the first passage applies to Lehmann, for he shows almost no sign of self-contentment in the first few months of his journal entries. In this respect the second passage is rather typical of his mood. In the autumn and winter of 1901 he is so full of self-deprecation as to appear on the brink of insanity, so desperate as to be almost suicidal. And yet there are just enough contradictions set down in writing that, ironically, some semblance of balance begins to creep in.

The problem lay in his extraordinary sensitivity, a sensitivity which the adolescent is able to detect and describe rather well in the unduly harsh "Selbstkritik" (as he terms it) in which he engages on 19 November:

> Kann ich es denn allein helfen, daß ich nichts bin sondern nur eine Empfänglichkeit mit zur Welt bekam, die alles was ihr Freude machte—denn auch die Gabe hat sie: zu wissen oder zu fühlen, was schön ist [—] in sich aufnahm, gierig, hastig: alles, alles, bald dieses, bald jenes. Ich habe bis jetzt *nichts* geleistet: gar nichts....denn auf mich, auf mein eigenes Gefühl, auf dem ich bisher gebaut, kann ich mich nicht mehr verlassen: auch es ist ja garnicht mehr mein eigenes.

Here there are not so much two souls within one breast as two distinct entities at odds with one another. His rare sensitivity and receptivity work independently; his "normal" self is incapable of any form of control. Small wonder that, within the year, he was to read Büchner's *Lenz* and find the work

> ...göttlich und genial...es berührt mich seltsam—wie wahr, wie furchtbar, armer, armer Lenz!—beneidenswerter Lenz! Friederike—o Elsaß—nirgends ist Glück und doch möchte ich dort sein in Straßburg, in Tübingen, weit weg, im Sommer zwischen blauen Bergen—im Schwarzwald. Wo bist du, Zeit, wo bist du Glück? Wo? Wo? "Das Glück ist dort, wo du *nicht* bist!"[17]

The quotation at the end of this passage is from Schubert's "Der Wanderer." Schubert was another composer Lehmann was particularly fond of at this time.

A few days before he wrote his November "Selbstkritik" Lehmann had also belittled his "Empfänglichkeit" as he took stock of his qualities:

> Welchen geistigen Besitz nenn ich mein eigen, als höchste Empfänglichkeit, höchstes Gefühl für Poesie und Kunst—was ist aber das? Weltengebären, aber— parturiunt montes nascetur ridiculus mus![18]

The use of the quotation from Horace's *Ars poetica* makes it quite clear how he viewed his passive appreciation of art at this particular moment.

Even before Lehmann arrived in Berlin he was frequently trying to put his thoughts into poetic form. Had he been more successful he might have been happier, but his poetic sensitivity, combined with his uncompromising capacity for self-criticism, continually brought home to him that his poems were eclectic in the worst sense of the word: "nachgefühlt, anempfunden...die Worte anderer."[19] Indeed, he is quite specific and points to the authors and works to which he was indebted in particular instances:

> Das Gedicht: *Ein Abendgang,* das ich kürzlich schrieb, und das ich für gut hielt, für schön sogar, ist nichts als eine verwässerte Nachempfindung der schönen Kirchnerschen Übersetzung von Paul Verlaines überherrlichem Liede: "Ein Waldhorn hör" u.s.f. Ebenso ist das "Gedicht" Herbst nur Reminiscenz an Hermann Conradis wundervollen "Herbstabend."[20]

Despite this sad admission, Lehmann realized that all art has a mimetic character, and this is some consolation to him. He quotes Rosegger: "Alles Dichten ist ja nur Nachahmung: Zuerst ahmt der Dichter den Dichter nach dann die Natur." But even this is scant consolation, for he immediately and rather bleakly adds: "Wann aber werde *ich* überhaupt in *allem* zu Letztem kommen?"[21]

At this stage in his life there is no doubt in Lehmann's mind that he wishes to be a poet. His despair as he reads each new attempt and subjects it to his scathing critical scrutiny steadily mounts. It is not simply that he sees through his eclecticism, however. He also sees that he is still captivated by the beauty of the word *per se,* and that his poems are as yet devoid of any sustaining thought: "Alles, was ich bisher geschrieben, ist Rhetorik—'Schöne' Worte...."[22] He twice seizes on a passage from Hebbel's *Tagebücher,* which he was avidly reading at this time, and uses it as a yardstick for his own poetic character. Hebbel (in 1839) wrote: "Es ist ein großer Unterschied, ob das Wort den Gedanken erzeugt oder der Gedanke das Wort." Lehmann sadly reports that his own "Reimschmiederei" stems from an inability to proceed from the thought to the word, which is what a true poet would automatically do.[23] Much later, in his essays, he was often to reiterate this view: "Von den Dingen zur Sprache, nicht umgekehrt, nicht mallarméisch."[24]

Unfortunately, Lehmann not only sees himself as lacking in true poetic ability; he finds no personal qualities to redress the balance. He frequently uses words like "Wertlosigkeit," "Nichtigkeit," "Schlechtigkeit," and "gar nichts" in summing himself up as a person. "Ich bin müde und kalt und so klein.... Mir fehlt es an glutender Kraft," as he puts it on 20 November, and this feeling of personal worthlessness convinces him that he has no friends, indeed, *can* have none: "Ach—Freunde! Ich habe keine, kann keine haben."[25] He compensates for the lack of friends by cultivating his loneliness, his solitariness; talking of "ein stürmender Wunsch allein zu sein,"[26] and notes a tendency to remain aloof from companions, a tendency not to share experiences with others, like Rudolf Franz, whose company he convinces himself, he hardly tolerates:

> wo zufällig unser Gespräch auf tiefste Probleme kommt, *schweige* ich aus innerem Drang, während er eine [sic] ganz andere verkehrt lächerlich dumme und gänzlich die Sache verkennende Worte machend, dieses *Tiefste* gar nicht einmal sieht.[27]

Such people, he says, "die sogenannten 'Freunde' sind mir nur Ableiter und Ablenker, weiter nichts."[28]

Given such psychological barriers against people in general, it is scarcely surprising that the adolescent Wilhelm suffered agonies in his continual yearnings for love. With regard to Therese Rougement, who really belonged to the past at this stage anyway, he would like "von ihr geliebt werden und allein sein, allein, ganz allein."[29] He repeatedly stresses that he has had no experience of love (although he occasionally contradicts himself): "...die Liebe zu einem Weibe kenne ich nicht. Zweifle, ob sie etwas so Schönes ist und werde wohl niemals lieben."[30] He doubts whether he is even capable of love, and catches himself in the pose of a misogynist: "Ebenso spiele ich mich gerne als Weiberfeind auf: dabei laufe ich den schönen Gesichtern wie Waden nach, wo ich eins sehe. Also auch Heuchelei."[31] Nonetheless he desires love with a deep and pathetic longing, as can be seen from numerous passages concerning Therese ("ich liebe Dich, sei mein, liebe mich wieder"[32]), as well as other more general statements ("Ich möchte wohl lieben, vom ganzen Herzen"[33]). But, as his "relationship" with Eveline amply demonstrated, what is unattainable in Lehmann's real life can easily be transferred into his inner world of phantasy. There are many passages in his journal from this period where he slips into such extravagantly romanticized prose that he ends up in a fairytale-like approximation of what he would wish his reality to be:

> Ich freue mich auf das Zusammensein mit Altenburg [an old school friend] wie auf das Christkindlein; ... aber man muß sich nicht zu viel vorausdenken—Trotzdem ist es mir, als ob wir zwei Hand in Hand miteinander durch ein weites weites schweigendes Land schritten, die Dämmerung sinke in die Tannen, es weht leise— gerade so als ob ein süßes deutsches Mädchen an meine Seite schritte, dessen reines Herz mir gläubig und stürmisch entgegenschlüge. Ich fühle die kleine, zarte weiße Hand: wir wandern, wir wandern, es wird immer dunkler, die Füße immer müder aber immer glücklicher das Herz, die Herzen—einst muß das Ziel erreicht sein— Das klingt pastoralisch, aber warum schreibe ich denn auch das?—Es ist aus wahrer Gesinnung hingeschrieben. Ich möchte, ich möchte wohl zusammen mit jenem

Mädchen mit dem feinen, stillen lächelnden Gesichtchen—Phillip Otto Runges Schriften lesen, seine Arabeskenmalerei durchstöbern und die roten Farben der Sonne und der Gestirne holdselige Pracht bewundern—mit ihr, mit ihr.[34]

There are other passages where Lehmann imagines himself together with an idealized female companion. The virtue of such a companion and the purity of their love always shine through.

To what extent his mother's admonitions as he left home influenced his flights of fancy is impossible to ascertain. It is, however, clear that she continued to play a forceful role during his Berlin period, so that Lehmann was obliged to consider his relationship with his mother again and again. He was still not able to resolve that early diagnosed problem stemming from what he saw as the essential difference between them: their divergent views of life and art. His mother's ties to bourgeois normalcy and his artistic leanings still could not be reconciled to Wilhelm's satisfaction:

Nicht wissen, worüber man mit seiner Mutter sprechen soll. Denn sie würde über das, was ich schreibe mit dem Herzen erschrecken und sich grämen, denn sie kann mich nicht verstehen. Also muß ich Phrasen und leichte und billige Redensarten machen, die mir der Kopf auf Befehl zurechtlegt. Das ist sehr traurig—ist es auch eine Folge von Willens- oder Charakterschwäche oder Schlechtigkeit bei mir?[35]

He was still far from reconciled to his mother's desire that he quickly complete his studies and begin his professional career: "ich zwinge mich zur Arbeit, es geht eine Zeit lang, dann versenke ich mich in müßiges Grübeln und Träumen."[36] Her own bourgeois ideas were so abhorrent to him that he continually and anxiously looked to see whether they were rubbing off on him. He was delighted to find, for example, his own form of "Selbstkritik" was, according to Julius Hart, "ein Zeichen des Nichtphilisters." He was, however, sufficiently fair-minded and suspicious of any smugness that might creep in that he could add the phrase "Ein Nichtphilister zu sein, als ob das schon etwas wäre."[37] Berlin was at this time full of the very businessmen and Philistines that he found so suspect, and they escaped neither his gaze nor his vitriolic pen: "Ich hasse sie doch furchtbar, diese satten Kaufleute und Philister, die die Zeitung lesen und die Börsennachrichten studieren."[38] At this point it is interesting to note just how much more confident and verbally effective Lehmann is when he hates or attacks.

With so little in his life from which to draw comfort and so much that nauseated him, it is hardly surprising that this sensitive, introvert student's thoughts often turned on leaving the life he so heartily despised. It would be an exaggeration to say that he was suicidal, and yet, for someone not yet twenty, he was often preoccupied with the thought of death. Sometimes it was expressed harmlessly enough:

Es ist wohl zu früh zu sterben: die Genies wandeln noch leibhaftig unter uns: ich muß erst sehen, was Hermann Stehr noch schafft. Hugo Wolf möchte ich noch ganz hören und Philipp Mainländer genießen. Auch Emil Strauß lebt und irgendwo auch—Ella Heuberger. Könnte ich sie noch einmal spielen sehen! Auch Hans von Volkmann malt noch, malt so schön wie Eichendorff und Moritz von Schwind.[39]

Such are the writers, painters and musicians who sustain this would-be poet in his Hölderlinesque pose. At other times he is more desperate—even if not yet actually suicidal:

> ich glaube es war Sünde meiner Mutter, mich zu gebären—und ich war ein Stück der geheimnisvollen Natur, nun bin ich losgelöst und sehne mich ewig zu ihr zurück und finde mich nicht mehr.[40]

From this statement it may be seen that the real seat of Wilhelm Lehmann's anguish was none other than the mythic expulsion of man from former paradise. It was soon to become the germ of his Weltanschauung and poetic philosophy.

But Berlin did not prove to be unmitigated misery for Wilhelm Lehmann. He had come here because he had felt attracted to the city of the books, journals, and authors he knew he could find in this metropolis with over 600 bookshops and over 400 periodical publications. It would have been strange had he made absolutely no effort to establish contact with some human being connected with the writings he so venerated. As much as two years earlier, on 30 November 1899 when he was still a Primaner, Wilhelm Lehmann had written a postcard to the Fischer Verlag asking for Moritz Heimann's address. On 6 December 1901, when the Berlin winter weather was most depressingly bleak, he wrote a neatly penned two page letter and included fair copies of five poems. The letter opens thus:

> Demjenigen, der die Betrachtung "Friedrich Hölderlin" geschrieben, (Juni 1899) in Verehrung und Bescheidenheit.
>
> *********
>
> Wenn ein junger Student einem Manne, der jene Betrachtung "Friedrich Hölderlin" gedichtet hat, der einen Hermann Stehr Freund nennt—sich zu nähern wagt, so muß er um Verzeihung bitten für seine Kühnheit. Aber lesen Sie, ich bitte Sie, vorher das Märchen "Der Kobold und der Höcker" von Hans Christian Andersen— vielleicht zürnen Sie mir dann schon darum nicht, weil ich eben ein—Student bin!

Lehmann here identifies with Andersen's student who sits alone in his garret, goes hungry, but devotes himself to the study of poetry. Later he was often to refer to Heimann as a "graues Männlein" and liken him to some benevolent kobold. Heimann, short in stature and with large, protruding ears, was not without a certain resemblance to the little people. In his letter Lehmann goes on to praise Hermann Stehr's genius. In paying particular attention to the opening of *Leonore Griebel*, he quotes the well-known passage from Schelling "Die Natur soll der sichtbare Geist, der Geist die sichtbare Natur...," and expresses his awe at Heimann's Hölderlin essay. The letter ends as follows:

Und gegen diese Worte sende ich Ihnen—zürnen Sie nicht—das Folgende. Ich empfinde es wohl, Schweigen ist das Schönste, unendlich schöner als sprechen—aber einmal lassen Sie mich reden! Und wenn Sie die Herzensgüte besäßen, mir ein ernstes Wort, sei es begütigend, sei es ablehnend, zu erwidern, Sie würden ein fröhliches Herz in jedem Falle machen
      In großer Verehrung und Bewunderung
              Wilhelm Lehmann,
stud. phil.

The five poems Lehmann sent Heimann indicate that those that we can read in his journal are but rough drafts. These polished versions, however, no doubt prepared especially for Heimann, possess exactly those weaknesses Lehmann often alluded to so bluntly in his journal: they are eclectic, they are "Reimschmiederei." The poem "Am Rhein" exemplifies these faults and demonstrates that Lehmann was still writing his poems from generally acquired knowledge rather than from direct and specific experience:

> Schön war die Welt, mir glänzten ihre Blicke,
> In sehnsuchtsvolle Ferne floß der Rhein—
> Aus grünen Höhen drang wie Abendschein
> Ein Waldhorn klagend, selge Melodien tragend;
> Ich spannte weit die Flügel und mich trug der Wind—
> Wie süß er taucht vom Fluß zu mir herein!
> Schon fällt der Thau, es schlummern schon die Reben,
> In sehnsuchtsvolle Weite floß der Rhein—

Lehmann was, of course, deeply immersed in Eichendorff and Brentano at this time, and their influence shines through glaringly.[41] Then we have the alliteration, cheap rhymes, pathetic fallacies, and the weak ending with a repeated line—sixty years later Lehmann was to advise an aspiring young poet that a repeated line was no way to end a poem![42]

Moritz Heimann quickly replied in all brevity, and he did not comment on Lehmann's poetic attempts. He simply suggested that the young student drop by quite informally and see him one evening. So on 19 December Lehmann went across through the slush to the Knesebekstraße just off the Kurfürstendamm and climbed up to the third floor of a Gartenhaus. He was received by a man, a veritable "Menschenfischer" as he himself described Heimann,[43] who was at least as curious to meet this strange fish of a student as Lehmann was to ascertain the identity of the man behind the Hölderlin essay. They immediately launched into a conversation touching not only upon Hölderlin and Stehr but on just about every other author currently in the news. For the first time in his life Lehmann was conversing with someone who had read and knew intimately all the works and authors he knew. For the first time in his life there was a sustained dialogue which pulsed with ideas and insights. Heimann, moreover, did not just know the works; he knew the writers themselves and was Emil Strauß's and Max Marschalk's brother-in-law.[44] He did not just work for Samuel Fischer, he was on visiting terms with him; he knew Gerhart Hauptmann, Hermann Stehr, Oscar Bie and Alfred Kerr—all writers whose names and work were familiar to Lehmann even while he was still at school. Present at this first meeting was Efraim Frisch, the writer, reader and, later, editor of the *Neue Merkur*.[45] Heimann, in short, knew just about everyone who counted in the literary world.

A few hours in the Heimann house opened up a whole new range of human relationships for Wilhelm Lehmann. These people shared his interests and showed none of the pettiness and narrow-minded bigotry of, for example, his mother and her friends, of his teachers, or of those ubiquitous Philistines clutching the *Börsenblatt* in their pudgy fingers as they swarmed full of self-importance all over Berlin. At last, in Gertrud Heimann, he met a woman who looked upon him in kindly fashion and neither ignored him nor laughed at him. Gertrud Heimann proved that not all women were like his mother; she could convincingly dismiss slight inconveniences as if they really did not matter. The way she said "Macht nix," for example, when Lehmann returned to pick up a magazine he had left behind at this first meeting showed a friendly understanding which he had never met in his mother's circle.[46] Could things be so uncomplicated? It really seemed so. Gertrud Heimann apparently found intense young men brimming over with enthusiasm for literature perfectly normal. Lehmann recorded his joy in all brevity, but nonetheless evocatively: "Moritz Heimann kennengelernt: Wundervoll!—Seine Frau!"[47]

Immediately following this occasion both Lehmann and Heimann wrote letters indicating that this first meeting was mutually regarded as a success. Heimann had helped Lehmann in his fight "mit unsichtbaren Geistern..., die mich und meine Gefühle (Tautologie) zu verspotten scheinen."[48] Heimann sent a postcard suggesting a second meeting the following day. This duly took place, and Heimann wrote again to say that there was obviously a bond of mutual sympathy between them and suggested that Lehmann come and visit him as often as he pleases. Thus began a friendship which was crucial for Lehmann's development as man and poet and which ended only with Heimann's death in 1925. Lehmann was to attempt to repay the debt owed to Heimann with several articles and editions of Heimann's essays over the years.[49] He was virtually the only person to seek to keep the memory of this remarkable man alive.

Lehmann's return to Wandsbek for the Christmas vacation served to throw into sharp relief how different these two worlds were. Lehmann also continued to think about many of the ideas brought up in the earlier conversations. Back in Charlottenburg again after the holiday, he wrote a lengthy letter to Heimann, appending in the neatest of hands a few bars of Schubert's Piano Sonata 10, in B Major with the words:

—Und so
Im uferlosen All versinkt mein Geist,
Und süß ist mir's in diesem Meer zu scheitern.—

The letter begins

Verehrter Herr Heimann!
Da Sie mir so gütig und vertrauend schreiben, und 'von innigsten Plänen' sprechen, lassen Sie mich reden, wie ich denke.

Wenn man sich an einem Herbstnachmittage, wenn es schon recht kalt ist und fast kein Blatt mehr am Baum, in einsame Wege hineinverliert, an deren Rändern noch an rötlichen Stielen die Brombeerblätter sitzen, blutrot zur Hälfte und goldgelb vorn und hinten in ein grau betüpfeltes Schwarzblau auslaufend, daß es aussieht, als ob ein grausames Geschick einen Schmetterling totgespießt hätte, darob der Wind seufzend über die Hecken geht —dann entschleiert sich mir des Lebens tiefster Sinn.

Und wenn man sich in den verlassenen Wald hinein verirrt, wo alles feucht und naß und grau ist, und sich auf einen vermoderten Baumstumpf setzt, aus dem das Holz gelb-schimmelnd herausguckt, die Gräser jenseits des dampfenden braunen Ackers wehen im Winde hin und her und die Dorfgänse schnattern—dann ist das Leben wirklich, nicht bloß in holdester Gestalt etwa, sondern das Leben überhaupt: in trunkenen Rythmen [sic] jauchzt es vorbei und zündet die heiligste Glut an.[50]

Lehmann is at last able to express such thoughts to someone without any fear of ridicule. What he has previously somewhat hesitantly confided only to his journal can now be stated openly and with self-assurance. This passage shows that Lehmann is already at nineteen years of age able to make the greatest sense of existence when he is wandering alone in nature. It shows that his powers of observation are fully developed and that his capacity for minute and exact description is well-advanced. The scenes here described are innately poetic for Lehmann and, as such, deeply inspiring. All that remains is for him to develop two further skills: one is his capacity for mythologizing a landscape, for breathing the life of anthropomorphic culture into the natural—his ability to civilize nature; the other is his ability to take only the essence of the image and to depict it in concentrated form. Of the former quality there is more than just a hint in this very letter. Lehmann picks up a remark of Heimann's from their very first meeting to the effect that his own Hölderlin essay was merely "Gerede" and disputes it:

Sie sagten mir, ich dürfe nicht vergessen, daß der Inhalt Ihrer Aufsätze doch bloß 'Gerede' wäre und nicht 'die holde Kraft, aus der das Leben springt.' Aber ich glaube, wenn Sie über diesen Unterschied einmal etwas schrieben, Sie würden ihn noch ganz anders fassen und begründen, ihn jedenfalls nicht so ausdrücken.—Als ich Ihren Hölderlin-Aufsatz gelesen, dachte ich, hier sei, weil aus stürmischem Herzen geboren, höchste Stille, reine Feierlichkeit und tiefinnerlichster Ernst. Aber das war nicht genug. Vielmehr so: nicht etwa so, als ob ich in pfadloser Finsternis umhertaumelnd, plötzlich auf eine sommerlich glänzende Wiese gelangte, die klar und ruhig athmend daliegt, die Wege gehauen, die Hecken im Wuchern gemäßigt, und man nun mit einem Frohgefühl sondergleichen wie in einen sonnigen Herbsttag hinein durch sie hindurch schreiten könnte—nein, es war vielmehr wie endloses weites Rauschen unabsehbarer grüner Wipfel in ungestörter Stille, nur in Lüften jenes Sommerconcert der unablässig schwirrenden Insekten, indessen in den leise zitternden Buchenblättern blaue Glockenblumen stehen, Schmetterlinge fliegen hin und her, und Käfer hasten von überwachsenem Grund zum Stein. Dort, in tiefster Einsamkeit, sitzt Moritz von Schwind und malt am Melusinencyklus—dort teilen sich die Büsche, der Bach rauscht lauter, die Amsel pfeift—Friedrich Hölderlin tritt mit glänzenden braunen Augen hervor —zum Greifen nah, und man fühlt keine Scheu, ihm die Hand zu reichen—

> Da ich noch um deinen Schleier spielte,
> Noch an dir wie eine Blüte hing
> Noch dein Herz in jedem Laute fühlte,
> Du mein zärtlich bebend Herz umfing

In feierlich grüne Stille das Bild einer heiligen Seele so hinein zu zaubern, so quellend, so innig, so tief—ist es wohl etwas Kleines? Wer kann das so schön wie *Sie?*

This is a remarkable way for someone so young to sum up Heimann's Hölderlin essay (the way he coolly places Schwind and Hölderlin in the natural scene), and it points to the future poet's propensity for finding cultural correlatives in nature. Given the minute vignette of beetles, butterflies and bluebells, all observed with such surrender and intensity, and at such close proximity, it is particularly apt that Heimann presented Lehmann with a volume of Goethe's *Werther* when the latter left Berlin some six months later.

The letter ends with Lehmann's fervent repetition of the beneficial effects of the atmosphere of the Heimann house and all who move therein. Having already met Efraim Frisch on his first visit, Wilhelm Lehmann was soon meeting many of the friends and acquaintances who congregated around Moritz Heimann, "das Gewissen der deutschen Literatur" as Gerhart Hauptmann so aptly called him.[51] Of particular importance to Wilhelm Lehmann at this time were Hermann Stehr and Heimann's brother-in-law Max Marschalk. The latter instilled in Lehmann a little self-confidence and made the young student feel more at ease with the world, his newly won friends, and himself. The former, just beginning to make a reputation with books such as *Der Schindelmacher* and *Leonore Griebel,* not only provided the young Lehmann with a first-hand acquaintance with a living writer (very important to this shy, aspiring poet), but also with some provocative conversation concerning the function and character of the written word.

Lehmann had always been fascinated by words. His interest in philology, awakened by Zupitza, grew out of this fascination. His first poems, as we have seen, stemmed from words rather than thoughts or objects. Periodically throughout his Berlin journal there are isolated statements which indicate that he was still pre-occupied with the essence of the word: "Sinnlichkeit ist gleich Poesie—aber das sind Worte, nichts als dürre Worte, 'umnebelnd Hundsglut'"[52] and "Es ist ja unmöglich, daß ein Geist den anderen versteht! Was denkt sich wohl der andere unter 'hübsch,' da ich selbst nicht weiß, was ich unter 'hübsch' denke!"[53] The more he thought about the subject, the more perplexingly obvious it became that there were no absolutes:

> Es ist sehr wahrscheinlich, daß alles, was ich hier schreibe, *Un*sinn ist, gewiß. Wie unwahrscheinlich ist alles, was man sagt. Was sagt man eigentlich, kann man überhaupt etwas *sagen?* Was ist 'sagen'?[54]

Some three days after he wrote this, Lehmann received a postcard from Heimann telling him that he had tickets for a Hubermann concert, but that it was conceivable that he, Heimann, might not be able to go. In this case he would give his ticket to Frisch. But later the same day he sent a second postcard suggesting that Lehmann might prefer to give his own ticket to someone else and visit Heimann—if he wanted to meet Hermann Stehr! Bronislav Hubermann or Hermann Stehr! Today one might opt for Hubermann, but Lehmann found it easy enough to settle for Stehr, having admired this novelist almost beyond all others for the past two years or so.

The experience was a strange one. Immediately following the meeting Lehmann wrote the following note in his journal:

> das *Genie* Hermann Stehr: daß er real da [?] ist, hat mich nicht so entgeistert, wie ich dachte. Er war ja schon *in* mir, ohne daß ich ihn leibhafts sah.[55]

There was no disappointment, however, as countless subsequent allusions to Stehr indicate:

> Hermann Stehr—die urgeborenen Genie Worte versagen—steht da und glüht mit seinen Augen und streut seine genialen Himmel und Hölle umfassenden Gedanken umher.[56]

and

> Mit Stehr, diesem Titanengenie—viel mehr ist, viel gewaltiger ist als Goethe; nur mit Shakespeare—der mehr Fülle hat als er noch—kann man natürlich nicht lange zusammenleben.[57]

They talked about everything imaginable, but the topic of words and things kept creeping in, and since Stehr at this time was still a schoolteacher, he often referred to the attitude of children to things and words as they grew up:

> Die meisten Menschen lesen d.h. verstehen den mechanischen Sinn der Worte, der ganzen Sätze: aber die Vorstellungen bluten ihnen nicht. Das kommt, weil man als Kind gezwungen wird, in einem Jahre 100 neue [?] Zeichen zu lernen aber nicht die

Vorstellungen damit. Man müßte als Lehrer die Worte immer vornehmen, die dem Kinde selbst kommen, woran das Blut der Vorstellung klebt! Lehrt man sie "Eine Burg steht auf dem Berge"—ja sie lernen es; oft aber haben sie bei dem Worte "Pferd" nicht die Vorstellung.

So mit allem. Die Menschen verknüpfen sich mechanisch mit Schriftzeichen Vorstellungen: setzen sie sich hin, Blut strömt nicht auf das Blatt.

Diese ungeheure Scheidung zwischen dem Leib und dem Wort ist es: der Dichter hebt beides sich auf, da geht ein elektrischer Strom durch den Arm hindurch auf das Papier: das ist der Dichter.

Die meisten Menschen sprechen auch so: nur mechanische Laute. Ich habe Mißtrauen gegen flüssige Redner. Ein Stammler giebt mir ja fast garnichts; aber was er giebt, ist sein Blut.[58]

It is striking that Lehmann, who usually reported conversation in very fragmented fashion, here sets everything down in rather full and clear sentences. It was obviously a topic of such importance that Stehr's words remained long enough in his mind for him to re-formulate everything in the privacy and quiet of his mansarde room. The ideas expressed in the above passage continued to occupy Lehmann for the rest of his life. As was usual whenever he found striking ideas in other people's writings or statements, he applied them to himself. And, as was usual, he found himself wanting and squeezed into the margin a sentence to this effect: "Ich bin nicht immer so geistig, so lebendig, daß meine Worte immer [?] von Vorstellungen begleitet sind." From "Worte" and their "Vorstellungen," the conversation turned on general aesthetics and the nature of "Schönheit." Lehmann's notes continue:

Schönheit ist im tiefsten Sinne *Nützlichkeit*. Denn daß der Baum so Knospen ansetzt—nur der Schöpfer weiß warum so—ist für den Baum das Nützlichste. Seine Schönheit ist seine *Lebensnotwendigkeit*.

All Stehr's ideas as formulated by Lehmann and quoted above have a familiar ring to them. They are expressed in one form or another in many of Lehmann's later essays. The most striking example concerns the "Lebensnotwendigkeit" of a plant. The important essay "Bewegliche Ordnung" (1948), although most obviously indebted to Goethe and his two poems "Die Metamorphose der Pflanzen" and "Metamorphose der Tiere," is also indebted to this Stehr-Lehmann meeting. In his essay Lehmann writes of the wild anemone: "Ihre Schönheit ist ihre Notwendigkeit."[59] The reported conversations with Stehr are full of similar examples: "Worte sind ja Abkürzungen..." and "Es ist die Wissenschaft der Tod der Poesie." The tension between the thing and its word abbreviation and the poet's concern with the same crop up in many of Lehmann's essays, while Lehmann brings the latter idea to its best expression by quoting the revered Blake: "The tigers of wrath are wiser than the horses of instruction."[60] With regard to the relationship of "Wissenschaft" to poetry, Lehmann's horror may well be imagined as he sought to find some kind of interest in

"Wissenschaft" to hear that it killed his one great love, poetry. But Stehr had some encouraging words for Lehmann in this instance, too:

> Stehr sagt ja—o tröste dich—eine Seele, die eine Seele—denn in sie kann nichts hinein, was nicht in ihr ist—ist, kann *nie* untergehen: ich glaube, sie wirft dann, wenn ich 4 Jahre lang Phonetik und Grammatik eingepaukt [?] habe, alles ab und ist sie selbst!!
> freue dich![61]

Stehr, this "Titanengenie," was an overpowering personality so that, despite all the stimulation, comfort, and sense of importance that he often gave Lehmann, the young student was just as often overawed and left feeling decidely inferior. Moritz Heimann's uncompromising cerebral approach to matters also often irritated or crushed the insecure young man, and it was accordingly left to the genial Max Marschalk to restore the balance somewhat. Marschalk understood the problem. He, too, suffered from the "unausgesetzte geistige Arbeit Heimanns, ewig drängend und denkend," and said as much to Lehmann.[62] Marschalk was, as Lehmann put it, a "Blüte des reinen schönen Menschenthums," the "Froheste göttlich unbefangene Naivität."[63] He was "einfach schalkhaft und offen und vertraut,"[64] and very kind and helpful to Lehmann. They would go to concerts, walk home together, and chat unrestrainedly about everything and everybody—for Marschalk was a bit of a gossip. Lehmann would be invited back to the Marschalks in Halensee to drink grog and warm himself by the tiled stove before going back to his simple garret. It was Marschalk who later encouraged Lehmann to go to Agnetendorf and visit his brother-in-law Gerhart Hauptmann, Marschalk who would willingly sit down at the piano and play his latest compositions (such as his songs from Hauptmann's *Hannele*) for the admiring student, and Marschalk who trustingly confided his marital difficulties to him.

There were others whom Lehmann met through the Heimanns. Jakob Wasserman, for example, was an occasional visitor, and Lehmann was struck by his remark concerning dreams and dreamers—a frequent topic in the Heimann circle (Freud's *Traumdeutung* appeared in 1900): "J. Wassermann hat *sicher* Recht: die Träumenden sind die wahren Wachen...."[65] The dreamer is a character who reappears continually in Lehmann's fiction, while the dream condition is one which later enables the poet to attain that state of intimate communion with nature from which the poem springs.

Meanwhile the conversation often touched on Emil Strauß, the author of *Freund Hein,* a work which Lehmann particularly admired. Like other contemporary authors such as Thomas Mann and Hermann Hesse, Strauß was much concerned with the state of German schools at the time. His novel depicts the sufferings of a sensitive schoolboy in the rigid and repressive German Gymnasium. Hein is unable to cope with mathematics and is brought to such a state that he kills himself. Just how sympathetic to such a hero Lehmann was, after almost having failed his Abitur because of his own weakness in this very same subject, may readily be appreciated. Lehmann was also particularly impressed when Heimann told him that Strauß would get up early, look to his apricots in his garden, record the weather conditions in his journal, and observe the birds through his field-glasses. He was to develop similar habits himself as he became more settled.

Partly, no doubt, because of Simmel's lectures and partly because of general interest, the conversation often turned on philosophical subjects. Much of Lehmann's reading was necessarily in philosophy at the time, and his journal records his pre-occupations and thoughts as the semester and the weeks passed. Sometimes it seems as if Lehmann, as he railed against the limitations of "Verstand" ("Mozart hatte keinen"[66]), passed from Kant through Fichte ("Nichts kann vom Anderen kommen, *alles* nur vom ich"[67]) to a hesitant grappling with Hegel, who was now, partly through Dilthey, enjoying a renaissance at Berlin:

> Wenn Hegel sagt, jedes Ja gebiert sein Nein, jeder Begriff, jeder Inhalt seinen *Gegensatz:* Was heißt dann Gegensatz, ist es dasselbe wie Gegenteil? ... [68]

Certainly some aspects of Hegel's thought, in which "Geist" replaces "Verstand" and enables a progression beyond mere reason, appealed to Lehmann. The Hegelian dialectic began to suggest intriguing solutions to those hitherto warring opposites of "Natur" and "Geist," realism and idealism, the object and its designation, the "All" and the "Nichts." At the same time it connected nicely with the aesthetic of *leicht-schwer* which Simmel had so tantalizingly presented to the student.

By the end of February, then, the diffident letter written to Heimann just before Christmas had yielded so much fruit that Lehmann, faced with the prospect of Easter in Wandsbek and another change of university, seriously began to consider staying in Berlin for the summer semester so that he could continue to meet these fascinating people. Frightened to ask Moritz Heimann for advice, he confided in Max Marschalk, who encouraged, indeed convinced him to return to Berlin for the summer. Immediately a good deal of his dread over the Easter vacation in Wandsbek disappeared: "Was für Ferien werden das sein, *diese* Ostern! Immer mit dem seligen Gedanken zu *diesen* Menschen zurückzukehren nach der Frist. Wie Sonne das Bittere durchleuchtend."[69] As he saw how his mood fluctuated so violently between the extremes of happiness with the Heimann circle and despair at home, he began to apply the Hegelian dialectic to his own personal outlook on life. Thus it is possible to find passages, like the following one, where the mood oscillates markedly:

> Nun bin ich so warm von Euch empfangen—an Eurer hellen warmen Flamme o wie wärm' ich mich! Habt Dank, habt Dank—vorher ging ich zweifelnd im Zimmer herum und war der Raub meiner Gedanken—laßt mich los, liebende Kreise, laßt

mich los und laßt mich wieder frieren in den öden—wenn es im Herbst Abend wird, der Wald dunkel und kalt wird—Räumen meiner Herzensheimath und laßt mich den Winden, die über den fahlen Acker säuseln, der einem fernen Lenze entgegen die Schollen hält—ein Staub sein und meine Blicke wieder in hoffnungslose Ferne schweifen!

o du Mensch, du Mensch—wo werd ich sein in den nächsten Tagen, in der dämmernden kleinen Stadt und ich werde warten, worauf, worauf? Die Zeit geht und nichts blüht primelgleich aus Tiefen heraus und ich bin trostlos, trostlos; was hilft es mir, daß Menschen mich freundlich aufnehmen? Wie grausam rächt sich *alles,* alles an mir. Und den Flug meiner Gedanken tötet vorahnende Kälte und die Frühlingswinde, die großen wahren ruhigen Feierlichen, hauchen dereinst nur an meinen Sarg.

Winde wehen und Wolken wandern
Nachmittags geh ich zur Heide hinaus
Dämmernd krochen die Hügel, die Sonne noch leuchtet.
Und im Abendregen liegt zweifelnd der Wald
Kalt ist die Wange mir, schaudernd horcht mein Ohr
Und aus vermoderndem Laube dröhnt mir ein Leichenchor
Wo ist das Veilchenlicht denn der Wonne
Wo der Garten mit schimmerndem Wein
Über das Filtern [?] weint blaß die Georgine und die Winde ziehen höhnend herein
Triumpf [sic]. *Trotz alledem.*[70]

Here Lehmann's bliss paradoxically causes him to desire the sorrow of solitary exclusion. From such melancholy his thoughts may dialectically formulate a rescue in the form of art—hence the poetically expressed and unpunctuated final section. Having produced something out of nothing, a poem out of barren alienation, Lehmann's twice-underlined "Triumpf. Trotz alledem" is totally justified.

Despite his relief now that the decision to return to Berlin for the summer semester had been made, Lehmann was still aware of the real problems lying ahead. How was he to explain his decision to his mother, whose impatience and frustration at her son's lack of progress were steadily growing? Full of foreboding he set off for Wandsbek where the mood was indeed somber. His diary, after the excited and passionate utterances of the past few weeks, takes on a tone of resigned melancholy during his time in Wandsbek:

Lauwarm erscheint mir hier und in diesem Augenblick das Gleitende um mich und ich lebe so und lebe nicht und ich mag nicht schreiben. Ich gedenke eurer, ihr Gastfreunde und warte sehnend auf deinen Brief Moritz Heimann und auf die Worte, die du *mir* senden wirst.

Und nun ist es schon halb Frühling. Doch lebe ich hier halb und ich muß meine Seele erst auf weiten Wegen nach Primelwiesen bei Ahrensburg und in düsterer melancholischer Binsen- und Heideeinsamkeit weit hinten bei Kiebitzschrei hinter den Dörfern an einsamen Wegen wiederfinden....

und ich möchte leben nur um noch Worte von Moritz Heimann zu hören und noch einmal von einem reinen schönen verliebten Mädchen mild geküsst zu werden—und sonst möchte ich tot sein und die Leere meiner Seele vernichten durch Tod in der Stille morgens 4 Uhr an einem Wald oder auf einer jungen Wiese....

Und ich schaudere kaum in dem Dunkel des Kirchhofes, denke an das Rauschen des grünen Kleids der Todesstille im schwäbischen zitternden schwülen Walde, versuche ein süßes todesaufregendes Lied zu hören und ich versinke, versinke—und

Angst habe ich zuweilen vor dem Nichts, Angst nicht, nichts, nichts—und dunkel und gleichgültig ist alles und meine Seele verebbt in ihrer armseligen Leere. Wäre ich tot! und nicht mehr hier, wäre nirgends, nirgends.[71]

Here in Wandsbek, with the family who meant so little to him at this stage, he had a series of vivid dreams. The hated teachers from the Matthias Claudius Gymnasium figure prominently: a mathematics test is returned with masses of comments in red, including "Schillerpreis" sarcastically scrawled across the bottom! Almost sixty years later Wilhelm Lehmann was indeed to receive the *Schillerpreis,* but for work of a different kind. But his dreams were not all of a frightening nature: Heinrich Lehmann appeared in one dream and talked in friendly and reassuring fashion to Lehmann; and then there is the Hölderlin dream:

Heute—Frühlingsanfang—träumte mir ich sähe ein neues mir ganz unbekanntes Hölderlin-Bild: ein gezeichnetes großes von dunklen Locken umgebenes Haupt, schön und feierlich (etwas Ähnlichkeit mit Rubenstein) nach deren Blick und Augen mir seine Dichtung kühn und rein menschlich viel vertrauter erschien und erscheint. Wo ich dies niederschreibe, sehe ich den scharfen, reichen, dunklen, schauenden schwermütigen Kopf und Blick noch.[72]

Somehow the leap from Hölderlin to the temporarily absent and much-missed Heimann is an easy one. It was one which Lehmann himself made, for he added the sentence "ob es ein Vorzeichen war, daß ich heute morgen von Moritz Heimann einen Brief erhalten werde?"

The contrast between life in Berlin with his artist friends and his home life with the pettiness of his mother and her world comes out most strongly in a letter Lehmann wrote to Heimann on 16 March:

An Moritz Heimann.
Wie sich alles so seltsam spiegelt, alles sich kreuzt und ich davor, unbewußt einem Ungeordneten gegenüber, das mich trifft, mich bestürmt, mich hochemporträgt, mich zu Boden senkt, mich fragt. Die unsichtbaren Mächte, die uns so dahintragen, rätselhaft und verschwiegen, bald kalt, bald warm! Und des Nachts wacht man auf und möchte den tiefrauschenden silberklaren, das ahnt man, und doch so verworrenen Quellen des Lebens lauschen—aber so selten höre ich sie, so selten, wie heiß man auch fleht: 'Deute Muse, mir die Nachtgeräusche, Die ans Ohr des Schlummerlosen fluten!'—In diesen öden Gassen, an deren Ecken ewig der Wind weht, ist es entsetzlich kalt und schwer. Wenn die Dämmerung kommt, ist es tot und verzweiflungsvoll, hier zu leben. In den Häusern zünden die Leute Licht an und ein

heimlicher Strahl fällt in das Dunkel. Dann kann ich den Hut ins Gesicht ziehen und freue mich, daß ich die mir Begegnenden nicht zu grüßen brauche. Aber am Tage, da ziehe ich höflich den Hut: all diese anständigen , so sehr anständigen Leute, die so 'fromm', so ordentlich sind; die Lehrer, die so große Hoffnungen auf den Abgehenden setzen, sich so jovial nach dem Gang der Studien erkundigen, so freundlich sind, daß ich oft den wilden Wunsch hege, *nichts* zu 'werden', diesen Schurken und Ehrbaren und Geachteten, die so talentlos sind, daß sie nicht das Talent haben, 'nichts' zu 'werden'; ich möchte mir wohl einmal eine Kugel durch den Kopf schießen und am Morgen, wenn sie aufstehen, quer über dem wohlgepflegten Gartenbeet bei der Pforte liegen, daß sie den Appetit für einen Tag verlieren, sie, die denjenigen, der um *eines* schönen Liedes willen dem Leben mit frohem Lachen Valet sagt, unfehlbar ins Irrenhaus sperren würden.—Die Äquinoktial-Stürme sausen um das Haus, es regnet und der Wind weht den Regen schräg seitwärts, ich möchte mit lautem Schrei losbrechen und hinausstürmen in die ewig reizende Ferne: 'Doch die Katheder im Gebirge nah, Der Meister unsichtbar, doch laut Hurrah Ihm Wälder Strom und Sturmsflügel rauschen, Matrikel ist des Herzens frischer Schlag, Da will zeitlebens ich bei Nacht und Tag, Demütiger Schüler seinen Worten lauschen!'—Augenblicklich ist es ganz still um mich herum, nur der Stieglitz und das Canarienweibchen, die mein Bruder, der künftige Theologe, zusammengethan, zwitschern leise. Kommt es mir dann vor, als ob die Luft wie ein bunter Sommervogel die Flügel wohlig zusammenlegt, als ob alles gut und herrlich sei—geht dann die Thür und meine Mutter tritt herein, so fällt mein Gedanke wie eine tote Schwalbe zu Boden. Und nachher sitzen wir dann zusammen und rühmen unser behagliches, feines und friedliches Heim, das jeder leiden mag, für das sich jeder interessiert. Weil es so garnicht schlimm scheint und gerade weil ich mir zuweilen selbst einrede, es sei garnicht schlimm—gerade deshalb ist es so bitterlich schlimm.

Dann gehe ich wohl hinaus, ruhige Wege suche ich auf, an deren Rändern im Sommer die weißen Camillen üppig blühen, von den Hummeln umschwärmt, draußen an den großen Gärten vorüber, die im Juni wahre Rosenbetten sind, in denen die warmen Nächte zu ruhen, das schönste Mädchen sich nicht scheuen würde—jetzt ist alles grau und kalt, die Stakete sind schwarz und naß und gramvoll heult der Wind über alles hin. Dort zwischen schwarzem Geäst taucht das rote Schindeldach des 'Pächterhofes' auf, des Hauses, wo meine schöne, schöne Knabenzeit ruht, die nur zu bald ihre unbekümmerten Märchenaugen geschlossen hat. Gerade dann, wenn ich bei Ihnen gewesen bin, fällt es mir schwer aufs Herz, wie heimatlos ich bin, wie heimatlos. Ich darf Ihnen schon jetzt schreiben, weil es jetzt noch ein ruhiges Plätzchen im Hause giebt: in der nächsten Woche müssen wir fort aus Wandsbek, wo wir zwölf Jahre gewohnt und wie eine selige Fügung kommt es mir vor, daß ich in der Zeit, nach der ich zum letzten Male hier her zurückkehre, Ihre Hand gefunden. Seien Sie so gütig, wie Sie immer sind und zürnen nicht, daß ich Ihnen all dies belanglose Zeug schreibe. Und sollte ich jemals ein Wort sagen, das Ihnen zu nahe tritt, so bin ich mir bewußt, daß ich doch nur ein Eindringling bin, dann lassen sie mich sein wie das Klingeln der Bahn, das Ihnen ein Bach-Motiv bringt oder lassen Sie mich wie das Summen in den Telegraphenstangen, an die Sie auf Spaziergängen das Ohr beugen, Fröhliches und Gutes in Ihren Gedanken hervorrufen und nichts Bitteres und Trübes; denn nichts mehr bin ich als ein

Athemzug, gehaucht auf den Spiegel Ihres Lebens, ein Käfer, der in der Dämmerung unbequem gegen Ihre Wange prallt—Haben Sie Dank dafür, daß Sie mir erlaubt, über Ihre selige Schwelle zu treten, daß Sie mit mir sprechen. Wenn ich bei Ihnen sitze und Ihre gütige (dies Wort, im tiefsten Grunde sei's gedacht) Gattin mich freundlich-verwundert ansieht, habe ich das Gefühl, als ob sie sagte: 'Es ist alles nicht so hart und rauh, fühlt nur den Duft des Lebens!' Ich höre dann nicht mehr das Lärmen der Nachtvögel und das wütende Gebell der Dorfhunde stirbt in der Ferne, der nasse Rock trocknet am Herdfeuer und aus der Mitte ziehender Regenwolken fällt Mondlicht durch's Fenster

> Von dem lang vernommenen Axthieb
> Schwingt ein nachgeborenes Echo
> In des Feiernden Ohr
> Schwächer und schwindet.
> Der vergangenen Pein
> Denkt er mit stolzem Befremden,
> Und aus reinerem Herzen
> Schweben seine Gefühle
> Willig empor wie Rauch
> Vom gefälligen Opfer.

Confirmationsbesuche werden gemacht, man schüttelt die Hand und wünscht Glück—was für eine Kluft! So sehr, daß ich mich vor mir selbst schäme, wenn ich einmal weil sie stets gähnt, wähne sie sei nicht da und mit breitem Lachen drüber will.—Gerade jetzt fällt ein karger Strahl der Märzsonne auf die ergrünenden Fluren durch einen Wolkenspalt—wie ein Gedenken an Sie ist es, wie alle Last (Last?) des Lebens. 'Und jeder Widerstreit des Lebens und alle Zweifel sind versöhnt' ich vergesse, daß es das Los der meisten ist, sich ewig im öden Nichts herumzutummeln. Mir klingen im Ohre Ihre Worte, 'Auf gutes Wiedersehen!' und ich freue mich unmäßig auf den kommenden Sommer; ich wollte Ihnen so gern nur noch von hier, aus der Matthias-Claudius-Stadt schreiben, und bitte Sie, dies alles für nicht mehr als einen bewegten Gruß zu nehmen.

In der größten Verehrung
Ihr
Wilhelm Lehmann

Wandsbek, d. 16 März 1902

This letter effectively demonstrates what paradise Lehmann's childhood in the Pächterhof had been, what Heimann and his circle meant for him, the degree of frustration the stolid middle-class citizens of Wilhelmine Germany occasioned in him, and how intolerable he found his mother and life at home. The apparent readiness for death expressed so dramatically in the letter was not an isolated instance and indicates that Lehmann, despite the newly found happiness in the Heimann circle, was by no means a totally changed man. His contact with "genius," for want of a better word, served only to heighten his despair at his own worthlessness in moments of ill-humor. At such moments the most obvious solution to the problem was death. Whenever he was feeling particularly low because of this sense of inadequacy, because of the world of mediocrity he seemed unable to escape, or because he seemed destined never to find love, we come across such phrases as "Wäre ich nur tot." The encounter with Heimann gave him a degree of self-assurance, encouraged him in his hesitant gropings towards art, and helped him to focus his thoughts in a more disciplined fashion than hitherto. All this was of untold value in his development, but the old problems would not go away, and they continued to trouble him.

On 8 April, Lehmann returned to Berlin for the summer semester. Once back among his friends, once escaped from the choking strictures of his mother, he relaxed considerably. On 10 April, in glorious warm sunshine, he went on a little outing with Heimann. They took the Stadtbahn to Potsdam and wandered around the palace and grounds of Sanssouci:

> Herrlicher Tag, blauer Himmel, dicke Kastanienknospen, weiße Statuen: was hat Heimann mir nicht alles gesagt, Wundervolles, Unsagbares, Großes und Entzückendes.[73]

Two days later they went to a concert given by a men's choir; the music, its rendering, and the somewhat unsophisticated audience left Lehmann almost speechless "Welch Publikum—welch Concert!"[74] But in the company of Heimann and, probably, Marschalk he was able to take such matters in his stride, finding them amusing even; a few months earlier bitter scorn would have spiced his commentary.

About this time Max Marschalk came up with the idea that Lehmann should visit Gerhart Hauptmann. The very thought of it filled him with both excitement and doubt. His subconscious reacted accordingly, and on 18-19 May he dreamed of visiting "Grete Hauptmann. Ich war zu Besuch bei ihr. Aber sie war Emil Straußens Frau, Veranda, Lachen erregtes Sprechen."[75] At the same time, he worried about Moritz Heimann's reaction to Marschalk's suggestion, such was his desire to find approval in his master's eyes. Whatever the reaction may have been, the visit to the Wiesenstein in Agnetendorf duly took place in June. Lehmann was familiar with the outside appearance of this remarkable domicile, having received a picture postcard of the place from Heimann three months earlier. Despite his genuine desire to meet Hauptmann, whose work he had long admired, the visit was less than successful. The palatial Wiesenstein overawed him, as did the imperial presence of its master—although, to be fair to Hauptmann, he did engage the young visitor in conversation and did give him some encouragement. Unlike her sister Gertrud, Margarete Hauptmann did not take him seriously—she judged by appearances, and Lehmann looked decidedly out of place in the elegant surroundings, for his shabby old brown suit was now a size too small for him. The other lady present, the "Schöne Frau des Berliner Archäologen Kekule von Stradonitz,"[76] also made no effort to get to know him, but Lehmann at this time generally fought shy of beautiful women, such was his insecurity still. The painter Ludwig von Hoffman more or less ignored him and devoted himself to the ladies (Anne Kekule von Stradonitz was his mother-in-law), but he had brought along the English painter William Rothenstein, and Lehmann, making good use of his as yet still limited command of English, spent most of the time speaking to him. It was the first time Lehmann ever had the opportunity to hear someone talk about contemporary English literature. Rothenstein dismissed Florence Montgomery's *Misunderstood* as so much sentimental trash—not without some justification.[77] The encounter with Rothenstein proved to be a useful one, as we shall see.

Once again the experience played upon Lehmann's sensitivities, and on 17-18 June he dreamed of

> eine laute Gesellschaft, eine Frau wollte Ludwig von Hoffman, weil er "nackt" oder ähnliches gesagt, zu Bett bringen...Nachher war der widerliche Herr Franz da, der Klavier spielen wollte und spielte. Ich haßte ihn, beschimpfte ihn und sein klägliches Spiel und Affektieren. Nachher aber schien sich alles leider in gutes Vernehmen (weil er eigenthümlich ruhig blieb) aufzulösen.[78]

Once again the fears of open sensuality driven into him by his mother and his equally inhibiting school experience combine and surface in a dream.

Four nights later there was another dream, but this time Lehmann failed to note the details before they faded. It is a pity, for this dream seems to have all the potential of some psychedelic experience worthy of an E.T.A. Hoffmann or a Novalis. He was out walking among bushes and was about to break off some twigs or branches when he noticed that each bush had different colored leaves—blue, yellow and so on. He remembered nothing more, but even this fragment allows intriguing possible interpretations. Is nature here doing what Lehmann continually longed for in real life, namely revealing to him her inner secrets and hidden splendors?

From Agnetendorf Lehmann travelled on to Waldenburg in Silesia to visit Hermann Stehr. Together they walked through the countryside of this mining district, and Lehmann was struck by the way Stehr was continually open to everything which went on around him. The sight of a man straining with every sinew as he pushed a heavy wheelbarrow before him was enough to make Stehr cry out "Ich wollte, ich wäre ein Maler!" Stehr read Lehmann some of his latest poems, and they talked about literature and life as was their wont. But Stehr was in poor health at this time and was not the ebullient figure that Lehmann knew from Berlin. He saw how bothered Stehr was by the extra attention forced upon him by his anxious wife, and he privately wondered what had become of the "Titanengenie" of a few weeks earlier. As Lehmann was about to leave, Stehr gave him a piece of advice: "Sorgen Sie sich nicht zu viel. Das Leben macht; lassen auch Sie das Leben machen!"[79] Although Lehmann saw the good sense of this advice, he was constitutionally unable to follow it. Such cares and worries as plagued Lehmann were not to be so easily shaken off.

Despite being back in Berlin and despite many happy hours with Heimann, Marschalk, and occasionally Stehr, Lehmann was still subject to his old depressions. He was still frustrated by lack of female company, he was still plagued by the fear of inadequacy, he was still lacking in any real drive to complete his studies (and a further semester in Berlin was, as he knew only too well, absolutely out of the question). On Saturday 5 July, his classes over for the week and with no motivation to do anything in particular, Lehmann began to brood on his situation. Realizing that he was no nearer to his goal—or rather his mother's goal—of completing his studies and embarking on his teaching career, he began to lay the blame on the hours spent at the Heimann's. Should he not break off the relationship and spend every available minute on his prescribed studies? Was his mother not right to expect this from her eldest child, this same mother who had been treated so ill by the world in general and by her husband, his father, in particular? Suddenly it all seemed so clear. Leaving his room, he set off down the Scharrenstraße, where he had moved for the summer semester, left the Charlottenburger Schloß behind him and turned into the Berlinerstraße. Branching towards the left at the so-called Knie, he continued on into the *Tiergarten.* Here the sight of so many normal Berliners enjoying their Saturday afternoon underlined his loneliness again, and he once more began to see himself as not of the normal bourgeois world but as set apart. He fell deeper and deeper into a black depression as he wandered "wie ein Verzweifelter" past the ponds, flower-beds, statues, and "Zelte." To whom could he turn? There was no one apart from Heimann:

> Es war sehr, sehr schlimm—Aber dann ging ich zu Moritz Heimann (den ich am Morgen in "Arbeitswut" hatte sogar abschreiben wollen) und er sprach mit mir— und es war sehr schön. Und noch jetzt, Sonntag morgen, wo ich dies schreibe, ist alles gut.[80]

Heimann was, by now, totally indispensable to the young student, and Lehmann knew it. He was not just a willing ear in matters of a literary nature, nor just an antidote for Wilhelm's bouts of depression brought on by over-exposure to self-doubt or the bourgeoisie. He was a great example to the youth, his only support, his trusting confidant, and a safety valve for all manner of tensions. He was, in short, the perfect father-figure, the figure so long missing in Lehmann's life. The latter sensed this relatively early in the relationship, writing in his journal on 1 February 1902 "Wie...die Empfindungen glutend süß in mir überstürzen, wie ich Ihnen die Hände küssen möchte und sagen: Wären Sie mein Vater!" The acquisition of a new father, so to speak, was a great help in the youth's development, but did nothing to erase from his psyche the old father and, in particular, the image of his real father that his mother had implanted in him.

As the division between the world of art and that of Philistinism became clearer, and as the gap between his aspirations and his mother's expectations grew, his conscience and psyche suffered accordingly. The night following his desperate peregrinations in the Tiergarten and Heimann's subsequent comforting words saw yet another vivid dream:

> Mir träumte von meinem Vater: ich ging glaube ich mit meiner Mutter, da sahen wir ihn eine Gartenstraße gehen: er sah aus wie ein abgerissener Künstler mit wirrem Barte oder wie Johannes der Täufer. Ich beruhigte meine Mutter—Das meiste (ich muß noch viel *mehr* geträumt haben) habe ich leider wieder vergessen.[81]

Such were his mother's admonitions that his hankering after art reduced him to the level of irresponsibility associated in his mind with his father's dissipation.

The summer semester was coming to an end and, with it, his time in Berlin. In the mellow and reflective mood which overcame him on such occasions, Lehmann sat down at his desk on his last day in Berlin and considered his situation. Sad as he was to be leaving the Heimanns and their circle of friends, he was nonetheless glad to be starting a new phase of his life, glad to be retreating, as he thought, into utter solitariness, to be leaving this huge, for him, desolate city for the quiet beauty of heath, moor, and sea:

> ...nun muß ich fort, gehe ich gern? Ich gehe gern. Rein und nicht nur urbar [?] zu machen breitet sich mir wie das Meer mein Dasein. Ich freue mich auf die Einsamkeit, auf ihre Freuden, nicht auf ihre Kämpfe. Behüte mich—nein ich bitte so garnicht—vor der Sinnlichkeit, die mich so stramm am Bändel hat....Hinaus, hinaus, an mein Ohr tönt das Rauschen des Meeres—Stille, Weite, Ferne, Wiese, Deiche—ins nackte weiße dunkle Leben stürze ich. Tod komm *da* zu mir, wenn mein Inneres nichts gebären sollte! Wen soll ich anklagen als mich selbst.... Wäre ich erst in Kiel und könnte dies mein Seelenleben, wie es so *jetzt* ist, gleich dahinströmen. Aber erst kommt England und fremde Menschen, vorher zu Hause. Die Gegensätze.[82]

Before Berlin and the Heimann friendship, Lehmann was only dimly aware of the many "Gegensätze." Now, with all his problems, with all the crises into which his complex psyche dragged him, he was at least aware of a means of reconciliation, of playing off one extreme against the other. This was to be both his pattern of life and his art in future years. Meanwhile one year in a city had demonstrated, despite his friends, that a large city was not the milieu in which he could thrive. He needed "das Rauschen des Meeres—Stille, Weite, Ferne, Wiese, Deiche." Leaving the city, however, would not mean the end of his relationship to Heimann, for he was to need this surrogate father desperately in the next few years. Although, on the surface, it may have seemed otherwise at the time, Berlin had proved to be a crucial experience for the young student, and Lehmann had made a definite break-through into a realm of new possibilities. The experience was indeed a "Triumpf. Trotz alledem."

3

Kiel (1902-1906). "So schlagt denn zu, ihr alle...."

ON HIS RETURN from Berlin Lehmann spent a week or so at home in Hamburg-Uhlenhorst and then took the "Schnelldampfer" from Hamburg to England. After a miserable 24 hour crossing he found himself in Harwich. Hardly recovered from a nasty bout of seasickness, he took the train to Liverpool Street Station and timidly asked his way to Salcombe, a seaside resort in Devon. Like most students of a foreign language on their first visit to the country in question, he was at once bewildered and depressed to find that he could understand practically nothing of what the natives said. But fortunately, a kindly old man with a white beard had the time and patience to take him to the correct station and put him on the right train. His good fortune continued as a lady in his compartment took pity on what was all too clearly a confused and shy young foreigner and provided him with the inevitable cup of tea and cakes. By the time he reached Salcombe he was feeling considerably better and this first, good impression of England remained with him for the rest of his life.

Through friends of his mother, he had arranged to stay as a paying guest with one Mrs. Twining, the widow of a country doctor in Salcombe. The house overlooked the sea and was full of children and young people all bent on enjoying their summer vacation. Lehmann was free to join in the fun more or less as he pleased, and he soon found himself at the Salcombe Regatta watching the boat-races, swimming, water-polo, and other carnival activities. Then there were picnics and various social engagements. But the combination of Lehmann's innate shyness and lack of self-confidence, together with the language difficulties, made the first few weeks somewhat miserable.

Nevertheless, he did his best to join in the activity of the moment. The older Twining children did not go out of their way to make him feel at home, but the younger ones were more agreeable. Dan Twining (1885-1970) did his best to put the German guest at his ease, and his younger sister, Winifried (1893-) distinctly remembers how Wilhelm patiently tried to teach her how to swim. She also remembers that Wilhelm was not particularly good at climbing trees—quite a shock to a nine-year-old who was accustomed to think that grown-ups did everything better—and she singled out the "kindness and gentleness" of Willie, as he was known in the family.[1]

The Twinings were a musical family, and most evenings there were informal house concerts. Wilhelm, like his father, possessed a pleasant baritone voice, and with his days in the school choir not so very far behind him, overcame his shyness and sang both German and English songs accompanied by either Kathleen Twining or Winifried. On 25 August, a Monday, there was to be a concert in the Town Hall in aid of the Church Institute, a charity organization. Kathleen, who was herself on the program, arranged for Lehmann to appear not once, but twice. The review of the concert in the *Salcombe Times* described Lehmann's performance as follows:

> Herr Lehmann, a German gentleman who has been in England a fortnight, undertook the somewhat difficult task of singing an English song "Rocked in the Cradle of the Deep"; when he came to his native language and music, in Schubert's "Wanderer," Herr Lehmann evoked, deservedly, great applause. The Wanderer is almost, if not quite, the best of all songs, and everyone who heard Herr Lehmann render it, felt its power.[2]

The success (and trauma) of the concert behind him, and with unusually pleasant summer weather, Lehmann began to relax and even enjoy himself. Finally, towards the end of his stay, came that memorable occasion in the life of anyone who learns a foreign language, the linguistic counterpoint of the first depressing day, when one suddenly begins to fully understand what has hitherto seemed gibberish. Up until this day he had hardly thought the expense of the trip worthwhile, and he had written home to this effect. But then it suddenly seemed that "bei Gelegenheit eines Picknicks auf thymianbekleideter Klippe gleichsam ein Bausch aus dem Ohr gezogen wurde und mir die fremde Sprache, die ich bisher nur in Stücken verstanden hatte, als Ganzes verstanden zuströmte."[3]

While still in Salcombe Lehmann dropped a line to the painter William Rothenstein, whom he had met at Gerhart Hauptmann's a few months earlier, and asked whether he might visit him in London on his way back to Germany. Rothenstein responded enthusiastically, and Lehmann found himself invited to Sunday lunch on 5 October 1902. Over the meal they discussed where Lehmann should go and what he should see, and Rothenstein sent him off to Westminster Abbey that very afternoon. In the evening Rothenstein sat down and wrote Lehmann a letter suggesting further sights and the most important galleries and museums. In the course of the conversation Lehmann mentioned his new-found interest in Irish literature, especially Yeats's *The Celtic Twilight* (1893), which he had just read. Rothenstein, who knew Yeats well, offered to meet Lehmann again the following Tuesday and take him to see the Irishman. Unfortunately

THE "GREEK TEMPLE" IN THE DÜSTERNBROOKER GEHÖLZ, KIEL, WHERE
LEHMANN LIVED IN 1902-1903. IT IS SHOWN HERE AFTER ITS (MINIMAL)
CONVERSION TO A WAR MEMORIAL. THE BUILDING WAS DESTROYED IN WORLD
WAR II.

Yeats was not at home and the encounter, which might have meant so much,
never materialized. Instead, they wandered around the secondhand bookstores
and narrow streets of inner London, and Rothenstein bought and presented
Lehmann with a copy of Mitford's collection of Japanese fairytales. Just before he
left for home, Lehmann sent Heimann a postcard in which he said how
impressed he was with Turner's "seligste Gedichte" and G. F. Watts's "feierliche
Todesallegorien" in the Tate Gallery.[4] On 9 October he left London and was back
in Hamburg late the next night.

It had been decided that Lehmann would move to Kiel and complete his
studies there, not far from home. Kiel University had been founded relatively
early (1665) but was even smaller and more provincial than either Tübingen or
Strasbourg. Furthermore, it could boast none of the illustrious names of Berlin,
and Kiel itself had no Heimann to whom Lehmann could run for guidance and
encouragement. But it was not the alienating metropolis that Berlin, in its bad
moments, had been. Here, at last, Lehmann was able to find himself a room such
as he had longed dreamed of.

Up on the wooded cliffs stretching away northwards from the University and
the Botanical Gardens on the west bank of the Kiel Fjord, was the highly
desirable Düsternbrooker Gehölz, with its picturesque villas dating from the

great expansion period when Kiel was designated a Reichskriegshafen (1871). Here, at number 91 Düsternbrooker Weg, Lehmann found a room in a modest and isolated pavilion like "a Greek Temple"[5] tucked away among the trees. It was owned by a strange old forester and his wife whom Lehmann likened to Philemon and Baucis, and this, together with the fact it was rumored to have seen the action of a Storm novella, made it appear "eine rechte Dichterwohnung."[6]

The University offered him no more than he had come to expect, which was little enough by now, and Lehmann stolidly set about fulfilling the bare requirements while contentedly going his own way with aspects of comparative philology, zoology, botany, and the learning of Gaelic. On 24 November he wrote to Heimann, heading the letter with a poem entitled "Novembermond," which is as Eichendorffian as ever. Now that he had settled "in diesem runden grüngestrichenen Zimmer, in dem zur Zeit Christians III von Dänemark eine geschiedene Königin wohnte," he could describe his situation at some length:

> Ich habe ein brennendes Interesse an der vergleichenden Grammatik.... Und das zoologische Praktikum erfüllt mir einen Jahre lang gewährten brennenden Wunsch meines Wesens, und meine Mutter hat es mir gern zugestanden. Ich finde nicht die Ruhe, um Ihnen von England viel berichten zu können—ich glaube zuversichtlich, daß ich in den 8 Wochen soviel gelernt habe als überhaupt zu lernen in der Zeit möglich ist (und dies glauben alle, die mich kennen, nur ich selber glaube es nicht ganz gewiß).

So far, after a little more than a month in Kiel, Wilhelm Lehmann seemed somewhat calmer and more contented than he had been in Berlin. Was the worst over? Had he found himself? The letter goes on:

> Ich arbeite jetzt gern und viel, oft nutzlos und oft hoffnungslos, weil mir 'dahinter' zu kommen oft vergeblich erscheint. Und dazwischen kommt dieser oder jener von meinen ehrlichen fleißigen praktischen Conabiturienten und gleiten und fahren über die schlimmsten und drohendsten Klüfte des Seins mit ein paar Worten hinweg und keinem von ihnen sprüht je Feuer aus den Nüstern. Wenn aber der Mondschein wie vergebendes und verzeihendes Lächeln unbekannter Güte auf den First des Hauses flimmert und auch aus den kahlen Buchen ein süßer Traum hernieder rinnt, weiße Nacken blinken und goldene Blätter am Stamm hervorschießend knistern und singen—dann wird mir schlecht zu Mute und ich kann niemand um Rat fragen, und wenn ich in die einzige Weite, die Beruhigung leuchtet, wieder hineinschreite, die Arbeit—der Stachel bleibt: zwischen dem Ungeheuren All und einem kalten nicht einmal kalten Nichts hin und herdrängend, von den Mächten des Leibes bedrängt und mit dem zehrenden Wunsch nach Schuldlosigkeit, friedlicher Stirn, fruchtbarem Herzen und schaffendem Geist, gehe ich dahin und merke es mit Wollust, wie der Novembernebel mich ganz einhüllt und mein Gesicht mitleidig verhüllt....

Not much, then, has changed. He is still alone, alienated from his Philistine fellows and oppressed by the meaninglessness of his studies. Even nature is of only limited comfort to him, and there is no Heimann close at hand. He is lost in a divided and alien world, caught between the "All" and the "Nichts," desirous only of "Schuldlosigkeit." This situation will remain more or less as it is, will become the background of all his written work, and will be graphically described in his essays 40 years hence. As for being oppressed by the powers of his body, we may appreciate that his yearnings for love, for contact with the opposite sex, had not vanished with his move from Berlin.

The letter goes on:

> Und manchmal schreibe ich, glaube ich, nur aus Angst vor der Unproduktivität Verse, wie die obigen, die, wenn sie das können, Ihrer Seele einen reineren Gruß bringen mögen als all mein unfrisches Geschreibe.

Everything is the same, then, right down to his desperate attempts to write poetry.

But no matter what his general mood was, Lehmann was now seriously striving to finish his studies. Accordingly, he cast about for a dissertation topic, and since he had become particularly interested in Jakob Böhme, he decided to visit the philosopher and oriental philologist, Professor Paul Deussen. A friend of Nietzsche's at Schulpforta, Deussen was now almost blind, and Lehmann found him puttering about his library clad in his nightshirt. Lehmann asked him whether he would direct his dissertation and mentioned Böhme, but Deussen, himself somewhat of a mystic, absent-mindedly dismissed the student with a wave of his hand.

Meanwhile, having received no immediate answer from Heimann to his letter of 24 November, Lehmann soon wrote again chiding him for not having written for so long! Heimann's justifiably nettled but humorous reply of 30 January 1903 put matters into proper perspective:

> Lieber Freund. Sie finden, daß ich Ihnen spät antworte? ich finde das nicht. Ihr Brief datiert sich vom 24.November, das heißt: 3½ Monate nach Ihrer Abreise von Berlin, und ich antworte nach wenig mehr als 2 Monaten! Denken Sie nur. Aus dieser Rechnung schließen Sie, daß ich Ihre Postkarten nicht mitzählen lasse und Sie schließen sehr richtig. Ich will es nicht verhehlen, daß mir, nach der Art unseres Verkehrs und unseres Abschieds, Postkarten kein Genüge gaben; Und ich zürnte Ihnen deshalb.
>
> . . . .
>
> Immer geben Sie zuviel oder zu wenig, oder, was die Regel ist: zuviel *und* zu wenig. Doch nun genug, sonst denken Sie am Ende, ich sei Ihnen nicht mehr gut, und das wäre ein Irrtum. Ihr Brief war mir eine große Freude, er war stärker, heller, klingender von Gemüt als früher, und ich wünsche Ihnen den Fortgang, den er andeutet. Schreiben Sie bald wieder, aber bald! hören Sie! Lehmann!

Those last words must have rung in Lehmann's ear to good effect, at least momentarily, for he replied to this letter by return post on 1 February and did his best to placate Heimann. He was able to report that he had in the interim found an alternative field for his doctoral dissertation, namely English philology, and that Professor Ferdinand Holthausen, a philologist with a special interest in comparative etymologies, would be his supervisor.[7] He describes his dissertation topic somewhat wryly as follows:

> Zu meinem Thema gehört also redliche und schwitzende Arbeit und kaum mehr, wie ein Sack mit tüchtigen gelben Steckrüben, in den nicht einmal *ein* Apfel als lachende Zugabe gesteckt werden kann—ich habe zunächst 2935 Verse Angelsächsisch sinngemäß zu übersetzen, dann das betreffende Syntaktische herauszusuchen, dann das Material zu sichten und anzuordnen—vor die Tugend setzten die Götter den Schweiß....

But later in the same letter he confesses to being particularly depressed, although he gives no reason for this condition and couches everything in rather balanced terms. A few days later, however, he sent a most disturbing, undated letter:

> O Heimann in diesen Tagen ist mein innerstes Sein gestorben und ich werde nie mehr leben. Zehn grausame Tage haben mich am Boden hin und hergerissen—und mit mitleidsloser Hand hat etwas die innersten Herzblätter mir aufgerissen—sodaß alle Hoffnung auf ein "Leben" vorbei ist. Fragen Sie nicht, was es ist. Ich kann und darf es nicht sagen, nur daß das Schicksal über mich gekommen ist. Heimann Heimann seien Sie so heiß bedankt wie niemals für Ihre Zeilen am Montag und ich flehe Sie an, was auch bei Ihnen geschehen, daß Sie noch nicht wieder schreiben—schreiben Sie sobald Sie irgend können das, was Sie haben mir schreiben wollen. O Heimann gestern Nachmittag um eben diese Stunde stieg der Wahnsinn in meinen Kopf—wem soll ich danken, das er wieder abgezogen ist....

Something about the tone of this letter deeply disturbed the Heimanns, and they both wrote with anxious inquiries as to what was wrong. Little did they suspect that the "Schicksal" which had overtaken him was, at long last, love. The woman in question was a certain Martha Wohlstadt, and she was 35 years old.

While the Lehmann family was at the beach at Schönberg two years earlier, Agathe Lehmann had struck up a friendship with an older lady from Kiel, who, after the death of her first husband, had married Sanitätsrat Dreis. The couple lived with Martha, Frau Dreis's daughter from the first marriage in a house in Gaarden on the eastern side of the fjord not far from the ferry. Now that Wilhelm lived in Kiel Agathe suggested that he pay Frau Dreis a social visit. This, shortly after Christmas, he had done. Greeted at the door by the daughter, Martha Wohlstadt, Lehmann remembered her as an understanding person who, two years earlier at Schönberg, had smiled reassuringly at the shy boys. The same sympathy was patent on this occasion, too, and her parents received him in no less kindly fashion. Frau Dreis, a woman not devoid of a certain ironic humor—although inclined to hypochondria—soon confidingly expressed her anxiety that her daughter was still unmarried, little suspecting as she prattled on how events were soon to develop. Lehmann showed every sympathy for Martha, who was covered with embarrassment as she listened to this homily, and a bond of friendship sprang up between the couple which soon flared into uncontrollable

MARTHA WOHLSTADT (1867-1947) AROUND THE TIME OF WILHELM LEHMANN'S
BIRTH.

MARTHA WOHLSTADT, c. 1901, AT THE TIME WILHELM LEHMANN MET HER
FIRST.

MARTHA WOHLSTADT, c. 1905, SHORTLY BEFORE THE MARRIAGE.

passion. But it is typical of Lehmann that, when he finally did fall in love, he should see the whole business in the darkest light possible, invoking words like "Wahnsinn" and feeling that this will be the end of him. In his diary for 1903-1905 he likens his love for Martha to Hölderlin's doomed love for Diotima.

When he came to reply to the Heimann's worried letter, Lehmann spoke about his problems in very general terms:

Ich kämpfe immerfort und beständig auf Leben und Tod, mit dem Wahnsinn und mit dem Selbstmord—ich wollte, ich hätte keine Angehörigen, dann wäre es schon aus.... Meine Seele windet sich oft so furchtbar, in so blutigen Geberden [sic], daß Sachen entstehen wie das Folgende:

Mann und Weib
Wo nun die blutige Johannisbeere blüht
Und die Pappel wird gerührt die roten Raupen auf die Wege streut
Versinke ich in einer heißen Wollust ganz in dir!
Daß du, o Traum, der mir am Herzen fraß, Gestalt genommen
Und aufgebrochen bist als Quell der Schmerzen und der Wonnen;
—So werd' ich doch, wenn du, grausamer Tag, vorbei, dahin getragen
Wo an die Küste weiße Wasser schlagen—
Wo ich, in einen Vogel gewandelt, die brandrote Brust den nutzenden
Strahlen hingegeben,
Ton für Ton an dich die Seele verschenke,
Nur schweigend, um dem Echo nachzuhängen,
Daß du, hoch auf den goldenen Haaren einer Esche sitzend
Tropfen auf Tropfen in mich gießt—

Oder, in noch schlimmerer Lage und noch tiefer versagend, heute früh:

O du herausgerissenes Stück des Ganzen! Für eine Weile bist du erlöst.
Wie jetzt der Nabel des Himmels glüht
Und von den langsam athmenden Hügeln ein klingendes Licht zieht.
Und halb im Traum noch eilt der Tag herbei mit glühenden Gedanken—Ich
sitze am Haus und sehe, wie die Sonnenstrahlen wanken,
Und horche zu wie die Kastanie sich auf ihre weißen Flammen freut.
Des Lichtes goldenes Kreisen schreitet vor und es erholt sich mein Leben,
mit Beben.
In ein wunschloses Meer strömt alles hin
Und jede Geberde [sic] der Seele findet ihren Sinn.
Küssend umhüpft mich der letzte Strahl und wie er rückt, Zittern die
Buchenknospen beglückt.

If the Heimanns were not able to divine from the first poem, in particular, that Lehmann was in love, there was a brief sentence squeezed in at the very end of the letter which was a little more explicit:

Die Leidenschaft für eine im Beginn der Dreißiger stehende geniale Frau, die tief unglücklich ist, hat mich hier zurückgehalten: ich *muß* damit brechen, ich *darf* sie nicht wiedersehen.

For various reasons the Heimanns were unable to respond at length to this letter, but, in a birthday letter sent on 3 May, Moritz Heimann again gave him encouraging words regarding his poetic ability:

Lieber Freund. Mein Brief an Sie muß noch liegen bleiben: ich habe gar viel zu thun und zu arbeiten. (Fischer kehrt morgen von der Reise zurück; und ich bin Korrespondent für Theater an der Wiener "Zeit"—seit vorgestern.) So sollen Sie Grüße und Wünsche zu Ihrem Geburtstag haben,—von Trude und mir; herzlich, freundschaftlich. Wir fühlen Sie uns immer verbunden. Ihr Brief macht mir nicht Kummer! Es wird Ihnen Alles zum Segen werden; denn Sie sind ein Dichter. (Lesen Sie Hölderlins Dichtermut, das ist mein Trost und Stecken gewesen in mancher schweren Zeit.) Ihre Verse sind! Sie leben! Sie tönen nicht mehr bloß. Schreiben Sie bald.

Treulich Ihr

Heimann

Even though these poems are still not very good, Heimann is right: there is a great improvement. The dreadfully imitative sounds and images of Romanticism have all but disappeared. The rhymes are no longer the conventional Baum/Traum rhymes of earlier attempts, and Lehmann has started to use the long line characteristic of Whitman which was now finding its way into German poetry and which was to pervade much of Lehmann's published verse. His passion for Martha has jolted him out of an epigonal rut into a freer and more individual mode. Heimann nonetheless shows remarkable insight to be able to assess Lehmann's capabilities so well on such dubious evidence.

In April 1903, about the same time that he wrote the poems contained in the letter above, Lehmann wrote a poem in sonnet form entitled "Thränenweg"

So schön wie in der Leberblume
Das Blau sich in das Rot ergießt
So bitterlich ist jede Thräne,
Die auf mein Aug von deinem fließt.

Im wilden Wald ein weißer Schauer
Umschwebt uns und ein dünst'ger Kreis.
Es versinkt um uns, es versinkt in uns—
So daß ich keinen Ausweg weiß.

Doch siehst Du im Zwielicht den Brückenweg?
Das ist der letzte, der Thränensteg.
Siehst du dort hinten die zitternden Seen?

Wo so viele blanke Tropfen stehn—
Laß uns zu ihnen die unseren thun
Und süß an diesen Wassern ruhn.

This poem also stems from his new-found love for Martha, and indicates his feelings of helplessness and sorrow in the face of impending family and societal pressures. But, as Hans Dieter Schäfer has convincingly shown, the poem does not break out of the pattern of "Stimmungswerte wie 'bitterliche Thräne' und 'zitternde Seen,'" or facile alliterative effects.[9] The one positive factor which bodes well for the future is that Lehmann is already as a 21-year-old avoiding the cliché of flowers like the rose and the violet and using a somewhat more "natural" and less artistic flower for his image.

More at ease with Gertrud Heimann on subjects of a personal nature, Lehmann was encouraged to write a little more specifically about his situation to her:

> *Martha* Wohlstadt ist *ihr* Name: sie ist ein bis an die Fingerspitzen leidenschaftliches Geschöpf mit einem *Freiheit*sdurst und einer Lebenssehnsucht ohnegleichen.... Ach, verzeihen Sie mir, daß ich nun *Hoffnung* habe, wirkliche Hoffnung trotz alle—alledem.[10]

In *Mühe des Anfangs* Lehmann describes Martha Wohlstadt thus:

> Sie war schweren, ungeschickten Körpers. Ihr Gesicht war oval, großlinig, ihre Augen schön und gütig warm, ihre Augenbrauen stark. Ihr Haar lag als mächtiger Turm auf dem Kopf oder fiel in starken Zöpfen.[11]

Photographs confirm both the beauty and the striking hair. A letter Lehmann wrote to Gertrud Heimann on 27 June fills in the picture somewhat. Lehmann first of all recants all previous disparaging remarks about his studies: "mir selbst erscheint es als kindisch und schwächlich, daß ich jemals über mein Studium geklagt: dieses Studium ist gut!" He goes on to describe Martha in more detail, and tells how it all came to pass:

> Also, diejenige, von der ich schon schrieb, ist frei, sie ist ein 35 jähriges früher vielumworbenes und noch jetzt begehrtes und schönes, merkwürdig schönes Mädchen. Als ich harmlos, unbefangen, nichts erwartend und ruhig hier in Kiel in das Haus *ihrer* Eltern kam, sprachen wir eines Abends am Klavier über dieses und jenes, sie kramte ihre Ansichten aus und ich stimmte dem [?] zu und bewunderte die Moral ihrer Seele tief. Und damit war denn auch schon alles geschehen. Nun sagen die Umrisse ihres Gesichtes schon mir, der ich es hören kann, wie diese Liebe gebettet liegt. Ich suche mich mit Gewalt über die große Kluft der Jahre zwischen uns hinwegzubäumen und sie ängstigt sich, daß diese Kluft uns nicht "glücklich" machen kann; ...

Now the gulf of almost fifteen years difference in age, although a matter which caused them some worry, was in itself less a problem than how others, and in particular the parents, would react. And all Lehmann's anxiety began, gradually, to center on this one problem—the very same problem, no doubt, which had caused his initial despair when he first realized that he was in love with a woman almost old enough to be his mother.

Carefully the couple did their best to hide their passion from all three parents and were obliged to resort to desperate subterfuge in order even to meet. In fact, they managed to meet relatively often, and, in defiance of all Wilhelmine codes of decency, Lehmann even received his beloved in his Düsternbrook pavilion. Such flouting of society's rules would have been nothing for a rebellious youth living a Bohemian life. But Lehmann, with his family background, and conditioned as he had been to feel guilty should he so much as steal a surreptitious glance at a girl on the street, was painfully wracked with pangs of conscience. No matter where he went or what he did, he felt exposed and threatened, and was even less an integral part of his surroundings than he had ever been:

> Ich sehe mich und alles in einem so schiefen verzerrten unwahren Licht, ich komme mir so unwahr forciert auf Stelzen gehend so übertrieben vor—wo soll das enden? ... Es ist doch unmöglich, daß meine Mutter von dem allen erfährt, bevor ich irgendwas erreicht.... [12]

Whenever they were out together, he was convinced that the whole world was observing them and laughing at them behind their backs.[13] But even this vulnerability paled into insignificance whenever he thought of his mother's reaction. By mid-July, Lehmann was able to write to Gertrud Heimann and inform her that Martha's parents now knew of their liaison, and, predictably disapproved of it:

> Nachdem der Vater davon wußte, kam er zu mir und sagte, seine Frau müßte es sofort auch wissen. Sie erfuhr es denn: und von beiden bekam ich denn den Bescheid, es ginge nicht: Martha würde das alles nicht ertragen können und ich sei zu jung. Das haben Martha und ich ja im Grunde vorher gewußt. Ich habe noch viel zu den beiden Eltern gesagt: es war ein Beginnen als wenn ich mit 1000 winzigen Steinchen nach einem in den Zweigen hochhängenden zarten Pfirsich würfe, nichts fiel dabei herunter es waren denn Fetzen von Marthas (die alles hörte) und meiner Seele. Und so ist denn den Eltern gegenüber alles aus. Martha und ich aber *können* und wollen nicht verzichten—abgesehen vom tiefsten Leid, was hätte es denn für einen Sinn, was hätte es für einen *Sinn*? So sehen und schreiben wir uns denn wie zwei verängstete Vögel— und wenn alles zuletzt doch nicht gehen wird (doch warum sollt' es nicht gehen?), dann lockt uns beide der selige Tod.... [14]

Problematic though the opposition of Martha's parents undoubtedly was, it inspired nothing like the apprehension, fear even, that Lehmann's mother did. He could well imagine how she would react, how the tears would flow, how she would be convinced she was ill—if not dying—and how the recriminations would come as she once again accused her son of weakly falling into his father's wayward and irresponsible life-pattern. His feelings were ambivalent: on the one hand she must not hear of his relationship with Martha, so fearful was he of the reaction; on the other hand it was absolutely essential that she hear if the relationship was genuine and lasting, and it seemed to be. Moreover, it was essential that she hear from his own mouth soon, for she might otherwise hear from Frau Dreis, with whom she was on friendly terms, and that would be disastrous. If only there were no age difference; if only Wilhelm had completed his studies—that is to say dissertation *and* Staatsexamen. But, alas, there were those fifteen years, and Lehmann, a mere 21 years old, could not be expected to qualify for full professional life for several years yet.

There were other problems, too. Lehmann well knew his own emotional instability; Martha, it seemed, was equally unstable and equally ungifted in practical matters. Lehmann saw the dangers and was on some occasions driven to consider parting from her—the word "Entsagung" crops up in numerous instances. And then, in his letters to Gertrud Heimann, who was acting more and more like a mother or elder sister, he often alludes to Martha's "Stolz":

> Aber dieses Wesen tritt auf meinem Herzen herum und sie ist unbändig und viel zu stolz, viel zu grausam stolz, als daß ich ihr all die tausend Demütigungen zumuten könnte, deren sie sich aussetzt, wenn sie sich mit mir verbände.... Und Sie wissen, was ich sonst noch alles sagen möchte.... Ich will mich von ihr trennen und dann heilt vielleicht einmal noch alles aus. Sie sagt manchmal Dinge, die mich wie Peitschenschläge treffen. O dieser bodenlose, ruchlose Stolz—so entsetzlich stolz so wie ich ja auch![15]

Towards the end of July Lehmann travelled to Hinterzarten in the Black Forest for a holiday with the whole family. It was a miserable time, and he looked forward with some dread to having to spend the remainder of the vacation with his mother in Hamburg. Meanwhile Martha's parents, at a loss as to how to deal with their willful daughter's passion for this mere lad, decided to send her to Breslau to spend a year with her married sister helping out with the household chores. Separated from his beloved and faced with the prospect of two months with his mother, Lehmann looked around for some means of escape. At very short notice he accepted a position as tutor at Schloß Penkun, not far from Stettin. On the way to Penkun, idyllically set in the midst of Fontane's Pommerania, he stopped off in Berlin to see Heimann on 31 August. The month of September he spent at the Schloß coaching the son of Kammerherr von der Osten. This boy, as Lehmann wrote to Gertrud Heimann, had "ein sehr träges Gehirn,"[16] so Lehmann was later particularly gratified to hear that he was not obliged to repeat the year. Kammerherr von der Osten was, however, "ein gütiger Mensch"[17] and it was, on the whole, a pleasant month. He received full board and lodging, and 75 Mk, and enjoyed, in effect, a pleasant late summer vacation in most attractive countryside. Most important, he escaped his mother.

On his return to Kiel he found lodgings at the "Villa Lindig" in Voorde, just outside the city. His only contact with Martha now by letter, he settled down to serious work once more—that is to say he applied himself to his dissertation, which was once again progressing well, read a great deal, and merely went through the motions of attending class. His Irish interests now encompassed "ein celtisches Unternehmen"—probably a translation of Yeats's volume of essays *The Celtic Twilight*—as well as the learning of Gaelic. His correspondence with Martha left him for the most part calmer than he had been, although the thought that his mother might discover or be informed of what was going on continued to plague him. On 2 December, however, while paying the University one of his relatively rare visits, Lehmann received some unexpected and shattering news. Professor Holthausen approached him and somewhat shamefacedly informed him that he would have to find a new dissertation topic, since his subject had already been covered. The next day, when the shock had somewhat subsided, Lehmann broke the news in, for him, rather subdued language to the poor, long-suffering Heimann:

> Ich weiß nicht, wie es Ihnen geht, in welcher Stimmung Sie etwas von mir trifft—
> aber ich habe das Bedürfnis Ihnen zu schreiben, daß mich gestern ein doch nicht
> leichter Schlag getroffen hat. Meine Dr-Arbeit, von der ein Drittel so gut wie fertig
> und übersichtlich vor mir liegt, an der ich doch lange gearbeitet und an der immerhin
> allerlei Saures klebt, ist umsonst und nichtig geworden, indem eine schon [18]97
> fertige Arbeit, umfassenderen Titels, mein Gebiet miteinschließend, in America
> jetzt erschienen ist. Ich war gestern Abend sehr böse dran und kann mich auch jetzt
> noch einer gewissen Bitterkeit und des Gefühls von Hilflosigkeit nicht ganz
> entschlagen. Der Docent, von dem ich das Thema bekam, teilte es mir mit einem
> Verlegenheits-Lachen mit. Das Schlimmste ist die verlorene Zeit. Ich fühle doch
> eine Pein darüber. Es bleibt mir nichts, als das Ganze sofort in einer neuen Arbeit zu
> ersticken, und ich stürze jetzt auch gleich nach Kiel, um gleich Gewißheit über
> Neues zu haben. Gerade zur Weihnacht.[18]

This reaction to a genuine disaster is an unusually sober and balanced one. But the letter continues rather more predictably. The world is again full of "verknöcherten ewig satt lächelnden Männlein mit ihren abgezirkelten 'Lebens-Bahnen' und ihrem stumpfen Gehirn." Then he wonders how he can break the news at home. It seemed he was back in the old mood of despair, in isolation and up against the whole world, but there was a difference, as the end of this same letter revealed:

> Nein, ich will nicht traurig werden, denn es bleibt mein anderes Teil: ich bin jetzt
> *darin* klar und fest. Ich meine, in meiner Liebe. Es ist mir und ihr das Große und
> Unsagbare und es wird nicht zersplittern.

When this letter reached the Heimann abode, the mood there was already somewhat bleak. On the same day that Lehmann wrote to Heimann, Gertrud wrote to Lehmann to ask him why he was not writing and to tell him that Heimann's latest play (*Die Liebesschule*) had been turned down by Otto Brahm and was not so far meeting with any more success elsewhere. But Lehmann was now full of his love for Martha, and knowing that she was coming home from Breslau to spend Christmas with her mother and step-father, he was full of anticipation at the thought of seeing her again. More than that, he was, despite the setback in his work, more seriously thinking of a permanent bond between them, or, as he somewhat obliquely wrote to Gertrud Heimann: "die Eltern ahnen und sollen auch nicht ahnen, daß wir gewillt sind, unseren Willen durchzusetzen."[19] After all, it was their life, why should they renounce happiness? Gertrud and Moritz Heimann both responded to this letter (on 14 December 1903), remarking how much calmer and happier Lehmann clearly was from the tone of his letter, and expressing their happiness at the opportunity to meet Martha, his "Verlobte," in Berlin as she returned from Breslau. In fact Martha was unable to stop off in Berlin and see them, but proceeded directly to Kiel, where she and Lehmann were re-united, and where they were able to meet, however fleetingly, over the Christmas and New Year period. Despite fears about his mother's reaction to the dissertation misfortune and his continued apprehension lest she find out about Martha, Christmas in the Lehmann family passed relatively quietly.

The year 1904 began quietly enough, too, but then, in February, came yet another family crisis. This time it did not concern Wilhelm directly, but it nonetheless caused him a considerable amount of worry. His sister Lita suddenly announced she wanted to become an actress, and her mother reacted predictably. The position of the actress in Wilhelmine German society had not improved much since the efforts of the Gottscheds and the Neuberin towards stage reform in the eighteenth century, and Agathe somehow saw Lita going the way of her father. The little drama in the Lehmann household occasioned a barrage of letters from Lehmann to the Heimanns as he described the situation and asked for advice. He, the first born, had been so conditioned into a feeling of responsibility by his mother, that he made Lita's problem his own. But there was worse news to come. His mother, perhaps in part because of the added strain and excitement, had a recurrence of the breast cancer which had already afflicted her once. There was an operation, which was successful, and then relative peace in the house as Lita bent her will entirely to the care of her mother as she recuperated.

It sometimes seems as if Lehmann had developed into such an apprehensive and unbalanced young man that one begins to wonder whether he was not exaggerating the potential difficulties with his mother. Yet there is no doubt that she had developed into a most unpredictable and difficult woman. There are numerous examples of strange, inexplicable displays of temper or emotion where no obvious reason for such behavior was at hand. In the rather sketchy journal for 1903-1905 which Lehmann intermittently kept, there is a sober, undated account of just such a tantrum:

> Ein höchst peinlicher Abend mit Mutter. Sie wird unwohl, setzt sich in die Sofaecke, weint nervös und giebt ungeduldige Antworten auf meine und Litas Fragen. Walter

geht fort mit Köster, vergißt einen Schlüssel, worüber Mutter in Aufregung gerät, wie sie in dieser Verfassung überhaupt sich in kleines derartiges festbeißt. Totenschweigend verzehrten wir das Abendbrot. Bis als wir fertig waren, sie wieder wohler wurde und in der Küche mit Lita geschäftig. Mir war es entsetzlich: Ich nahm mir Ernstes vor. Ich schreibe dies mir selbst als Fingerzeichen für die Zukunft. Ich vergesse zu leicht. Gewisses soll von mir nicht vergessen werden. Tod. Und der Moment verfliegt zu entsetzlich rasch.

Not that Agathe Lehmann was entirely to blame for all the tension in her relationship with her eldest son. His own peculiar sensitivities would clearly have taxed the patience of the most understanding mother. Lurking behind the scenes and undoubtedly contributing to all the tension was Friedrich Lehmann, whose careless treatment and ultimate desertion of Agathe and their children played a continual and significant role in the family's psychic fortunes.

Meanwhile Lehmann and Martha continued to correspond quite happily and planned an Easter meeting in Berlin at the Heimanns. By now their situation was, as Lehmann wrote to Gertrud Heimann, "himmelsklar"[20] and much of his previous anxiety seemed to have disappeared. They were planning for the future, and both were accordingly convinced that Martha had to find a position somewhere, which would enable her to escape the family clutches and be more independent. Inevitably, the Heimanns were asked to help in this regard, too. Doubtless because of his hope for a future together, Wilhelm Lehmann was able to begin to attack his new dissertation topic (on the prefix "uz-" in Old English) with some degree of concentration—despite the family problems. Not that his research was always a pleasure; as he wrote to Heimann on 25 February:

Ich sitze beständig an meiner gottlos widrigen, geistlosen Arbeit wie ein Sklave. Könnte ich mich entzwei schneiden und das Dichten wollende aus mir herausnehmen wie ein Geschwulst. Ich treibe oft hilflos umher und möchte in die Wände beißen.... Und habe oft den kindlichen Wunsch, etwas und seien es zwei Zeilen *gedruckt* von mir zu haben, es wäre doch etwas *Positives* und der Druckbuchstabe würde mich etwas heben.

Ironically, he had not been able to produce much in the way of poetry in the last few months. Precisely at the point when, with his new love for Martha, he had seemed able to break through to a poetic voice of his own, the opportunities seemed to recede more and more. The problem was that he saw the poetic soul within him as a threat to practical achievement. And now that professional security seemed to be the *conditio sine qua non* for a contented life with Martha, he tried to concentrate on the one almost to the exclusion of the other.

He was constitutionally unable, of course, to drop all thoughts of his own poetry and poetic growth even if he did produce fewer finished poems during the Kiel period. Nietzsche, in whom he had always had some interest both as a Primaner and as a student of Simmel in Berlin, began to interest him ever more. On 10 March 1903 he had written in his journal "Ich beginne jetzt also kurz vor Schluß meines 21. Jahres, Nietzsche zu lesen." We should add a word like "systematically" perhaps, for he had certainly read some Nietzsche before then. He was particularly attracted at this time by Nietzsche's views on death, and he copied out the aphorism headed "Tod" from the second volume of *Menschliches, Allzumenschliches:*

> Durch die sichtbare Aussicht auf den Tod könnte jedem Leben ein köstlicher, wohlriechender Tropfen von Leichtsinn beigemischt sein—und nun habt ihr wunderlichen Apotheker-Seelen aus ihm einen übelschmeckenden Gifttropfen gemacht, durch den das ganze Leben widerlich wird![21]

This positive view of death not only appealed to Lehmann as a young man prone to thoughts on suicide. It also settled into his world view and came to permeate much of his fictional work and some of his poetry later on.

Other interests from his Berlin days also continued to occupy him— the whole problem of the object and its designation, for example. This very problem was beginning to be of general interest at this time. For some time the Swiss linguist Ferdinand de Saussure (1857-1913) had been grappling with the problem of the "signifié" and the "signifiant" in Paris and Geneva, and the fruits of his investigations, edited by his students, were to appear posthumously as the *Cours de linguistique générale* in 1916 and be a major force in structuralist thinking about half a century later. In Berlin Lehmann had been preoccupied (primarily because of Stehr) by the relationship thing-word. Now he progressed a little way into the field of aesthetics: "Wie ist's? Giebt ein in Stein gemeißelter Löwe den lebendigen Löwen noch einmal?"[22] This problem, too, was to stay with him for the rest of his life, and the attempt at its resolution was to be a principal facet of his art.

His old interest in George Meredith too, although not yielding the fruit that he and Sefton Delmer had once planned, did result in a translation of Meredith's poem "Dirge in the Woods." The translation is no better than his Shakespeare translation had been, however, and serves to show only that he was still trying his hand at verse translation from time to time. The choice of poem, on the other hand, is more interesting in that it indicates that even now Lehmann is fascinated by seasonal change and by the apparent death of natural phenomena as winter approaches. Fifty years later he was to translate Robert Frost's poem "In Hardwood Groves," which shares a common theme with Meredith's poem.

An interest in the apparent self-sufficiency of nature and the exclusion of humankind also surfaces in his diary from time to time: "Der rote Sauerampfer wächst allein, jeder aber wird befruchtet und Wind und Regen und Sonne verkehren leidenschaftlich mit ihm. Ja, ja!"[23] There is later hardly a single poem that does not contain this notion as an implicit base to its content. And not unconnected with the idea of a unified nature is the knowledge of his own, and modern man's, exclusion from any kind of unified mythos: "Wenn ich dann ein Celte wäre und im Sonnentempel in gloriosester Morgenfrühe...betete, wäre mir da besser, wahrer, früher [?] zu Mute? Ich kann und darf darauf nichts antworten."[24] As time went on, he was able to equate nature and mythos[25] and resolve the Ich-Natur/Mythos dichotomy through the poem—at which point such questions as the above no longer demanded answers.

The crucial role that nature was to play in his later work is already clear: it was to provide the ideal, but lost paradise, towards which humankind and the poet would strive, seeking to regain the old unity. In trying to ascertain why his poems were still failing, Lehmann sought other reasons than the Berlin excuses that they were eclectic and that he was approaching the poem through the word rather than the thought. He was now able to re-formulate the second reason a little differently:

> Wenn ich bedenke, *wie* ich eigentlich durch *Kunst* und nicht durch *Natur* zum Dichterischen gekommen bin—da verzweifle ich und denke, daß ich im Dichter-Philosophischen im Unwahren, Verquetschten einst elend mein Lügenleben enden werde.... [26]

Later on, as a successful poet, Lehmann would be able to look at this statement and see that it missed the point. Nature and art would be involved in a mutual give and take, a true dialectic, and his poems would reflect this.

The poem was not his sole literary pursuit during his Kiel years. Around October, 1904 he wrote an essay entitled "Anknüpfung," which was, as he said, indebted to Matthew Arnold and George Moore.[27] The essay is unfortunately lost, but a lengthy first draft of a fairytale about a beautiful maid he calls Weissleib Dieterichsen dating from this time is still in existence. It seems likely that it was written some time in 1904. Unfortunately, the disordered manuscript is so difficult to reconstitute into a sequential whole that we can only guess what Lehmann's final version might have been. But there is a sufficiently clear story line for us to see that it contains the germ of so much later writing, and is, in a very real sense, the forerunner of *Cardenio und Celinde,* Lehmann's first published fiction. The story concerns a maiden, Weissleib, whose beauty charms all humans, all flora and fauna. She is a personification of the spirit of nature and, in the course of the story, finally disappears. Her disappearance is an allegorical representation of seasonal change. Lehmann was to put this nature spirit into something like allegorical form in his fictional work, and in poems like "Traumleib der Wärme." There is an authorial intrusion in the tale, and this *Ich* is left seeking the lost maiden at the end of the story.

Lehmann's intellectual interests and creative urges had not, therefore, changed much from the Berlin days. Neither had his emotional state, despite the fact that he had finally fallen in love, and despite Heimann's repeated written assurances that he was, indeed, a poet. The old insecurities still meant that Heimann was called upon for comfort, advice, consolation, and even material help. In the Berlin days it was not unusual for him to press a substantial coin into Lehmann's hands—in addition to all the free theatre and concert tickets. And now Lehmann's need to *see* Heimann, to travel to Berlin to be with Martha, meant that he needed money for the fare. And so Heimann found himself dipping his hand into his pocket for his protégé more and more, although he was, at this point, not at all well placed to help. Both he and his wife were plagued by illness and greatly overtaxed by work. Furthermore, they were about to move from the Knesebekstraße to Zehlendorf. Nonetheless, with typical generosity, Heimann invited the young student to come and stay for a few days entirely at his expense. The visit should coincide with Martha's own visit, of course.

The brief Berlin reunion at Easter 1904 was an all-round success. The Heimanns met Martha for the first time and took to her immediately. She and Lehmann were overjoyed to see each other again and looked forward to days together in Kiel now that Martha was returning home. Lehmann also met the writer Eduard Stucken and his wife, who were both to play a quiet but significant supportive role in Lehmann's and Martha's life in the near future. Everything seemed fine. But shortly after Lehmann and Martha returned, separately, to Kiel, Martha fell ill, and this fact, together with Lehmann's ever increasing apprehension concerning the urgent necessity of completing his studies before any real progress towards an open bond with Martha could be made, caused unhappy days. Heimann duly heard about it all and sent a short letter on the eve of Lehmann's 22nd birthday, once again encouraging him in his poetic pursuits:

> Lieber Lehmann, morgen haben Sie Geburtstag und Sie sollen nicht ohne Gruß und herzlichen Wunsch von den Zehlendorfern sein. Also—Glück!? Auch das. Geschick ist besser noch. Und daß Sie lernen, Ihre Teufel nicht zu lange zu begucken, ehe Sie sie verschlucken. Welch ein Trübsinn, Gewissensbisse zu haben, weil Sie Verse pflanzen möchten statt Wurzeln zu ziehen! Noch mehr Wurzeln—und mehr Verse! Ob Sie ein Dichter sind, das dürfen Sie nicht erwarten—soll Ihnen das Schicksal bestätigen, sondern Sie sollen es dem Schicksal. Und wenn das Ihnen glaubt, so thun wir es gewiß. Sind Sie ein Kerl und wollen ermuntert sein? Ich ermuntere Sie....[28]

The next few months saw a constant repetition of a well-established pattern. Lehmann poured his heart out, asked for more advice, encouragement, and money, and Heimann duly listened, reassured him, and sent him advice, encouragement, and money. But the new dissertation progressed, and Lehmann felt he might have it complete by the autumn. He was even confident he could attempt his Staatsexamen soon thereafter. Then Martha found a position for the summer as a nanny with a Berlin lady vacationing in Heringsdorf on the Baltic. Unfortunately she did not get along with the lady in question, complained of being badly treated, and ultimately left. Heimann's aid in finding another position was enlisted—perhaps through Frau Stucken. In September there was a momentary scare as Lehmann began to think that his dissertation overlapped with some published research by the Sanskrit scholar Johannes Schmidt. In fact Lehmann outlined the answer to the problem even as he wrote about it to Heimann.[29] The solution lay in the simple addition of a footnote or two. Heimann, who suspected, quite rightly, that a neurotic Lehmann was once again exaggerating and finding problems where there were none, quickly allayed his friend's fears. Meanwhile Martha had found a new position in Berlin, and Heimann invited Lehmann to visit them again. So towards the end of October he was back in familiar haunts, talking to the Heimanns and together with Martha. It was on this visit that he finally met Emil Strauß. But he was often in the library working on the last stages of his dissertation, only too aware of the urgency of the matter if he and Martha were to become engaged.

By Christmas 1904 it was clear to Lehmann that his dissertation could now be submitted and the date of his Rigorosum settled. This meant, in turn, that he and Martha could communicate their continuing relationship and their desire to legitimize their unofficial engagement to her parents. Heimann agreed that Lehmann should talk to Martha's parents, especially since, as he tells Lehmann in his letter of 13 January, 1905, Martha had already informed them of the situation. As regards Lehmann's own mother:

> Sie haben recht, es vor Ihrer Mutter noch zu verheimlichen. Ist es so weit, daß sie es erfahren muß, so erbiete ich mich, Ihre Sache auch meinerseits zu führen; denn ich werde Ihrer Mutter sagen können, daß ich Sie auf dem guten Wege glaube und weiß: Frl. Martha ist uns von Mal zu Mal lieber, angenehmer und wertvoller geworden. Ich habe mich darüber unendlich gefreut.

In fact, at this stage, Agathe Lehmann must have been the only person who was still unaware of what was going on. Lehmann had confided in his brother and sister, and Walter, in particular, was most supportive.

By mid-January 1905 Lehmann had written the last word of his dissertation and spoken to the Dean about his Rigorosum. But the stress had played such havoc with his nerves that there were no signs of elation. On the contrary, in a letter to Heimann of 8 March, he talks of suicide again—this time with somewhat more compelling reasons for his depression:

> Lieber Heimann, Es geht mir nich sehr gut, der Glaube an mein Können, meine körperlichen und seelischen Kräfte wird immer mehr wankend, daß ich oft ein Ende machen möchte, wenn ich denn doch die Achtung, die ich von ein zwei bestimmten Menschen möchte, einbüssen soll! Äußeres kommt hinzu: meine Dissertation (sie heißt übrigens: "Das germanische Präpositional-adverb uz, seine Entwicklung zum Nominal- und zum Verbalpräfix mit besonderer Berücksichtigung des Althochdeutschen und Angelsächsischen. Ein Beitrag zur Wortbildungslehre") ist seit langem eingeliefert an den Dekan der philos. Facultät. So harre ich jeden Tag, daß der Pedell, der die Arbeit zu den drei Professoren, die ihr Gutachten darüber geben, bringt, mich benachrichtigt: sie sei aus den Händen des ersten Totenrichters und wandere in die des zweiten, zusammen mit dem dritten, den beiden weniger gefährlichen. Anstatt dessen liefert Holthausen die Arbeit *wegen zu kleiner Schrift,* zu ¼ durchgesehen, zurück und ich muß sie jetzt für 20 Mk durch Schreibmaschine noch einmal abschreiben lassen und zwar ganz. Dies hält mich auf und macht mich unsicher. Das Wichtigere aber ist: der Mann kann meinen Stil nicht haben, er ist zu

überladen, zu viel Fremdwörter, zu lange Sätze, geschmacklose Ausdrücke etc. Ich kann da nur sagen: Meine Arbeit ist eine fließende lebendige Darstellung einer Entwicklung, auf die ich Wert lege; mag sein, daß mein Stil nicht ein glattes mechanisches totes Abwickeln sondern ein Geschehen ist: wie dem auch sein mag: meine Arbeit *soll,* so wie sie ist, *durch,* es sind Dinge darin, die an die wissenschaftliche Öffentlichkeit *müssen,* rein philologisch-grammatischer Natur. Schreibe *ich* in der Arbeit "auslösen," so schreibt *er* "ergeben" an den Rand u. dgl. Nun Montag wird die Arbeit sauber abgeschrieben in meiner Hand sein: *er* wird sich ein Urteil dann darüber bilden, und es wird hoffentlich noch gut gehen. *Er* hat ja die *Macht,* wenn er nicht will, wo bleibe ich dann?

Lieber Heimann, ich habe ein Gefühl, als müßte ich doch mit Selbstwillen fort, wenn die Geschichte nicht gut abläuft. Es ist mehr und kränkender, als man denkt. Ein Mann in meiner Situation ist unmmöglich ohne praktischen Erfolg etc. Es läuft mir kalt über den Rücken, ich verhärte mich in Bitterkeit und Trauer, ohne Absicht ohne Kraft. Und doch werde ich *niemals* von Martha lassen *können* und *wollen.* Sie ist ein ausgezeichneter fähiger und wollender Mensch: in dieser Hinsicht ist alles denkbar gut: und ich werde mit Qual das Böse erleben—*wenn* es doch bald mit der Arbeit in Ordnung wäre. Niemand weiß natürlich von dieser neuen Calamität.—
....

Nun also ist Montag das Erwähnte in Ordnung, so werde ich vergessen, was ich gestern und heute dachte und hier schrieb, und bitte Sie, es auch zu vergessen: ist das Schiff wieder flott und pfeift der Wind durch die Raaen, will ich mir einen Sang auf das und mein Dasein spielen. In den Schaufenstern liegen auch hier aus "Die Tobiasvase" und "Die Liebesschule," nie aber war mein Beutel leerer als jetzt, mein Sinn leerer und verwirrter, mein Dasein wie höchst schwankend aufeinander-getürmte Steine, die eine Kindeshand in einen Trümmerhaufen wandeln kann, so lebhaft nie das Gefühl davon: die gangbaren Werte sind mir bloßer Ton, auch das nicht mehr, woran soll ich mich halten, wenn denn mein Wille doch nicht geschehen soll. Entscheidet es sich nächster Woche, ob meine Arbeit acceptiert wird, so ist Anfang Mai spätestens das Mündliche.

Heimann replied to this letter quickly and offered, as usual, much comfort and sound, practical advice:

Liebster Lehmann, immer wenn ich Ihnen schreibe, muß ich damit beginnen, Sie auszuzanken. Was sind das für Worte, welch feiger Gedanken bängliches Schwanken! Das Schlimmste angenommen, so sehen Sie sich einmal im Spiegel: Sie sind jung, gesund, begabt, beglückt: und haben den Mut, so unmutig, ohnmutig zu sein beim ersten queren Balken!

Sehen Sie, Lehmann, ich mache mir einen Vorwurf: ich hätte daran denken können und sollen, daß Ihre Handschrift schwer zu lesen ist, zumal wenn Sie eng, klein und viel schreiben. Hätte ich Sie nur gewarnt! Denn der Professor hat gewiß mit diesem Tadel Recht. Nun, es ist repariert, und Sie haben noch keine Ursach zu glauben, daß seine Verstimmung seine Pedanterei so nähren werde, daß sie Ihnen Übles zufügen kann. Die Ausstellungen am Stil sind albern, und Sie werden sich dadurch nicht beirren lassen. Tritt das Schlimmste ein, woran auch noch nicht ein Hauchlein von Glaube in mir ist, so bleibt Ihnen nur eins: die andere Universität, Stolz und

Publizierung der Arbeit. Müssen Sie das auf eigene Kosten thun, so stehe ich zu Ihrer Verfügung für die ganze Summe. Aber kein thörichtes Geschwätze mehr.

. . . .

Meine Bücher werden Sie sich doch nicht kaufen! Die liegen natürlich für Sie bereit; ich habe sie nicht geschickt, weil ich Sie in dieser Zeit schonen wollte. Tragen Sie Verlangen danach, so bitte um eine Zeile.

. . . .

Hier geht alles vortrefflich. Wir grüßen Sie und Frl. Martha von Herzen.

Ihr

Heimann

(Zehlendorf,) 12. III. 1905.

Lehmann's lament that he cannot even afford to buy Heimann's recently published books was not a mere routine complaint. At this stage of his life, Lehmann was several times forced to beg a bowl of bread-soup or whatever was available because of lack of money.

But even as Lehmann became calmer and more confident regarding the achievement of his doctorate, other problems arose such as his military service which was particularly vexing to Lehmann because it would cost him both time and money. Now Agathe had very carefully kept back some of the insurance money she had received on the death of her husband specifically to cover the cost of uniforms and the like entailed in her two sons' military service. But since she was now obliged to retire early because of her health, she had conceived of another plan which would enable her to use this money for other, more practical purposes. She would utilize the fact that she was widowed and unable to work to have her eldest son excused from military service on the grounds that he was (or should be) the family's bread-winner. But for Lehmann nothing was as simple as this: "Komme ich da nicht in eine Schiefheit sondergleichen? Soll der Unterstützer der Familie sein und hole mir dazu eine Verlobte?"[30] Somehow the problem was forgotten for a few months, only to reappear periodically and continue to bother him for the next few years. For the moment he concentrated on his doctorate.

Owing to the delay occasioned by Holthausen's objections to the handwriting and style of Lehmann's dissertation, the Rigorosum did not take place until 6 May. But Holthausen asked all the right questions, the other examiners were all content, and Lehmann had cleared this hurdle. But the spring deadline was past, and he was obliged to wait until the autumn before the dissertation could be accepted and the doctorate officially conferred.

As October 1905 approached, tension in the Lehmann abode ran high, for there was to be yet another move: the family was going to leave the noisy apartment in Uhlenhorst and move back to Wandsbek. At the same time Agathe was coming to the end of her teaching career and viewed the prospect of her retirement with mixed feelings. But the move went well, and everyone, especially Wilhelm and Walter, was pleased with the new house. Agathe was delighted to be back in Wandsbek among friends and immediately began to wonder whether she would not be able to resume her old teaching job in Wandsbek after all. When, in mid-October, Lehmann officially became a Doctor of Philosophy, her delight knew no bounds: "...in meinem Herzen wallt's noch jedesmal süßfreudig auf, wenn ich dem Herrn Dr. schreibe und dabei denke, daß das mein Sohn, mein lieber Junge ist."[31] The flush of success did not leave Lehmann untouched: he suddenly had very positive feelings about scholarship—even though his hatred of examinations remained: "Freie Forschung ist herrlich— Examensarbeit ist mein Tod!"[32] He was particularly gratified by the immediate response to his dissertation. Holthausen accepted the first part concerning "Nominal-Komposition" as the official dissertation, and decided to print this part and a second section on "Verbal-Komposition" in the series "Kieler Studien zur englischen Philologie," which he himself edited. The confidence stemming from the knowledge that Holthausen was willing to accept his scholarly work led him to consider publishing other smaller pieces of philological research he had conducted over the years. He accordingly wrote to Heimann to ask whether he could help him through any of his contacts in Berlin. Heimann promised to do his best and thus began a brief period of philological research and publication, which was to last until he went to Wickersdorf.[33]

It would be unrealistic to imagine that Lehmann could exist without any crisis—real or imaginary—and a crisis was about to emerge, the magnitude of which he had never yet experienced, and which would abruptly change his life style. By the end of November 1905, he was so upset at the way Herr Dreis was treating Martha that he was again looking for some means of escape for her. Could Heimann find her a position in Berlin? Would he buy a rare edition of Pfeiffer's *Deutsche Mystiker* from Lehmann so that the money could be used to pay for the rent for a room in Berlin? Should they attempt to break into Martha's dowry of some 4000 Mk now, rather than keep it back for their marriage and for Agathe (who would presumably live with them once they were married and she was retired)? Such were the possible solutions he threw out to Heimann in his letter of 28 November. In fact, none of the questions needed to have been asked, and very soon no answers were sought in the face of a new problem of disastrous proportions: Martha was pregnant.

Throughout the month of December the couple was simply apprehensive that Martha *might* be pregnant, for there was no certainty as yet. But if there was to be a quick marriage, money would be urgently needed, and Lehmann would have to give up his studies before his Staatsexamen. All these thoughts ran through his mind, and he dreaded the thought of Christmas at home, knowing that he would now have to indicate their desire to marry to Agathe in case their worst fears were confirmed. On Christmas Eve all seemed set for an excruciatingly miserable time. Walter had not turned up, nor had he informed anyone of his plans. Agathe, as one can imagine, was complaining bitterly of his lack of consideration and responsibility. But then, just before Agathe had sullenly decided to go ahead with the gift ceremony without Walter, a horse-drawn cab drew up and a jubilant Walter appeared, having just completed his final examinations. And so the family gathered together for the festivities with no less than two freshly acquired academic honors. Agathe's seething anger changed to radiant joy, and everyone relaxed. Christmas and the New Year proved considerably pleasanter than anticipated, and Lehmann avoided broaching the dreaded subject for fear he destroy the atmosphere. He did discuss the situation with his brother, however, and the more practically inclined Walter advised finding a position immediately. As luck had it, there was a teaching position at a private school in Eldena in Mecklenburg and Lehmann wrote off straightaway. By 5 January 1906, it was clear that the job was his, and he accepted, provided that he could delay starting teaching while he sorted out his affairs. Meanwhile the peace of the Lehmann house had in any case been shattered by a row over pecuniary matters between Agathe and the three children, and so he resolved to break the news to her forthwith. On Sunday 6 January he told his mother everything except the possibility of a child. On the following Tuesday he wrote to Heimann and told him what had happened:

> Vorgestern Sonntag hat Mutter davon erfahren: Ihr Schmerz war grenzenlos. Gestern sind Martha und ich bei ihr gewesen und sie war die ewige Güte selbst. Nur beschwor sie mich, vorher Staatsexamen zu machen. Wir haben nichts Bindendes hier gegeben. Aus Gründen nämlich, die ich Ihnen in Bälde auseinandersetzen will und möchte, reise ich zunächst noch *nicht* in die neue Stellung. Was wir vorhaben, bleibt bestehen. Der Himmel verlangt noch ein Anderes.— ...

As it became more and more certain that they would be obliged to marry, and marry quickly, Lehmann hatched one new plan after another, each one designed ever more extravagantly to hide the truth from his own mother, Martha's parents, and the school authorities in Eldena. At one stage there was to have been a nocturnal elopement with a note left behind for Martha's parents. His imaginative and energetic efforts to arrange a marriage expeditiously and secretly over the next three weeks turned out to be a remarkable tragi-comedy of errors.

The problem centered on where to marry. Kiel was the obvious place, but this would entail publishing the banns there, which in turn would mean that Martha's parents would have to know. Now Martha's parents were gradually taking on a role of tremendous importance, for it began to seem to the over-sensitive pair that they, in effect, controlled Martha's dowry of 4000 Mk. If Lehmann alienated them still further, then his and Martha's financial position would be even more precarious. He accordingly resolved to marry in Berlin with Heimann and Köster (Walter's friend) as witnesses. In this way, he thought, the truth could be kept from all three parents—for the time being at least—and Eldena. When this suggestion reached Berlin, Heimann and Köster were both horrified, for in order to circumvent the various legal requirements, Lehmann would be obliged to invent one lie after the other. Köster took on the delicate task of trying to persuade Lehmann, who had meanwhile gone to Eldena to begin teaching on 15 January, to change his plans. In two weeks they exchanged a dozen letters and telegrams. Köster was blessed with a surfeit of energy and good humor—and he needed both to cope with Lehmann's over-reactions and bunglings.[34] He arranged for a room in Berlin for Martha—she was never there. He made out elaborate itineraries for Lehmann as he travelled from Eldena to Kiel or Wandsbek so that he could go via Berlin—but he never used them. He cancelled all his own plans so that he could substitute in Eldena for Lehmann, who insisted he would have to spend a weekday in Kiel arranging matters at the Standesamt— but Martha did it all without Lehmann's presence being necessary. Köster even took the train to Ludwigslust near Eldena to meet Lehmann and discuss the most important matters in person—but Lehmann did not turn up. Köster accordingly spent a few hours sitting in the waiting room before he could return to Berlin, and he took the opportunity to send an irate but surprisingly good-humored letter to Lehmann in which he catalogued all the problems Lehmann had caused him:

> Ich grolle Ihnen, lieber Lehmann!
> Erstens) schreiben Sie alles zu spät. Ich bekomme ein rätselhaftes Telegramm *um Mittag* (auf das ich sofort antworten soll) und am Abend erst die Interpretation
>   2) Sie schreiben und telegraphieren aus Kiel, ohne Addresse anzugeben, wohin die Antworten sollen
>   3) Sie beschweren sich deshalb, daß ich die Antworten in meiner Ratlosigkeit dahin schickte, wohin ich allein konnte, nach Gaarden! ... Die Warnung nicht nach Kiel zu schreiben, kam natürlich als alle 3 [Antworten] abgesandt waren....
>   4) Ich weiß ja nun nicht, weshalb Sie nicht hier sind....[35]

And so on. Lehmann meanwhile had lost touch with Martha, who was obliged to enquire of Köster where her husband-to-be was. Horrified to hear that Lehmann had advised Martha not to write to him, Köster wrote and pointed out that the inquisitive villagers would naturally expect to see letters from Frau Dr. Lehmann arriving from time to time. In order to rectify matters himself, and no doubt skeptical that Lehmann could ever do anything right, Köster straightaway sent a telegram to Lehmann and signed it with Martha's name. It was, he thought, "eine glänzende Leistung"[36]—although Lehmann had not found it so. But somehow, many misunderstandings later, the pure logistics of the marriage were all sorted out.

At various stages in the hectic back-and-forth of deliberations, circumstances obliged Lehmann to act in an uncharacteristically sensible and expeditious manner. On 14 January he confided the whole truth to Gertrud Heimann:

> Unsere Mutter *weiß* von uns, aber nicht—das dürfen nur Sie hören, hören Sie es an, wie nur Sie es anhören können, sagen Sie es Heimann, wenn Sie es für durchaus nötig befinden—daß Martha glaubt, die aller-aller ersten Regungen einer

Kinderzelle in sich zu spüren. Die drängende Not läßt uns das Glücksgefühl noch nicht so haben, wie wir es haben *werden*.[37]

He still held back from telling his mother, but since the Heimanns and Köster urged him with some passion to do so, he finally followed their advice. On Sunday 21 January, when he was supposed to be meeting Köster in Ludwigslust, and when he was back from Eldena to arrange matters in Kiel, he took the train down to Wandsbek and poured out the whole truth to his mother. In doing so he followed his brother Walter's advice and pleaded for her help rather than insisting on the importance of his own happiness as he had egotistically done a little earlier. Agathe, as Walter had rightly surmised, suspected the true reason for all the haste by now, and she took the news rather calmly, agreeing to do her best to help the couple both materially (furniture) and by talking to Herrn and Frau Dreis. Much relieved, Lehmann went back to Eldena and, two days later Agathe went up to Kiel to see Martha's parents. Forced to witness first hand what the typical reaction of respectable citizens was going to be, Agathe's calm was shattered, and she fired off a description of the encounter the next day:

Mein lieber Willy

ich bin wieder krank und stehe eben mühsam auf, weil ich muß. Mein Gesicht ist orangerot, hundert Messer reißen und stechen darin herum. Wie ich gestern nach Hause gekommen bin, ist mir nicht klar; ich wagte mich schon von Kiel aus kaum auf die Reise und riß mir beim Eintritt hier wie toll alles Zeug vom Leibe, um nicht zu ersticken. Furchtbares habe ich gestern durchgemacht, was ihr *nie* an mir gutmachen könnt,—um Euch etwas zu retten und der Tochter etwas zu ersparen, was ewig ein Glück unmöglich gemacht hätte—den Fluch der Eltern. Die beiden armen Alten waren außer sich über Euer Lügen und Trügen und heimliches Vergehen ohne sie zu fragen, mit vollem Recht; alles ist wahr und gerechtfertigt vor Gott und Menschen; die Mutter war noch härter als er, wohl, weil sie im Ganzen am tiefsten getroffen war. Den *wahren* Grund dieser unanständigen Hast sagte ich nicht, obgleich sie direkt fragten, und die Tochter log. Kann eine Ehe zum Glücke werden, die unter solchen Umständen geschlossen wird? Nachher waren sie plötzlich beide ganz weich,—zum Totweinen grausig—und sprachen von Geld und Möbeln und Anschaffungen. Natürlich wollen sie mit der ganzen Sache sonst nichts zu tun haben. Ihr müßt Euch allein trauen lassen und dann reisen, ins Haus zu ihnen darfst du nicht kommen; *schreiben auch noch nicht,* sonst verdirbst du alles. Unverantwortlich habt ihr beide gehandelt; betrügt Ihr Euch anständig, hättest du längst dein Examen, wie du der armen Mutter schuldetest, anstatt Jahr nach Jahr— —oh, ich kann nicht mehr—, *der* Vater hätte nicht als Gutes an Euch getan. All dies Reden ist nur umsonst; heiraten mußt du sie, und ich verbiethe mir jedes weitere Lügen; du gibst als deinen Wohnsitz Eldena an, wenn du nicht noch mit dem Strafgesetz in Berührung kommen willst. Und dann, machst du dann nicht dein Staatsexamen in kürzester Zeit, wie ichs gestern heilig auf mich genommen habe— ohne meine Überzeugung—dann—Gott im Himmel hört mich! dann vergesse ich auch meinen Walter und meine Lita, und du ladest deinen Geschwistern gegenüber furchtbarste Schuld auf dich, und deine zu Tode gequälte Mutter geht an einem fernen Erdenfleckchen still und leise aus der Welt; so lange bis ich die Nachricht von deinem bestandenen Ex[amen] erhalte, blutet mir das Herz, verblutet langsam; also beeile dich, sonst erspart mir ein gütiger Gott das Letzte, Schreckliche.

Ich habe Ungeheures geleistet und getragen; ich habe für deinen Vater, den ich liebe, gelogen und getrogen, ich habe für meinen Erstgeborenen gelogen und getrogen, ich bin am Ende. Was Ihr von meinen Sachen haben wollt, könnt Ihr bekommen, wie ich dir ja schon gesagt.

Deine tr. Mutter.

The ghost of Friedrich Lehmann was never laid to rest. In this instance he appears in writing—how much more often was he conjured up in Agathe's spoken words. Walter Lehmann, writing from Carolinensiel (Ostfriesland) where he had taken a teaching position, called his mother "eine furchtbare Egoistin"[38]—it was of small comfort to his brother.

By the end of January everything had quieted down somewhat, the marriage had been arranged, and Lehmann, feeling ill-used by absolutely everyone, sat down and wrote a rather woe-begone and ill-conceived letter to his most faithful friend and ally Moritz Heimann:

Scham, Bitterkeit, Trotz machten sich in mir gegenseitig das Dasein streitig inmitten einer traurigen Flachheit, die aber von einem rasend wollenden Lebenshunger in guter Stunde rauschend durchwühlt wird. Wohl "gab ich mich" der Mutter—aber ihr Schmerz bleibt und mit schwersten Vorwürfen beschüttet sie mich. In Mühsamkeit holte ich meine paar Verse hervor, die aufgeregte Perioden in mir gezeitigt, als schwache und elende Verführer zu dem Glauben, daß mein Wille, *diese* Liebe hinter mich gebettet zu wissen, damit ich wieder für Anderes und Andere ins Gleichgewicht komme, vielleicht doch auch für das Gesicht der Mutter—ach! wenigstens etwas—Farbe und Wert besäße. Vielleicht mit etwas Erfolg, vielleicht mit keinem, denn meine Mutter ist aus Eichenholz, und das blutet bloß und biegt sich nicht. Und gaukelte mir in lauer Luft, wenn die ersten Stürme vorüber, nicht doch ein Stern einen linden festen Glauben an mich selbst vor—wahrlich, ich ließe das Ganze fahren oder würde ein buchstabengetreuer Sohn meiner Mutter, die kein anderes Merkmal meines Wertes kennt als das bestandene Staatsexamen. Glaube doch niemand, daß ich mich "verteidigen" will! Bloß liegt mein Herz allen Vorwürfen, und nur weniges bedarf's noch, um mein Haupt aller Blütenblätter zu entkleiden. Wenige sind's, und blaß wird unter der Erde die Wurzel. So schlagt denn zu, ihr alle, die ihr ein Anrecht drauf zu haben wähnt und umbreitet mit drohender Wolkenruhe das ängstliche Stapfen des Menschenvogels, dem sich durch farbige Tranen hindurch die Welt als Liebesheimat nicht verwischen will! Schon einmal nannten Sie, daß ich meiner Mutter einst direct verschwiegen, ich hätte Hauptmann gesehen, "unanständig"—und "unanständige Hast" ist das Wort, mit dem auch meine Mutter diese Eheschließung nun brandmarkt. Obwohl Martha und auch ich von Anfang an nicht daran gedacht hatten, *nach* dem Geschehnis den Eltern ihrerseits ein Geringstes zu verschweigen—meine Mutter *wollte,* der Alte solle den wahren Grund *nicht* erfahren; sie ist mit Martha *selbst* bei ihm gewesen, hat ihn von unserem Wollen in Kenntnis gesetzt und er *wird* jenen Grund also nicht erfahren.

Mir scheint das gut: *scheint* dieser Mann auch gütig und all unser Gehabe darüber ein Häufchen Dreck: ich nenne den "Vater" ein Scheusal. Wenn es denn niemand glaubt, Martha ist ein blasser Vogel und meiner Seele ehrlich Thun und Vorhaben hat dieser Mann in rohester unsagbar roher Weise mißhandelt, mit Peitschen gezüchtigt wie ein Viehknecht, Nächte voll frohen Arbeitswillens in verzerrtes Brüten verrenkt: genug, genug, ich bin sein Sklave nicht, wir wollen seine Sklaven nicht sein. Mit Jubel möcht ich es in den Muttermund der gleichmut'gen Erde rufen, daß sie *fort* von ihm kann, der sich *jeden* Tag, mit *jedem* Worte, bemühte, das Farbengetupfe von meinem Vogel der Liebe mit heiserem Wohlbehagen abzureißen. Der Schierling ist giftig und die Erde ist ihm wohlgesinnt, so laßt auch mich giftig sein, die Erde wird mich nicht verdammen.

Hätte mein Bruder Walter mich nicht Weihnachten aus meinem Tag für Tag, endlos, sekundenfolgend sich in den eigenen Stachelschwanz beißenden Quälen zum Handeln vorwurfsvoll aufgerissen, nichts wäre geschehen; auch dieser Plan mit Eldena nicht, der jedem Verständ'gen in der That ein "Wahnsinn" sein muß. Sonderbar genug, daß diese Sache, die sich mit einer Komödie einleiten muß, dem Kopf meines Bruders entsprungen ist, der mir noch allezeit so rein wie eine Seemuschel und so unberührt wie Seetang vorgekommen ist! So muß denn zu Ende geführt werden, was ich begonnen; Köster teilt mir Ihren Ausspruch mit: "Wie er lügen soll, kann ihm niemand vorschreiben." Nun ja! Als ich den letzten Brief meiner Mutter las, da drohten mich alle guten Geister zu verlassen, mit Ihnen [sic] auch Sie; Auch Ihr Thun und Rat schien [sic] mich zu verspotten und wehmütig blickte ich Ihnen in graue Ferne nach!

Ihr
Lehmann

Am 10. Februar ist unsere Trauung auf dem Standes Amt; auf Wunsch des alten Dreis folgt eine Kirchliche am Nachmittage in der Dorfkirche zu Flintbeck bei Kiel von einem M. verwandten Pastoren. Die nötigen Möbel werden inzwischen von M.—aus ihrem, auch Mutters Hausrat zusammengesetzt—besorgt und hier angelangt sein, hier ist eine geräumige Wohnung zum Einziehen bereit. Das Staatsexamen suche ich dann so bald wie möglich zu beschaffen.[39]

This sad letter bears eloquent witness to Lehmann's depressed state following such a harrying period. The fact that he chose Heimann as the recipient of such a letter may be explained in part because he had just, through the honest Köster, heard that Heimann was wont to use the very apt word "Flackerbrünste" to describe his extreme oscillations of mood. Thus nettled, Lehmann attempted to get his own back and vented his spleen in the best way he knew—through his pen.

Thus, with his marriage to Martha Wohlstadt on 10 February 1906, ended Lehmann's student days in Kiel—for the time being, at least. And thus began a new period as he settled down to teaching and married life in the tiny and isolated village of Eldena, some 30 miles south of Schwerin.

4

Eldena (1906-1907). "Tausend äußere Widerwärtigkeiten"—and Worse.

ANY THOUGHT THAT the worst was now over and that the wedding would usher in a new period of agreeable domestic stability was soon dispelled by the actual events. Martha's parents insisted on a church ceremony in addition to the civil marriage, but then refused to attend either. Agathe Lehmann also stayed away and kept Lita from attending, too. So Lehmann and Martha had the support of only Walter and Köster, who were witnesses, and the Heimanns, who were unable to attend but lent their moral support from Berlin. The pastor at Flintbek, an "unsympathischer Mann, vollbärtig, mit dicken, rotvioletten Genießerlippen,"[1] was an uncle of Martha's and undoubtedly knew the background, because "eine versteckte Anspielung auf Marthas Zustand unterblieb nicht"[2] and, furthermore, he omitted the word "Jungfrau" on the marriage certificate— something which was to be of consequence later on. With wry humor in view of the past few weeks, Lehmann chose as their "Trautext" a verse from the book of Matthew which was particularly apt: "Kommet her zu mir alle, die ihr mühselig und beladen seid: ich will euch erquicken" (Matthew 11, v. 28).

After the wedding and the somewhat subdued celebrations, the couple travelled to Eldena (not Caspar David Friedrich's Eldena, incidentally) and settled into the roomy but drafty apartment which came with the job. Somehow they were ever conscious (probably justifiably) that the scornful eyes of the whole village were upon them. Martha, with her magnificent head of fashionably groomed hair, had stood out in Kiel and had made people there turn their heads. Here, she must have struck the citizens of Eldena as "eine Art großstädtische Kurtisane," as Lehmann himself later put it.[3] Neither she, nor the socially inept Lehmann were able to allay the innate hostility such closed communities as Eldena invariably feel towards newcomers breaking in on their isolation, and it was difficult for them both to relax. They had escaped, it seemed, from the malicious gossip and psychological pressures of relatives and acquaintances only "um wieder der Welt, den Leuten, ihrem Geschwätz, ihrer Ranküne in den Rachen zu gleiten."[4]

But Lehmann threw himself into his new career with some considerable energy. There were about twenty boys at varying levels above the Volksschule in the school, and he dutifully made up a teaching schedule with no less than 39 lessons so as to accommodate each one: "the busy bee has no sorrow" was Lehmann's ironic comment, slightly misquoting Blake.[5] Although he had earlier made it clear that he would not teach arithmetic, he nonetheless found himself obliged to do so—much to his alarm and later regret. The obligation to teach this hated subject turned out to be the thin end of the wedge: try as he might, he just could not put this alien discipline across to the village boys, and his success in other subjects seemed to diminish as he gradually lost his self-confidence.

If his lack of self-confidence made for a relatively unpleasant time in the classroom, it made life within the village community well-nigh impossibly miserable for the Lehmann's. Wilhelm Lehmann was so obsessed with the idea that Martha and he presented a strange and ill-matched couple that he felt persecuted wherever he turned. To compensate, he doffed his hat at the villagers whenever possible and was almost obsequious before the parents in whose direct employ he was. He found the family who lived in the apartment above him particularly inquisitive and was convinced that they were tampering with his mail. His oversensitivity in this respect may be judged from the fact that he had encouraged his brother Walter to seal his letters with sealing-wax during the few weeks he spent alone in Eldena before the marriage.

For the benefit of Martha, who was not particularly gifted in practical household matters, they hired a maid, Ida Verleih, whom they could ill afford considering Lehmann's meager salary. But neither Martha nor he were able to treat her in such a way that any mutual respect developed. Martha's initial gushing friendliness soon gave way to belligerence, and the maid responded with rudeness and chicanery until the whole affair came to a head in December 1906. Martha accused Ida of dishonesty and said as much in public. Such an accusation was bound to get back to the Verleihs in such a close-knit community as Eldena; and Lehmann, in his turn, soon heard indirectly that they were considering taking him to court for slander. But instead of rationally considering the situation and concluding that such a step would be exceedingly unlikely, he brooded on it and literally worried himself sick until the very day they left.

It seemed that the whole village was against them. There was one common entrance for the two sets of tenants in the house, and since the kitchen was separated from the entrance hall only by a partition which did not stretch to the ceiling, it was uncomfortably drafty. Lehmann decided to have the partition extended to the ceiling to keep out the draft, but was not wise enough to consult the landlord beforehand as to who would foot the bill. He proceeded in like manner with the installation of a laundry boiler, and was soon furious to find that in both cases he was expected to pay. He refused to do so, however, and was told that the boiler would have to be removed. He turned to the local squire Försterling for help and the threat was not carried out. Luckily the house changed hands, and in the confusion both partition and boiler became an issue between the new and the old owner, so he slipped out of one more problem—much to his relief.

To compensate in part for the almost complete lack of any pleasant human company, the Lehmann's acquired a starling. But here too—initially at least— nothing went right. The bird developed sore feet and Lehmann wrote to his brother, a great source of consolation at this time, for advice as to how to treat the unfortunate creature. Furthermore, perhaps because of the feet, it would not sing, and its silence seemed to underline their isolation. But then, as the Easter bells began to ring out, it suddenly burst into song and the house seemed to lose some of its oppressive darkness. Walter who had a dog and kept an assortment of birds, offered his brother a jay. But Wilhelm, who had in any case just acquired a kestrel, turned the offer down. It almost seemed as if the two brothers were seeking to recapture those halcyon days of childhood in the Pächterhof, but Lehmann was now all too aware of the meaning of freedom, and he soon let the proud and magnificent creature free.

Lehmann and Martha were not quite without friends or human contacts. The village physician, Dr. Möller, an agnostic and on war-like footing with Pastor Behm,[6] was agreeable company, as were the Schwerins who ran the inn just across from where the Lehmann's lived. The closest to a friend that Lehmann possessed in Eldena was the squire Försterling, and it was to Försterling that Lehmann came when in great need of comfort, as for instance at the time of the slander threat. The main source of comfort at this time was Walter Lehmann, however, and the brothers exchanged letters full of comments regarding the current state of the weather, the flora and fauna, and the various dramas in their respective narrow communities. In a position similar to Lehmann's in Carolienensiel, Walter had to face many of the problems which were so bothersome to his elder brother. But the future pastor was able to accept the irritating human failings and foibles he was faced with daily and could dismiss them with waggish humor. In this instance he had several advantages over his brother; not only was he blessed with that particular brand of humor (so often lacking in his brother) necessary to deal with such situations, but he had not been saddled with the responsibility of the first-born. He was thus able to avoid the additional aggravation of Agathe Lehmann's comments. As Lehmann put it in *Mühe des Anfangs,* referring to his mother's reaction to his hasty marriage plans, "Der Ausdruck 'Erstgeborener' wiederholte sich wie ein Triller."[7] He was always plagued by the notion that he was not living up to his responsibilities, and the resultant guilt colored his outlook on life in general. Walter, of course, was also at an advantage in not suffering quite the same material deprivation stemming from the marriage and a growing family.

In fact, the material circumstances of the Lehmanns rapidly became desperate.

Lehmann was paid 1800 Mk for his teaching duties, and this sum, although not at all princely (in the State schools he would have received twice as much—with his Staatsexamen behind him) should have been sufficient for them to live frugally but comfortably. Had Lehmann or Martha been married to someone else, it would have sufficed; but the combination of Martha's household ineptitude and Lehmann's lack of practical expertise was little short of disastrous. Martha was extravagant in small things, like tips, and careless in larger matters, like household bills. Since she did not keep receipts, it sometimes happened that the same bill was paid twice. Lehmann's request for financial help from Martha's parents was turned down, and they were soon obliged to break into what remained of the Mk 4000 which Martha had brought into the marriage. When Agathe heard of their pecuniary difficulties from her daughter-in-law (Lehmann himself hardly ever wrote to his mother during his marriage to Martha), she offered to lend them some money from Lita's savings. This generous offer was, however, tempered in typical fashion by her reminding Lehmann that she herself must soon rely on the support of her eldest son now that she was no longer teaching and receiving an income. Despite their sorry financial state, Lehmann was extravagantly irresponsible and cavalier in his continued acquisition of books. After a year in Eldena he was able to add up his outstanding book bills and somewhat smugly write: "Nicht erheblich viel. Trenkel ca 76.40 noch zu bezahlen, Lippold 240.25."[8] If he considered over 300 Mk, or 1/6 of his total income, "nicht erheblich viel," then the mind boggles at what his total expenditure for books at this time must have been. Small wonder that he was able to write somewhat ambiguously two months earlier: "Ob ich wirklich—ja!— immer an ein Wunder (Mäcen od. dgl.) glaube?"[9]

The tremendous proportion of their income spent on books was a result of two factors—apart from Lehmann's insatiable greed to possess his own books. Firstly, there was no library in the vicinity, and, secondly, Lehmann's new interest in scholarship—"Freie Forschung ist herrlich" as opposed to "Examensarbeit" (see p. 80 above). The positive reception of his dissertation had left him feeling particularly satisfied, and several smaller items of research were, in the course of 1906, accepted for publication: "Artikelchen zu machen ist ganz hübsch (zumal wenn sie wenig Zeit beanspruchen)," he wrote at the end of 1906,[10] once again revealing his deep-seated need for public recognition at all costs. True, the old ambivalence and doubt were still there. A day earlier he had written: "Hat *diese* Philologie noch ihr Leben, noch ihre Bedeutung für mich? Wehe, sie *muß* es doch haben," but in general the successful pursuit of etymological explorations at this time was an important and satisfying part of his life: "Wille ist alles, Arbeit ist alles, macht klar, groß, kräftig, hoch wie ein Baum."[11]

Hermann Stehr, Ernst Zupitza and then Ferdinand Holthausen had all played important roles in fostering Lehmann's innate interest in language. Zupitza and Holthausen were both primarily interested in comparative etymology, a branch of philology which was growing in importance at the time and attracting many significant scholars like Friedrich Kluge, Wilhelm Wundt, and the Pole Jan Rozwadowski. Kluge is, of course, still well known today for his *Etymologisches Wörterbuch der deutschen Sprache,* which first came out in 1881—one year before Lehmann's birth. Largely because of Kluge's pioneering work a spate of etymological journals and dictionaries arose during the first decade of the 20th century. One of these, Alois Walde's *Lateinisches Etymologisches Wörterbuch* (1906), quoted from Lehmann's own dissertation—much to his delight and satisfaction. Wundt was important for two reasons: first, one of the two essay projects Lehmann was faced with for his Staatsexamen was an investigation of Wundt's philosophy of language; and second, Wundt's recent and pioneering work *Sprachgeschichte und Sprachpsychologie* (1901) provided the source for Rozwadowski's *Wortbildung und Wortbedeutung* (1904). It was this book which gripped Lehmann's attention and helped him formulate a theory of language which was crucial in the development of his poetic theory and practice.

Rozwadowski perceived that the designation of the object reflected only one aspect of it, and that it was arrived at subjectively. Paradoxically, the designation which reflects only part of the whole and which was arrived at through the "Enge der Apperzeption" nonetheless allows the object to appear as "ein einheitliches Ganzes." This is because human consciousness is blessed with an "Einheit der Apperzeption" as well as an "Enge der Apperzeption." This dual aspect of human consciousness is matched by the "Einheit und Enge der Benennung." It is but a step from this formulation of Rozwadowski's to the almost leitmotiv phrase which appears throughout Lehmann's essays: "Des Totalerlebnisses werden wir nur mittels des Einzelerlebnisses inne,"[12] or "Es braucht in der Tat Erfahrung, um zu merken, daß man eines Ganzen nur teilhaftig wird, wenn man eines Teiles sich bemächtigt, daß das All nur als ein Etwas sich beschwören läßt...."[13]

In 1906 Lehmann was still far from producing such poems as were to appear in his mature years. Indeed, partly because of the constant harrassments and trials of life with the villagers of Eldena and the demands his teaching made on his time and nerves, his poetic production at this time was almost non-existent. He was, by the same token, also far from such theoretical statements as those quoted above. But his etymological studies at this time reflected the influence of Rozwadowski and are, in a very real sense, the forerunners of his later poetological writings. Most of his short papers deal with the etymological development of plant and animal names and show how the name reflects a part of the whole. It was with great delight that Lehmann was able to show direct links between old high German and Gaelic words. This seemed to demonstrate that Gaelic retained the character of the older languages in a way that German or English did not. And since he subscribed to the "Romantic" notion that the older languages were closer to the essence of things, Gaelic took up a position of even greater importance in Lehmann's private studies and sphere of interest. It was

Gaelic, he said in *Mühe des Anfangs,* "dessen Märchen und Sagen mich geheimnisvoll anredeten and das mir als *die* Sprache vorkam."[14] In the brief laudatory essay entitled "Irisches," which appeared in the *Neue Rundschau* in 1914, Lehmann asserts that the sound of the language itself and the remarkable sagas of Ireland make it easy to understand "daß die Irländer kühn genug gewesen sind, den Homer für eine Übersetzung aus ihrer Sprache zu erklären."[15] In the light of Lehmann's deep appreciation of the particularly primal nature of Irish and of his use of comparative etymology in getting back to the pure roots of language, it is now possible to trace a direct line from those conversations with Stehr in Berlin, through Zupitza's and Holthausen's lectures to his two dissertation topics (the first, it will be remembered, was a translation of and commentary on an Anglo-Saxon version of Genesis) and the collection of articles following the completion of his doctorate. The second, and completed, dissertation topic itself (an investigation of the old English prefix uz-, the equivalent of the German prefix ur-) is accordingly not a cranky piece of obscure philological research but flesh of his intellectual and poetic flesh.

The hours of linguistic research distracted Lehmann from the more unpleasant aspects of life in Eldena much of the time, and he was usually at his happiest while engaged on this work. Each day he looked forward with considerable impatience to the mail, which brought him books and letters from Zupitza, Rozwadowski, and various scholar-editors of linguistic journals such as the *Beiblatt zur Anglia, Zeitschrift für Celtische Philologie,* and others.[16] Meanwhile the birth of the child was imminent. Neither Martha nor Lehmann could enjoy the anticipation of the event fully, for they were both extremely apprehensive during the course of Martha's pregnancy. Old Dr. Möller reassured them as best he could, but they felt the need of the best facilities and medical attention and therefore enlisted the aid of the Heimanns to arrange for a room in the Berlin "Urbankrankenhaus," and asked whether Martha could spend a few days with them just prior to the confinement.

It was just before this that an occurrence in the village caused considerable alarm in the Lehmann household. Dr. Möller died, and Pastor Behm refused to officiate at this agnostic's funeral. It was less the loss of a physician-friend which worried Lehmann than Behm's attitude, which, together with the fact that Lehmann had been conditioned by his mother to an acceptance of the bourgeois moral code (even if he had not followed it), now made him fearful, as he admitted in a letter to Moritz Heimann, that the birth would reveal both the illegitimate conception of the child and the lies he had told to conceal the fact thus far:

Der kaum gefundene Boden wankt schon wieder unter meinen Füßen und ich befinde mich in seelischer Unruhe und Unsicherheit: jedes Kind wird hier nämlich beim Pastoren angemeldet wobei bei seiner genauen Art Trauschein notwendig ist und so muß, wie es scheint, die Lüge meinerseits doch ans Licht kommen. Der hiesige Geistliche ist ein engherziger Zelot, der mir sicherlich mein bißchen

Lebenslicht ausblasen wird, wenn er einen, der sich als "Lehrer und Leiter der Jugend geberdet" [sic], auf derlei Unmoral ertappt.[17]

Even towards the end of July, Lehmann and Martha both thought that the child would not arrive before the end of August or the beginning of September. The Heimanns, as usual possessed of a better grasp of reality, were convinced that the beginning of August was more likely, and urged Martha to come as soon as possible, which she did. On 28 July Heimann was able to write to Lehmann, quoting from Goethe's "Talisman," and tell him that the birth was imminent: "wie wär es, wenn Sie heut, am Empfangstag dieses Briefes, Sonntag, herkämen? Es ist so weit, möge Alles gut gehen! Bis jetzt sind alle Nachrichten günstig! Danke Gott, wenn er Dich preßt, und dank ihm, wenn er Dich wieder entläßt. Ich drücke Ihnen herzlich die Hand, kommen Sie freudig."

Everything went tolerably well, especially considering Martha's age and the fact that this was her first child, and on 2 August 1906 a son was born. Heimann, knowing of Lehmann's love for the Romantics, especially Brentano and Arnim, suggested the name Clemens Joachim, and the child was baptized thus. Agathe Lehmann came to Berlin in order to accompany Martha and Joachim back to Eldena, and Heimann was on hand to help them all into the train. Walter, who meanwhile had moved to Thuringia, sent them a beautiful, traditionally carved, and inlaid cradle. But the relief and joy over the birth were soon marred for Lehmann as his fears regarding Behm's reaction were unfortunately confirmed. He went to report the birth one evening and shrank back when Behm asked for the marriage certificate, compared dates and noticed that the designation "Jungfrau" was missing. Lehmann at first protested that the word "Jungfrau" was never included where he came from, but then, noticing that Behm was not to be that easily shaken off, he admitted the truth and played the humble penitent. Behm was satisfied and offered up a prayer of gratitude for the safe delivery the following Sunday. Lehmann's fear of Behm and desire to keep up appearances at this stage of his life were such that he regularly attended church services in Eldena—something he had not done since childhood and never did again thereafter.

In September school began again—much to Lehmann's chagrin, for his teaching had become pure torture for him. Unable himself to work out the mathematical problems he set his pupils, he was obliged to write to Martha's brother-in-law (who was the director of an office of weights and measures) and ask him for the solutions to some interest problems he had set. His omission of any geometry from the curriculum led one parent to protest vehemently, and Lehmann was obliged to introduce this subject in order to mollify him.

In early September Lehmann wrote to Heimann, using a botanical pun to describe his feelings: "Schule heute wieder begonnen mit Calluna vulgaris, recht mühselig."[18] The botanical name for heather enabled Lehmann to allude somewhat more subtly to the vulgar stupidity of his charges. Heimann, at home in both Latin and botany, would have had no difficulty understanding his young friend.

During his year in Eldena Lehmann continued to show an active interest in botany and scientific matters in general. But just as he emulated Zupitza's "kombinatorische Phantasie" in linguistic matters, so in science, too, did he seek out and absorb that which involved cross-references. *Das Sinnesleben der Pflanzen* (1905) by the biologist Raoul Heinrich Francé (1874-1943), whose works achieved some degree of popularity in the first decades of our century, was eagerly read, and it exerted a considerable influence on Lehmann.[19] It was now that Lehmann began to take long, solitary walks through the countryside, observing carefully all flora and fauna. It was a habit he never lost the rest of his long life. The desire to be alone was not surprising in a man of Lehmann's temperament, and it certainly afforded him some relief from his misery in the classroom. But Martha, meanwhile, was thrown back upon herself, and her husband's long walks underlined her loneliness in a hostile world. Lehmann's compulsive flight into seclusion began to take its toll on the marriage.

Back from Berlin with Joachim, Martha devoted herself to his care so exclusively that she neglected the household matters. Unable to cope with the more or less open hostility she encountered from the village folk, she sank into one depression after another. Lehmann tried to draw her out of such moods by "Liebenswürdigkeit," but in vain, and the shaky foundations of the marriage began to crumble. Aware of his own general selfishness and no doubt thinking of his father's irresponsibility in his marriage, Lehmann tended to blame himself for many of the domestic crises, and since the successful completion of his Staatsexamen seemed as far away as ever, his self-disgust grew.

In fact, Lehmann's dissatisfaction with self was nothing new. His diary for the Berlin years contains enough evidence of earlier disgust, as we have seen. At that point in his life it seemed that a combination of lack of achievement, lack of love, and constitutional shortcomings was the main source of his unhappiness. By the end of 1906, however, it might have seemed on the surface that he had progressed beyond his adolescent problems. He had fallen in love and married the woman he loved; he had completed a doctoral dissertation which had been published and had found favor with scholars, and he was turning out and publishing short scholarly articles in a satisfying way. But his problems were more deeply seated and by no means overcome. His initial love for Martha was seemingly unable to withstand the pressures of material want and societal disdain and began to fade. And his success in scholarship was a result of his own solitary endeavor and served only to point up his loneliness and his tendency to withdraw into himself.

The year 1906 was therefore not the beginning of a contented and stable marriage. Lehmann's relationship with Martha, which had earlier promised to inspire poems marked by depth of feeling and felicity of form, could not withstand the trials of financial hardship and village hostility. Had they been accorded the comfort and security of independent means, this marriage of two such demanding and idiosyncratic personalities might have stood a better chance of working. But unhappy in his work and only occasionally happy in his marriage, Lehmann found his desire and ability to write poems dwindling. He had neither the peace of mind nor the emotional excitement necessary for poetic creation. Instead, he applied himself ever more to his scholarly research, which was sufficiently structured to keep his attention and oblige him to channel his energies in a way that poetry could not.

By the end of the year 1906, Lehmann was in rather low spirits: his and Martha's finances were in a sorry state, and he had reached an extreme pitch of nervousness[20] which was exacerbated by both the tension in the marriage and his poetic unproductivity. So sensitive was he that the successes of even those near to him depressed and worried him. His brother Walter had written a story entitled "Das abendrote Haus" and had, at Wilhelm's suggestion, sent it to Heimann. The latter was impressed and wrote to Wilhelm and told him so. Lehmann's subsequent journal entry contains just a hint of envy: "Walter also *doch* ein Dichter? Heimann zweifelt morgen schon wieder."[21] It was at this time that Köster published his study of Pascal, and this caused Lehmann to note how small he felt next to his brother's friend: "Vor Köster—sobald was von ihm kommt, beuge ich mich unter ihm: er ist wohl fähiger als ich—liebens[werten] Brief bekommen."[22]

In this mood of depression there seemed to be little to hold him in Eldena and he began to consider resigning his position. The threat of a slander suit from the Verleihs was still hanging over him; the teaching situation was now such that one pupil, appropriately named Sauer, was, with watch in hand, openly checking that Lehmann did not leave the classroom a minute too early; he was doing little or no work towards his Staatsexamen; and domestic happiness came ever more rarely. He accordingly looked for another position and applied for a teaching post at the Evangelische Johannesstift at Plötzensee. He cast around for help from friends and relatives, and wrote to Gerhart Hauptmann, who agreed to help— though in what way remains unclear.[23] He even enlisted the aid of his Aunt Doris, who promised to try to help him get a university teaching position. But he was by no means sure of what his next step should really be and therefore he wrote letters to both Heimann and Köster in which he aired the possibility of leaving Eldena. Both responded quickly and urged him to do so: "Kündigen Sie, kündigen Sie!" wrote the ebullient Köster.[24] For his part, Heimann, knowing that Lehmann had applied for a teaching position at Plötzensee (with a five-year contract no less!), was a little more constructive with his advice. Lehmann should certainly resign, but he should, by the same token, not accept a five-year contract at a strictly religious boarding school.

Knowing that Lehmann's position would not improve until he passed his Staatsexamen, Heimann suggested that he borrow some money and spend a year concentrating only on his examination preparation.[25] He asked Lehmann to let him know how much he would need for such a year and promised to attempt to raise a loan to that amount for Lehmann's use.

Faced with this possibility, Lehmann began to waver. In almost pathetic fashion he had in any case totally ruined his Plötzensee application by electing to tell the chaplain at this institution, one Pastor Phillipps, about his peculiar marriage to an older woman. Realizing what he had done, he then attempted to rectify matters by explaining why he had felt it necessary to bring up the subject in the first place—a few days later he drafted a letter withdrawing his application, and the whole affair, doomed from the start, came to nothing.

But still he hesitated about a loan for a year to prepare for his examination, and Heimann was obliged to repeat his advice to do just this a month later, adding that he himself could guarantee "1500 Mk fürs freie Jahr."[26] Even now Lehmann hesitated—perhaps because his pupils, in a display of generous Christmas spirit, had showered him with gifts: "Jungens schenkten mir schöne Decke, Gummischuhe, kleine lächerliche Nippes (wird mir aber lieb bleiben, das fühle ich jetzt schon)."[27]

For this and other reasons, Christmas turned out to be a fairly pleasant occasion. Agathe and Lita came and were delighted with Joachim; there were gifts (Köster sent Joachim an edition of Plotinus' *Enneads!*—which undoubtedly pleased the father more than the son) and a prevailing mood of cheerfulness, not to mention Heimann's usual Christmas letter, with the guarantee of 1500 Mk. Things soon changed. On 30 December, Lehmann, still unsure whether to resign or not (although he had by now formulated his letter of resignation), was dismissed: "Mir wurde heute gekündigt!" but he took the news philosophically, "Auch darüber wird langes, grünes Gras wachsen."[28] Lehmann's overhearing the village washerwoman, Frau Krull, triumphantly telling his neighbor, "Wie hebbt em künnigt,"[29] served only to emphasize that there was no staying in the hostile atmosphere of Eldena.

Since the position at Plötzensee had not materialized, it was now, at least, clear that he would heed Heimann's advice, take a year off, and live from the loan which his friend had promised to procure for him. The question was simply: where should they move? where could he live economically and devote himself to study? Martha's parents suggested Malente in Schleswig-Holstein as a suitable place, and Lehmann went there on the weekend of the 2-3 February and arranged to rent "eine kleine Seewohnung in Holstein am Dieksee"[30] from a certain Kipp. It seemed as if it was just a matter of living out the remaining few months as painlessly as possible, and looking forward to a better future in Malente quietly preparing for his examination.

Meanwhile, with the end of his miserable Eldena year in sight, his thoughts turned to poetry again and he sought out some poems he had written around the time he was in Penkun a few years earlier, bundled them up and sent them to Oscar Bie on 5 January in the hope they might be published in the *Neue Rundschau*. The next few days saw him trying his hands at some new poems— the first for over a year. Not that he had much faith in their quality or his ability:

Ich bin wie ein Wahnsinniger: ganz aus meiner Bahn der eigentlichen Arbeit herausgerissen: kommt durch Dichten (ich schrieb einiges weiter), und durch Schule.

But, as the passage immediately following shows, his depression was general at this point: "Folgende Tage: Verzweifelt und krank in mir,...trieb mich sehnsuchtvoll verzerrt in Botanik und Biologie umher: empfand störend das Verheiratetsein."[31] In addition to this he was troubled by a nagging toothache throughout the month of February, and his spirits seemed to be at a particularly low ebb. Surely life could only improve? Surely he and Martha deserved a respite from all the buffeting Eldena had meted out to them? But worse was soon to follow.

On 23 February little Joachim's first tooth showed through. Over the next week or so there were several sleepless nights for the Lehmanns, and Martha, in particular, began to suffer from exhaustion. On 2 March, a Saturday, Lehmann disconsolately and with an uncanny sense of foreboding wrote in his diary "Was soll das Ganze? Mir scheint, es passiert noch was 'Übles.' Was, wag ich nicht zu schreiben." The same day he wrote "Kind weint Nachts, Zähne. Martha totmüde. Ich dumpf-verdrossen," and the following day continued "aber das Kind schreit furchtbar, armes Kerlchen, fieberheiß, Zähne." By 5 March they were so worried that they sent for the young doctor who had replaced Dr. Möller—after they themselves hamfistedly attempted to cool the baby's alarming fever by dipping it in cold water. By the time the doctor arrived the next day, it was too late; he "zündete ein Streichholz vor den holden Augen an: sie zuckten nicht mehr. Joachim war tot."[32]

It was the bitterest blow with which to end their lonely year in Eldena—their first year of marriage. The Heimanns rushed over to Eldena from Berlin and did their best to console the wretched couple. Moritz Heimann offered his young friend "über der geliebten Leiche das Du an und sagte zu Martha, sie könne nie mehr arm werden."[33] The grief-stricken couple decided to bury their child in Malente, away from the accursed Eldena. They accordingly quickly wound up their affairs, packed their belongings, and set off for their native Schleswig-Holstein. Even now, after the tragedy of Joachim's death, the people of Eldena did not shrink from taking off some Mk 50 from his salary, on the grounds that he had started teaching at Eldena a week later than the terms of his contract demanded. In vain did Lehmann protest that he had made up this lost time in the intervening months. The whole world seemed devoid of feeling; as Lehmann accompanied the tiny coffin to the station and then on to Malente, he clutched, as it seemed to him, an all too stark reminder of the callous world they lived in: "'Vorschriftsmäßig eingesargt', sagte das offizielle Schreiben, das mich als Begleiter der Leiche auswies."[34]

5

Malente and Neumünster (1907-1912). A "vollkommener staatlich geölter und geschmierter Schulmeister."

THE ELDENA EPISODE saw the beginning of a rather unhappy marriage, a turning away from poetry to linguistic scholarship, and a disastrous start to a teaching career. Faced with the unhappiness of his domestic and professional situation, the introspective Lehmann withdrew still further into his inner self and suffered in his self-enforced isolation. His poetic ambitions persisted, though how he was to realize them remained unclear. All these problems were not going to resolve themselves, and he knew it. It was absolutely clear that his priority was now more than ever the attainment of his Staatsexamen, and, in the hope that all other problems would disappear with the achievement of this next big step, Lehmann looked forward to applying himself systematically and consistently to study. As it turned out, the next few years did indeed see a resolution to most of his problems, but the manner of this resolution turned out to be typically arduous and taxing.

Once they had buried Joachim in the cemetery at Malente-Gremsmühlen and spent a week or two with Lehmann's mother and Lita in Wandsbek, he and Martha did their best to settle into a new life, a new routine in the Holstein spa. Situated on a narrow neck of land between the Dieksee and Kellersee, Malente had been "discovered" in the 1860's as a resort by an enterprising hotelier who capitalized on the current fashion of holidaying in Switzerland by designating his area as the "Holsteinische Schweiz." The decision to move to the gentle, wooded hills and picturesque lakes surrounding Malente had left Lehmann with ambiguous feelings right from the start: "...ich begebe mich jetzt aus dem Wirken—relativ—zwischen und in Menschen ins Wirken außerhalb und ganz *ohne* die Menschen. Ob das Wasser und die Bücher mir tönen werden?"[1] The water certainly exerted its fascination on Lehmann and often kept him from the very books he intended to study. Despite a meticulously worked out program of examination preparation, which he committed carefully to paper in the hope that he might thus be better able to resist the temptation to follow more congenial pursuits, Lehmann all too frequently went rowing on the lake or hiking through the woods and fields. As in Eldena he thus avoided human contact in general, although there was one exception in this regard.

His landlord, Kipp, was an agreeable and pleasant-natured type who was always willing to stop and chat with his young tenant or oblige him by taking him into town or to the station in his pony and trap. Whenever Martha was away, Lehmann would eat with the Kipps and enjoy talking with these simple and uncomplicated people. Kipp, moreover, was understanding in the matter of rent and was always willing to wait a few days or even some weeks if the Lehmanns, as was usually the case, had no ready cash at hand. Lehmann was exceedingly grateful for Kipp's kindness and friendly manner, but was incapable of appreciating it without, as was his wont, drawing some self-destructive moral from it: "Wie gut," he wrote in his diary, "wie liebevoll gut immer Herr Kipp mir vorkommt. Wie reich gegen mich. Wie bin ich arm!"[2]

The isolation into which Lehmann had now withdrawn by opting for a year of private study simply pointed up his inherent self-doubts again: "Wie *nichts* besitze ich! Keine Kenntnisse" and "Was weiß ich von Dichten? Weiter bin ich davon entfernt als je" were the self-deprecating remarks that found their way into his diary at this time.[3] His depression was not much alleviated by any warmth and sympathy within the marriage. Martha could not recover from the blow of Joachim's death. She visited the grave often and planted it with flowers, but then returned in such a tearful state from her visits that her husband, finding it impossible to console her, gradually became resentful of her continuing overwhelming grief. There were pleasanter moments. Lehmann, out walking one day, came upon a family of ducklings in the lake near their house. He gathered them up in his hat and brought them along for Martha to see, and suddenly the clouds of depression rolled back at the sight of such young and carefree life.

Martha, happily for them both, soon became pregnant again, and the grief at the loss of one child gradually gave way to happy anticipation of the next. But her pregnancy, alas, brought on varicose veins. A maid was absolutely necessary, but the one they hired was not altogether reliable, and Lehmann lived in dread of her frequent absences and the sight of Martha painfully standing in the kitchen washing up. A husband in the year 1907 just did not help in the kitchen. "Wir sind nicht gut fürs Leben gerüstet. Martha und ich nicht" was his wry and all-too-accurate comment in his diary.[4]

The maid was really a considerable extravagance for a family whose resources were meager and whose inability to deploy such resources carefully was pathological. Heimann had managed to secure a sum of money in loans from various people, including Eduard Stucken the writer. But in light of Lehmann's continued frenetic acquisition of books, the cost of the recent move and now the imminent birth of another child, this sum did not stretch far. Throughout 1907 Lehmann was continually "borrowing" sums of money from Heimann, and revealing details of the expenditure which demanded the loans. Heimann thus came to hear of the exorbitant cost of printing Lehmann's dissertation (which had appeared the previous summer) and was so shocked that he advised bargaining with the printer before paying the bill. In the event Heimann might just as well have advised Lehmann to forward the bill to the Kaiser, for the printer, after much wrangling, was finally persuaded to take over the grand sum of 50 Mk out of a total bill of 1337 Mk.[5] Lehmann's need for money also led him to consider a scheme for earning money which was, in the circumstances, all but insane. His friend had firm advice regarding this scheme too: "Jetzt Pensionäre nehmen und unterrichten, das wäre die Ökonomie eines Negers, der den Palmbaum umhaut, um die Datteln zu pflücken."[6] Lehmann assessed his debts at this stage of his life as in excess of 3000 Mk.[7]

Despite his domestic situation, his congenital dislike of examination work, and pressing financial demands, Lehmann did manage to forge ahead in his quest for the seemingly unattainable Staatsexamen. The first hurdle involved two major essays, which had first been set in 1905 and whose deadline Lehmann had continually deferred until now, when a final deadline of 1 August had been set. On this date he took the train to Schleswig, where he submitted an essay "Über die Principien der Sprachphilosophie bei Wundt" and an "Übersetzung der Paragraphen 11 bis 28 (S. 10-20) [seiner] Dissertation in das Englische." With this requirement behind him, Lehmann heaved a huge but momentary sigh of relief, set his sights on the oral examination, and planned his reading for the next few months. At the beginning of September, however, almost as a belated celebration, Lehmann arranged to go to Berlin to see Heimann. His brief postcard describes his frame of mind succinctly and effectively:

> Liebster Heimann.
> Ich komme morgen Freitag 12:56 Mittag in Berlin an. Ich komme nicht aus 'praktischen Gründen'. Gott verdamme das Praktische. Ich möchte nur etwas mit Dir über Kunst und Wissenschaft reden. Zur Erhebung. Ich hungere hier aus. Ist es verständlich? ...[8]

His moving away from Eldena had meant considerable change and should have made for an improved situation. But the isolation Lehmann so compulsively sought also entailed artistic and cultural loneliness. He himself saw the irony of his situation: "In Eldena hatte ich 1000 äußere Widerwärtigkeiten. Hier ist es kühl, ruhig, quasi 'ungestört', keine äußeren Pflichten: Und wie schrecklich doch auch hier alles wieder."[9]

Lehmann's final examinations had been postponed from October 1907 to 31 January 1908, and as autumn gave way to winter and this date grew nearer he began to worry again—even though he was working rather well during this period. The reason for this improvement in his working habits was not only the pressure but also, in part, the fact that Martha, whose confinement was expected around the New Year, had left Malente for Kiel early in October and was preparing for the arrival of their second child while staying with her parents. Everything seemed to be building towards a climax: the new child and Lehmann's Staatsexamen both promised a busy start to 1908. Meanwhile, as he began to worry about his military service again and to read up on child nutrition for fear that their second child might also die, the financial situation was steadily moving towards a climax of ever higher debts and continually increasing requests for ever greater sums of money. There was no coal left for the winter, for instance, and most of the borrowed money was spent. Recorded in his diary is the pathetic but telling phrase "Wollen mit Palmin (70 Pfg.) kochen und braten."[10] Then the hospital costs for Martha's confinement would have to be met, and, worrisome though the Staatsexamen itself was, there was no sign of a position thereafter. Faced with a bill of 50 Mk Gemeindesteuern, Lehmann wrote obsequious letters to the authorities seeking dispensation—and got it: such grotesque proportions did legitimate worries attain in the vivid and neurotic imagination of Wilhelm Lehmann.

The problem of a teaching post had clearly been a topic of conversation while Lehmann had been in Berlin with the Heimanns. Heimann and Samuel Fischer were both involved in the new "Freie Schulgemeinde" which Paul Geheeb had founded the previous year in Wickersdorf near Saalfeld. Lehmann now pressed Heimann to find out whether there might be a position for him there as an English teacher, and . . . could Heimann please be so kind as to send him some 900 Mk?[11] Heimann, as usual, obliged on both accounts, encouraging him with the notion that he and Wickersdorf were made for each other and finding the 900 Mk through Max Marschalk and Samuel Fischer.

December came and went, and then in the evening of 6 January 1908, after "ein Sturm draußen zum Bangesein,"[12] Martha gave birth to a boy, Berthold. The account continues: "Am 6. Januar 08 Abends 9:20 ist mir ein süßer kleiner Sohn geboren; fand heute, 7. Jan. Morgens 4 Uhr das Telegramm, fuhr hin. Martha geschwächt, Gott wird sie wieder gesund werden lassen." Upon his return from Kiel Lehmann was immediately confronted with a flood of advice from his mother regarding how he should comport himself as a husband and a father and how Martha might this time be a better mother. Meanwhile his examination was drawing closer, and the pressure was beginning to wear on his nerves. Receiving no word from Martha for almost a week, he suddenly wrote not one but two extraordinary letters full of bitter recriminations which, in the circumstances, were not only totally unjustified but also cruelly thoughtless. The shorter, more extreme, and probably second letter is given in its entirety:

Liebe Martha!
Meine Kraft und meine Geduld sind am Ende. Die frech empörende Rücksichtslosigkeit gegen *mich,* den Hausherrn, der ich am Ende meiner

gemißhandelten Kräfte bin, raubt mir den letzten Halt. Ich reise morgen zu Walter, weil meine Nerven hier allein nicht weiter wollen. Mein Geld ist nicht dazu da, um mich am [?] von einer Wärterin bedeuten zu lassen, von einer Wöchnerin könne man keine Nachricht verlangen. Die Person hielt mich für blödsinning (ich bin es allerdings zur Hälfte schon): aber *du,* die du 10 Personen hast, die *jedem* Wink Deiner [?] befolgen, du läßest seit Dienstag *nicht* an mich schreiben. Da ich außerdem wahnsinnig werde bei dem Gedanken an den Aufstand mit dem Kinde in Eldena in zweiter Auflage, der *gewiß* wieder eintritt; wüßte ich es nicht so, so ist mir *dies* ein klares Zeichen. Mein Wort gilt *nichts* in meinem Hause, was *ich* will, geschieht nicht. Also Gott sei Dank, daß ich mich wenigstens nicht darüber zu grämen brauche, daß du mit deinem Kinde *meine Person* irgendwie entbehrst. Ich habe Kipp eine Summe eingehändigt, er wird dich abholen seiner Zeit. Am besten aber gehst du wohl zu den Eltern zurück. Was ich verdiene, werde ich schicken. Es ist *aus* zwischen dir und mir für *alle* Zeiten. *So* laß ich nicht mit mir spielen. Dr. Wilhelm Lehmann[13]

Even allowing for the fact that Lehmann had equipped his wife with a number of postcards to be sent to him during her confinement, and allowing for the fact that his Staatsexamen was now looming large before him, this immoderate letter is a lamentable proof of Lehmann's overweening selfishness and pathological sensitivity. Reminiscent of some of the angrier exchanges of his own parents upon their separation some two decades earlier, the letter indicates that the marriage was not at all stable and was likely to founder unless there was some change in attitudes—especially on the part of Lehmann himself. In this bitter and overwrought frame of mind Lehmann journeyed up to Kiel for his two days of oral examinations. The event proved to be a traumatic experience.

Friday 31 January began quite inauspiciously with a nightmare journey from Malente to Kiel, which should have involved changing trains in Ascheberg:

Ich fuhr Freitag Morgen 5:43 hier ab, taumelte mit Büchertasche ins Dunkle, blieb in Ascheberg sitzen in dumpfem Sinnen, und fuhr nach Neumünster, mußte von Ascheberg-Neumünster nachbezahlen und neu von Neumünster bezahlen. Der Zug sollte 7:34 ab Neumünster gehen, hatte aber ¼ Stunde Verspätung, sodaß ich in Angst 25 Min. ca. vor 9 Uhr erst in Kiel anlangte.[14]

Once arrived in Kiel he still had to rush by horse-drawn cab to an outfitters for the obligatory dress-suit before presenting himself at 9:00 a.m. at the university. The examiners at the first session were the Schulrat Brocks and Professors Martius, Löber, and Mühlau. It began with philosophy, and Martius asked him a series of questions concerning monism—"Ich war zufrieden, er schien auch so." But then came religion, and when Brocks continued with some questions on Luther and Melanchthon, Lehmann's memory began to fail him and, despite some well-meant and kindly encouragement from the others ("Sie wissen es, seien Sie nicht so aufgeregt"), he could not recapture his composure. He then had a miserable time trying to cope with Mühlau's questions on the New Testament, origins of the Easter celebration, and St. Augustine. By eleven o'clock, mercifully, this initial ordeal was over and Lehmann, fearful of what the evening might bring, rushed off to the nearest bookstore and bought *Othello, King Lear,* and Milton's *Paradise Lost* "aus Angst vor Mangel an meiner n[eu] e[nglischen] Lektüre...und las bis mir die Augen schmerzten." After wandering around the town for a few hours he reported to Professors Holthausen and Körting at seven o'clock in the evening. The former questioned him on Langland's *Piers Ploughman,* demanding the etymologies of a dozen or so words. Then he turned to *Macbeth* and other Shakespeare dramas. Lehmann fared better in this more congenial area, but did not do as well as he himself felt he could have. His self-confidence accordingly dwindled to nothing.

The first day of examinations was over and Lehmann took a cheap room for the night. Then he ravenously consumed three "Spiegeleier, Limonade und Bier" and slept until six o'clock the next morning. Taking a tram to the University, he settled down in an empty classroom to revise the early history of new high German—only to be chased away by the cleaning ladies. As it turned out, it did not really matter, since Professor Kauffmann decided to quiz him on proto-Germanic grammar anyway. The memory of the previous day's ordeal flooded back, and Lehmann became so nervous that he found himself unable to give the answers he really knew so well. Professor Körting sat in silence as Kauffmann first applied the dagger, then mercilessly gave it twist after twist. But finally this torture, too, was brought to an end and the chastened, drained Lehmann "ging total consterniert heraus." His diary account continues, jerkily giving the gist of the bizarre, embarrassing, and highly painful proceedings:

> Ich ward *nach langer, sehr langer Debatte* hereingerufen: Die Kommission teilt Ihnen mit, daß Sie [i.e. sie] noch *nicht* das Zeugnis gegeben hat. Ich brach zusammen. Hörte Kauffmanns Stimme: Hören Sie doch weiter. Nehmen Sie Stuhl (Brocks). Bleiben Sie. Sie haben einen bedeutungsvollen Schritt vorwärts getan. In 6 Wochen. Mühlau kam und tröstete mich. Ich sollte gleich zu ihm kommen.

After the others had gone, Schulrat Brocks motioned to Lehmann to stay for a while and told him not to worry about the formality of repeating the examination in Religion and Pedagogy in six weeks time. Then he, too, vanished. Lehmann tried to pull himself together: "Ich ging. Sturm im Herzen." After he had calmed down a little, he began to piece together what had just been said to him.

In effect, the upshot of the whole sorry business was that Lehmann was accorded a pass in the subjects English, German, and Philosophy, but failed Religion and Pedagogy. As a special dispensation they were allowing him to repeat the examination in the latter two subjects in six weeks time. When he considered himself sufficiently recovered, Lehmann paid a brief visit to Mühlau and Holthausen to apologize for his weak performance and found them full of understanding and sympathy. He then telegraphed Martha and Heimann and, totally exhausted, took the evening train home. Even then his troubles were not over. Some cattle dealers insisted on smoking in his non-smoking compartment and brazenly laughed at his protestations.

Upon arrival in Malente he went first to the Pastor, in contrast to Pastor Behm a kindly man with whom Lehmann enjoyed a friendly relationship, and described his ordeal. The Pastor comforted him, suggested that he stay away from his books for a week or so, and offered to help him prepare for his examination in Religion. Over the next few days more advice and encouragement flowed in from Walter, his mother, Heimann, and even his parents-in-law. Heimann was humorously reassuring: "Das Teufelsschwänzchen—wie niedlich und boshaft, daß grade Religion es sein muß—hat nichts zu sagen."[15] Lehmann soon settled down to work again, and, on 6 March (the first anniversary of Joachim's death), Lehmann returned to Kiel and successfully completed his examination in Religion and Pedagogy—"Das Teufelsschwänzchen," as Heimann had predicted, proving to have no real bite after all. But even after the event Lehmann was unable to see it thus, and he began his diary description of the experience in a tone of blank incredulity: "Ich habe also das Staatsexamen definitiv ganz bestanden! Wie ist es möglich?"[16] The same insecurity over his own abilities which dogged him in Berlin and thereafter, an insecurity which applied to his poetic ambitions, his social accomplishments, and his studies, still overwhelmed him—despite Heimann's continued reassurances regarding his talent, despite his recently acquired confidence in his scholarly capabilities, and despite the undeniably arduous achievement of his Staatsexamen.

Now, theoretically at least, there was no valid reason why he should not embark on a teaching career in the state school system—his mother's goal for him ever since the year 1900. The Lehmanns' financial situation demanded that he earn money and earn it quickly, for they were heavily in debt all round. Lehmann hardly dared approach Heimann yet again, and so he wrote to Köster, who was now working for Eugen Diederichs in Jena. But Köster could not help, and there was nothing for it but to turn to Heimann. Heimann's resources were not inexhaustible, however, and so, without Lehmann's knowledge, Heimann contacted Agathe Lehmann. Unable to help, she in turn contacted Martha's parents, who grudgingly dipped their hands into their pockets. 200 Mk materialized, but not without a biting remark from old Herr Dreis that it was about time Lehmann earned some money and supported his wife and child like a man.

Heimann, as usual, had been plying Lehmann with good advice: Lehmann should aim for a position at Wickersdorf rather than take a post in the state system where his earnings for the Seminar and Referendar years would amount to little or nothing; he should "borrow" money from his mother which he would in any case later inherit (this latter piece of advice was based on the erroneous assumption that Agathe still had in reserve some of the insurance money she had received upon her husband's death—she did not). But Heimann now came up with a definite offer of some well-paid work which Lehmann could independently pursue at home:

> Eine kleine Einnahme weiß ich Dir. Es gilt, meines Freundes Trebitsch Übersetzungen der Werke Shaws zu kontrollieren und mit pupillarisch lexikalischer Sicherheit die Mist-takes aufzugabeln. Mist-takes mit Tinte, bloße Mißtakes mit Bleistift zu verbessern. Es handelt sich um die Dramen und, zuerst zu erledigen, zwei Essaybände. Honorar: ca. 10 Mk für den Bogen; was für die Dramen ungefähr 1000 Mk, für die Essaybände 200-250 Mk ergeben würde. Die Essaybände müßten sofort, das andere im Laufe eines Jahres gemacht werden. Willst Du diese Arbeit übernehmen?[17]

Lehmann accepted this offer after only momentary hesitation as he wondered whether he was really capable of such work. But, as Peter de Mendelssohn wrote of this episode: "Es gibt keine schauderhaftere Arbeit als eine verpatzte Übersetzung zu polieren,"[18] and so it proved. Lehmann must have heartily regretted having taken on the job on numerous subsequent occasions. Although Heimann himself was initially satisfied with Lehmann's work, there was a second person involved, Max Meyerfeld (the Oscar Wilde translator), who objected to much of Lehmann's revision over the next two years. Heimann at first defended Lehmann, calling Meyerfeld "ein widerlicher Wurm,"[19] but gradually he, too, began to find weaknesses in the Lehmann corrections and ultimately had occasion to write rather sharply, though in his own inimitable friendly manner, to his young protégé:

> Lehmann, Du verdeubelter Schurke, gleich schickst Du dem Trebitsch die Arbeit, um die er Dich zu mahnen Ursach hat—Du bist doch kein Schuljunge mehr, der etwas, nebst Vorschuß übernimmt, was er dann zu Ende zu führen zu vornehm ist. Und mach die Arbeit ordentlich, das bist Du mir schuldig. Du läßt immer die saftigsten Fehler stehen, und verbesserst so um Gotteswillen an Kleinigkeiten herum, ut aliquid fecisse videaris. Ich kenne Dich Spiegelberg.[20]

The project involved, for Lehmann, a considerable amount of time and energy and forced poor Heimann into a desperately uncomfortable position. Be that as it may, it did bring in a little money which, inevitably, disappeared as soon as it came. Happily, Lehmann's relationship to Heimann was not spoiled, and he and Trebitsch also remained on amicable terms:

> Mit S. Trebitsch bin ich viel, viel später im Tessin und in Zürich zusammengetroffen. Ich schrieb, auf seine Bitte, ein—sehr diplomatisches— Vorwort zu T's höchst fragwürdigen Gedichten. Ich pflege aber die Erinnerung an T. als einen generösen Mann.[21]

The money Lehmann received from this "generösen Mann" was nowhere near sufficient for the survival of the three Lehmanns. Fortunately another source of income, although minuscule, suddenly turned up. As the Staatsexamen seemed within his grasp, Lehmann registered his desire for a teaching position in Schleswig-Holstein with the state authorities. He now found himself offered a position for his probationary year at the Königlichen Gymnasium in Kiel, which he straightaway accepted and where he began teaching on 8 April. His professional career in the public school system thus underway, Martha's parents agreed to loan the couple some 1800 Mk to help them over the move and their (it was to be hoped) temporary pecuniary difficulties. As impractical as ever, however, Lehmann decided that he, Martha, and Berthold should settle down in Voorde, where he had spent a year as a student, and this caused his father-in-law to question his sanity. Old Dreis's faith in his children's ability in financial matters may be judged from the fact that he extended his loan in monthly installments of 150 Mk and, since Lehmann was so far in arrears with the rent, this sum threatened to be insufficient. Fortunately Lehmann was spared the embarrassing necessity of approaching Heimann for yet another loan by Kipp's kind assurance that he could wait a while for his rent—several months later he was still waiting.

Armed with a great deal of advice (mostly good) from Agathe as to how to become a successful teacher, Lehmann rose early each morning and took the 6:36 train into Kiel. Alas, the Kieler Königliche Gymnasium proved hardly any better than Eldena, and Lehmann showed the same paranoia that he had two years earlier. The very names he encountered put him off: von Rheinbaben, Tirpitz, von Doehren, von Waldersee; teaching seemed to him "ganz sinn- und ziellos"; the Primaner were "große Kälber, dumm und bedeutungslos." In short "Unterrichten [war] meistens mit Holz auf Eisen schlagen."[22] But however Lehmann saw himself as a teacher, he must have favorably impressed his own class. After he left the school, the boys sent him a picture of the class with heartiest greetings. His colleagues were, to a man, self-important clowns, "sehr unfeine Leute, die Herren vom Collegium, hochmutig und dumm!"[23] He did his best to fit in: he was "devot, fromm, verehrend, gehorsam ganz wie das Provinzialschulkollegium und ein Königlich Preussisches Gymnasium das verlangt."[24] To appear thus before his pompous colleagues involved considerable play-acting: "Ich kann vortrefflich schauspielern, mein Gesicht ist eine geölte Lehmmaske: ich kann sie oft garnicht abkriegen wieder."[25] By the end of the year nothing had improved, and Lehmann, looking at his colleagues and then at his Oberprima, could see just how self-perpetuating is that breed of Philistines who upset him so much during his Berlin sojourn:

Fest gebaut ist das Haus der Philister. Schade, daß ihnen die Jungens so ausgeliefert sind! In der O I sieht man das Produkt: marinös inficierte, "aristokratisch wohlerzogene" Jünglinge, die sich, ohne mit der Wimper zu zucken, die kahlsten Trivialitäten und ausgelaugten Wortschalen an die Stirn werfen lassen von erbsengroßen Gehirnen gewissenlos angeschleudert, daß man sich windet und den bramarbasierenden rotwangigen Herren auf der Kathederbühne lasterlos dumm findet.[26]

If there seemed to be no real improvement over Eldena in his professional life, there was also little improvement in his domestic situation during this time. Martha's abilities as a housewife and mother did not change much and, although she seemed to have come to terms with the loss of Joachim as Berthold grew and filled the vacuum left by his brother's death, the continuing material hardship still made for tension between her and Wilhelm. The combination of her own extreme sensitivity and her husband's irritability often led to tears and reciprocal resentment.

In view of his financial and precarious domestic situation, it is hardly surprising that Lehmann's mental state in the first half of 1908 remained at a dangerously low ebb. He was out of the house at 6:15 and hardly ever returned before 4:00 in the afternoon. His teaching once behind him, he still had to attend the obligatory Seminar for those engaged on their probationary year of practice-teaching. For this Seminar there was a lengthy essay to be written (on "Der deutsche Aufsatz auf dem Gymnasium"), and there was always the onerous and frustrating Shaw revision. Unable to scrape through on the money he received from Trebitsch, on the paltry 77 Mk per quarter for the substitute teaching he did at the II. Oberrealschule in Kiel, and the 150 Mk per month from his father-in-law, Lehmann also gave private lessons.

Since his school duties prevented him from taking the long walks he had enjoyed even when preparing for his Staatsexamen, Lehmann sought to escape from the frustrations of his everyday existence through his reading. Now, at least, he was more or less free to read what he wanted rather than what the exigencies of dissertations and examinations demanded. His journal entries begin to take on the appearance of his Berlin diary in that reports of reading habits jostle with complaints about daily life and wishes for the future. His reading matter remained as varied as ever: there were the literary and cultural journals, of which the most significant are *Die neue Rundschau, März, Simplizissimus,* and *Der neue Merkur,* but also some English-language journals such as *The Arrow* (ed. by W.B. Yeats) which now began to figure in his reading and which were soon to exert a crucial influence on his development. Then there were the biological works, which continued to attract him—works like Friedrich Hempelmann's pioneering work on the frog and the Göschen volume *Das Pflanzenreich* by Franz Reinicke and Walter Migula or Koelsch's *Biologische Spaziergänge.* Philological works still figured prominently in his reading—though not quite to the same extent as during the past two years. But his main reading was directed to German and, to a steadily increasing degree, to English literature. Prominent among the works he read with enjoyment and profit at this time were Robert Walser's *Gedichte,* Borchardt's "Rede über Hugo von Hofmannsthal" and *Der Kaiser,* Verhaeren, Yeats, Turgenev, Dostoyevsky, Verlaine, Kürnberger's *Der Amerikamüde,* the Dane Johannes V. Jensen, Oscar Wilde, and Matthew Arnold. He was curious to know who this Max Brod was who was always writing in Julius Zeitler's catalogues,[27] and he had a nodding acquaintance with the work of Else Lasker-Schüler and Harry [sic] Walden "zum Lachen eine Gesellschaft" as Heimann told him.[28] But the authors who now appealed to him beyond most others were the Irish writer George Moore (1852-1933), the now fashionable Walt Whitman (1819-1892), and the Whitmanesque German hymnist Alfons Paquet (1881-1944), and the Austrian philosopher-critic Rudolf Kassner (1873-1959).

The mere fact of his nationality made the nowadays somewhat underestimated George Moore attractive to Lehmann. The Irishman's mildly Nietzschean stance against respectability (which he personified as the "Villa"), the egocentric and rather undisciplined ramblings through life, art and literature in his autobiographical writings,[29] his praise of capricious reading over earnest study,[30] and his avowedly pagan ideas all appealed to Lehmann, who had been reading Moore on and off since 1905. The appeal of Whitman lay largely in the power of his pulsing, long lines and the impressive way he was able to set down his interminable lists of ideas or impressions in poetic fashion. The "Augenkunst" of Alfons Paquet, a disciple of Whitman and a pivotal figure in the development of modern German poetry, impressed Lehmann for similar reasons, as Schäfer has pointed out.[31] The final poem of Paquet's volume *Auf Erden* (1906), which Lehmann read enthusiastically at this time, is entitled "Meine Augen" and begins:

> Ich danke Gott für meine Sinne.
> (O Ihr Gelehrten! laßt mir, der ich nicht euer Geschöpf bin, die Wonne der Dankbarkeit.)
> Ich danke Gott für meine Augen.
>   . . .
> O meine Augen, die mich aus der Enge befreien!

Such words greatly appealed to Lehmann (despite their religious pathos), who had been assiduously improving his ability to *see* over the past few years through a combination of scientific and linguistic studies, and who was later to write that "die Kunst einen sinnlichen Leib hat und daß Anschauung unsere kostbarste Fähigkeit ist."[32] They appealed to him ironically at a time when his eyesight was beginning to deteriorate due to the inordinate amount of reading he indulged in.

Rudolf Kassner also laid a great deal of stress on the sensual appreciation of existence. Of the above-mentioned writers, he was undoubtedly the most important for Lehmann's spiritual development. The ideas which had been fermenting in Lehmann's mind since his Berlin days—Nietzsche, the duality essential to true art, the capturing of the essence of things in concrete appearances and not vague abstractions—it all seemed to come together in the writings of Rudolf Kassner, which he now avidly read and continued to read for the rest of his life. Furthermore Kassner seemed to possess that polyglot wide-ranging curiosity and knowledge which Lehmann himself so admired and hankered after. Kassner's first book, the influential *Die Mystiker, die Kunst und das Leben* (1900), contained a challenging appraisal of many of those English poets Lehmann had long read and admired—Blake,[33] Keats and Shelley, for example. Kassner saw them as essentially mystical, but more in the tradition of Jakob Böhme's sensual, earthy, open-eyed mysticism. Like Nietzsche and Moore before him, Kassner also attacked non-aesthetic man, calling him a "Gliedermann" or "Dilettant," and he had formulated a personal view of the history of mankind along the lines of Nietzsche in which he saw a split between a magical "Identität," where a paradisiacal unity of man and his world pertains, and "Individualität," where all is divided and where the aesthetically aware are obliged to try to restore unity through art. What Kassner termed the "Raummensch" has given way to the "Zeitmensch." Although one cannot say that Lehmann simply took Kassner's evolving philosophical view and made it his own, it is nonetheless clear that his reading of Kassner at this point was of influence in the moulding of his own aesthetic credo. Almost sixty years later he admitted as much in a letter to Hans Dieter Schäfer:

> Ich verdanke Rudolf Kassner (seit 1900 mir bekannt, sozusagen vertraut) sehr viel, er tut zuweilen tiefe, ausrufsreiche Blicke in Welt und Geschehen (ich weiß zwar auch, daß er ein *gefährlicher* Wegleiter ist mit dieser ewigen Spiegelung von Dingen und Begriffen in einander.)[34]

As the year 1908 progressed and the horror of his examination receded, Lehmann relaxed a little. The threat of military service all but disappeared when he heard in July that he was assigned to the reserve, to the "Landsturm.... Also ich brauche nicht zu dienen!"[35] Moreover, the long summer vacation gave him the chance to get out walking again, and a combination of more time for himself, stimulating reading, and pleasant landscape gradually put Lehmann in the mood for writing poetry again. The poems from 1908-1909 which survive generally bear witness to the effect of Whitman's long line.[36] They are for the most part unrhymed and are remarkable for an acuity of perception. The relationship of man and nature is now central, while the phenomena from the world of nature which Lehmann seeks out are far removed from those of the traditional nature poetry of the nineteenth century. Gone are the epigonal mood pictures of the Berlin period. Instead we find poems which, although still not of high quality, contain the germ of what was later to so impress the readers of *Antwort des Schweigens:*

> Unruhe war und die Gedanken flogen wie Hornissen
> An ihren Schwingen lösten alle Dinge sich
> Wie Blätter die nur halb im Leben hängen
> Und mager sind mit ausgeglühtem Leib
> Scheu übten an der düst'ren Ecke sich Grasmückenbruten
> Mit roten Lappen gaukelte der Kirschenbaum

Ich ging dahin und sank wie Schrecken
Und fiel, wie Anfangswind in tiefgepfähltes Ende, in den Tod.

The relationship of thing and word still preoccupied him, however, as a
lengthy passage jotted down hurriedly around March 1909 demonstrates:

Wie im zeichnerischen Ausdruck der Anatomie zum Trotz das menschliche Herz
ein ♡ wird, gibt sich häufig auch das Wesen der Dinge im lautlichen Ausdruck,
entwissenschaftlicht, d.h. entlogisiert, entrationalisiert. Manchmal sind
*neben*sächliche Züge bei der Benennung eines Dinges ausschlaggebend...
manchmal aber 'der Zusammenhang'. Hat der Mensch vorher und lange bestimmte
Dinge gesehen, so wird er ein neues diesen altgewohnten Bildvorstellungen hitzig
eingliedern: einen braunen Käfer rot sein lassen, weil ihm meistens 'rote' Käfer über
den Weg gelaufen sind. Dem Indianer sind daher 'Haar Zweige Strahlen' sozusagen
identisch. Es scheint auf den oberfl. Blick, daß Logik und Natur eine alte Feindschaft
zu einander hegen. Der Dichter entlogisiert die Sprache: er eint alles, was dem
Nichtgehobenen in viele nur nüchtern-logisch in Beziehung setzbare Sachen
zerfällt, zerfallen ist. Er wird zuweilen wahnsinnig vor Hunger nach Analogien. Oft
ist das 'Alles in Eins sein', das συνοᾶν [synorán] nicht stark genug: wenn die
Begeisterung in ihm lischt.
  Im Gemüt aber hängen die Dinge doch noch wieder anders zusammen als
draußen. Whitman allerdings zählt einfach auf und bezaubert: die Erdteile z.B.
(andere Dichter). Für den Tagessinn ist alles ein schleiervoll grau dunstiges Rätsel:
der Dichter entsiegelt. Die Einheit schaut man nur auf Minuten (vgl. Lichtenberg).
Die ganze *eine* Einheit: nicht nur ein paar Dinge als Eins setzen. Geduld und Mut
z.B. Wenn einst alles *eins* sein wird, dann wird damit alle Bewußtheit
zurückentwickelt sein: im dunklen Bewußten verschmolzen sein: wir werden Tier
sein oder Pflanze. Und die Bewußtheit quält uns nicht mehr, macht uns nicht mehr
zu schlechten Poeten. Man sagt häufig als [?] Dichter gefährlich 'zu bewußt' (vgl.
Kleists Aufsatz): Ist denn Bewußtheit ein Fluch?
  Das noch nicht reife B[ewußtsein] des Kindes *begreift* (greift zusammen) noch
nicht, daß Levkoje, Goldlack und Cardamine den Begriff *Crucifere con*/stituieren.
Ich sehe es seit einiger Zeit: schaue sie aber mehr zusammen. J Rozwadowski spricht
von anderer Entstehungsweise der Gattungsbegriffe. Oder doch ähnlich?
Hinwegsehen des Un-wesentlichen. Also käme die Logik hier in der Bildung der
Gattungsbegriffe wunderbar...hier mit der Mystik zusammen?[37]

This passage contains in embryo the gist of Lehmann's later poetic formula and
shows how he had continued to think through the ideas which came to him via
his linguistic studies and through Jan Rozwadowski above all (see p. 91 above).
Together with a confused prose sketch devoted to the beauty of the mallow,[38] a
fair copy of which Lehmann sent to Heimann for his comments, this passage
indicates that Lehmann had at this point in his life reached an aesthetic crisis,
whose ultimate resolution when it came would needs result in a finished literary
work. Lehmann's questions in effect centered on expressing the beauty of an
object as he personally experienced it. The expression should be fitting and

should lead to a restoration of the lost unity of man and the environment. Heimann could see that Lehmann was becoming trapped within the confines of his one-sided approach to the problem. He discerned the "Lebens- und Angstgefühl ganz persönlicher Art"[39] which the problem brought forth in Lehmann, but was pained to detect the "wollüstige Zerzupfen, Aufräufeln, Spinnenzähmen und die Linse durch das Nadelöhr werfen" which characterized his search for answers. For Heimann the root of Lehmann's problem was

> daß in Dir die produktive Mitgift Deiner Natur und die produktive Ader Deines Ehrgeizes über die Maßen lebhaft und rebellisch sind und Du hast das Objekt nicht für sie. Es drängt Dich, zu schaffen, etwas aus Dir hinauszustellen, und Du findest nichts in Dir als Dich selbst. Der deutsche Zustand an sich und nicht nur von heute! Was ist zu thun? Du hast, wovon ich innigst überzeugt bin, alle Elemente einer so ächten wie starken dichterischen Begabung in Dir, nur nicht die Begabung, den Trug und Traum, selbst; und die mußt Du Dir schaffen und aus allen Fäden: Gefühl, Phantasie, Leidenschaft, Liebe zum Lebendigen, Wortkraft, Schwärmerei, Melancholie und Heiterkeit—die alle Du reichlich aus Dir zu spinnen geschaffen bist—das Gewebe machen, darin Du Dir die Welt fängst. Ein großes Stück Welt, das ist die erste Bedingung, wenn Du zur Jagd gehst. Sieh um Dich, ergreife mit einem dreisten Griff einen Klumpen Erde und bilde! Schreibe einen Roman! Wage es! Ich prophezeie Dir: wenn er Dir nicht gelingt, wird Dir der zweite aber gelingen.[40]

Lehmann read this letter and was duly influenced by it—though not quite in the way Heimann hoped, as we shall see. Meanwhile there had been a development in Lehmann's life which was to have far-reaching effects, and which also played an immediate part in the artistic development of this would-be poet so eager to start on a literary career.

At the end of 1908 Lehmann found himself faced with an agonizing choice. Heimann had continued to mediate a position for Lehmann at Wickersdorf, and a semi-official offer to start at Easter 1909 now found its way to him via Heimann.[41] At the same time Lehmann was offered a position, also starting at Easter, at the Städtische Höhere Mädchenschule und Lyzeum in Neumünster. The former position was attractive, of course, but so was the latter. The Neumünster school lay within the state system, the position involved was that of an "Oberlehrer," and there was a chance that his second probationary year might be waived. By New Year's Eve he had made his choice, and he wrote to Heimann that he had "...die Tür zur Freiheit [i.e. Wickersdorf] zunächst noch zugeschlagen."[42] In the same letter he also informed Heimann that Martha was not pleased with his decision: "Meine Frau legt Gewicht darauf, Trude und Dir zu sagen, daß sie am allerliebsten schon April nach Wickersdorf gegangen wäre und an meiner Annahme der Neumünsterstelle schuldlos ist." Did she have a premonition of what was to result out of accepting the position in Neumünster?

A somewhat depressed Lehmann (he had badly sprained his ankle just before Christmas and had been rendered immobile) was initially not at all sure he had made the right decision. But in March came a positive review of his teaching by the "Herrn Geh.-Regierungs- und Provinzialschulrat Dr. Brocks"—the same who had watched Lehmann suffer through his oral examination. This meant that he was now, as he went on to tell Heimann, a "vollkommener staatlich geölt [sic] und geschmierter Schulmeister."[43] Somewhat cheered by this news, he moved to a handsome but somewhat neglected villa situated on the Einfeldersee just north of Neumünster and began teaching the fifteen girls of the sixth grade. Almost to his surprise he found himself enjoying the experience. Hardly had the first few weeks passed when the Direktor, who was in charge of a small group of senior girls training to become teachers and attached to the school, fell ill, and Lehmann found himself teaching four girls aged 16-20.[44] By the end of August 1909 he was able to somewhat ironically write in his diary: "Der Mädchenlehrer wie er im Buche steht: begeistert verehrt von seinen Schülerinnen: Mädchen im Alter von 16-20 Jahren."[45] Suddenly teaching was fun, and all complaints vanished from his diary. Gradually one of the four, Frieda Riewerts, began to emerge as the one to intrigue and attract Lehmann above all others, although his shyness and anxiety prevented him from showing it openly. Frieda Riewerts was a strong-willed girl of average height, of dolorous mien, and with striking, almost unkempt, thick reddish-brown hair. She was the oldest of the four students, and Lehmann soon realized that there was a strong, mutual attraction. His diary is full of statements carefully analyzing the situation: "Reizt es mich wirklich, bei Frieda Riewerts Leidenschaft zu wecken?"[46] Certainly he was arousing a deep passion in the twenty-year-old Frieda, who soon began to respond. On a school trip, for instance, she managed to sit next to him at both lunch and coffee, and one of the four girls, Helene Aeschlimann née Pahl, who was sixteen years old at the time, remembers the elaborate manoeuverings during a walk the four girls took together with their teacher one day, as Frieda worked her way between the other girls and ended up triumphantly at Lehmann's side.[47] Lehmann basked in the attention and in the invidious but delightfully warm passion that began to rule over their existences. In his diary he describes the above-mentioned school trip, typically invoking Goethe while doing so:

> Wie war diese unschuldige-schuldige Fahrt doch schön, menschenhaft schön, sündhaft schön!—O wie schön dies geistig-wollüstige Schweben! Dieses ungewiß-lassen! Das nicht drängende! ... Welch Genuß! Wie lang ist's her, so etwas nicht gespürt!—Jeder, viele würden's spüren! In der Novelle wird's mit schön-feierlichen Worten—als Neues Leben, frisches Blut "beschrieben" werden. Es flimmert in der Luft und während ein engl. Extemporale geschrieben wird, flimmert es.[48]

Just as, six years earlier, his emerging love for Martha had given rise to a number of fresh and original poems, so too did his growing love for Frieda Riewerts lead to poetic creation. But with Heimann's admonition to write a novel still ringing in his ears he forsook the lyric genre (while maintaining the lyric mood) and gave expression to this new love in prose. What resulted was not a novel, nor even the novella he alluded to above. Instead, he wrote a fairytale-like allegory of their relationship, remained true to his desire to describe natural phenomena precisely and strikingly, and sent this "Vorstudie" (as he called it) to Alfred Kerr in the hope that it might appear in *Pan*. Kerr accepted the piece, and Lehmann's first published poetic work appeared in the August issue of 1912.

Cardenio und Celinde has nothing in common with Gryphius's drama save the title. It is a highly lyrical and idiosyncratic celebration of Lehmann's love for Frieda and contains a number of autobiographical references which are, however, so disguised and transfigured as to be virtually unrecognizable. Just as Lehmann and Martha had given each other apparent fairytale names (Milesint and Lidselil) in the first flush of their new love, so now did Lehmann and Frieda take on Gryphius's names—*Cardenio und Celinde* probably being a work they read together in class. The place-names of Lehmann's story are purely fictitious and cannot be deciphered, but they undoubtedly refer to the isolated villages and farms around Neumünster where the lovers surreptitiously met and took their walks. The fairytale motif which introduces the story ("Das singende, springende Löweneckerchen"—Grimm) is, as Hans Dieter Schäfer correctly observes,[49] intended to create the atmosphere of a love story. But beyond this it will certainly have had a piquant and private tang to it for Lehmann and Frieda, for Lehmann was wont to use the Grimm fairytales frequently in teaching—even in English classes, where he would have his students translate them into English.

Beyond the autobiographical aspect however, the work is interesting in that it heralds Lehmann's exceedingly lyrical style and contains elements which are to remain his literary stock-in-trade for the next six decades:

> Der Wind wehte ihr an die Kehle, da spülte und spielte es um ihre Knie. Es war das zur Süßigkeit spannende Pfeifen des Amselhahns im Februar. Das kam, und beide mußten antworten. An seinem Barte hing ein Schein. In den Johannisbeerbüschen saßen kleine Knaben und wirbelten im Riesenschwunge hundertmal. Sie hatten Zwiebelblütenhüllen als Mützen auf, und die glänzten wie die Mutter der Perlen. Ein hohes Lachen hing wie Glasketten überall. Fremd sprach das Wasser.
> (SW I, p. 15)

This passage is notable not only because of the music of its alliteration and assonance, but also because of the anthropomorphisation of nature: the wind is assigned a major unifying role and is eroticised, as it is so often on later occasions;[50] the natural scene is peopled by "kleine Knaben" worthy of a Philipp Otto Runge or a Moritz von Schwind, and the water speaks. Whether this is still Romanticism, whether it is literary *art nouveau,* or whether it is already magic realism is a moot point. But it is certainly characteristically Lehmann. He had found his poetic voice, and it remained only for him to perfect it.

Throughout 1910 and 1911 the passion grew despite the obvious difficulties involved. Not only was Lehmann married and Frieda his student, not only was provincial Neumüunster in the year 1910 absolutely not the place for such dalliance, but Frieda Riewerts was the daughter of Probst Riewerts, a well-

NEUMÜNSTER LYZEUM, c. 1910: "DER MÄDCHENLEHRER WIE ER IM BUCHE STEHT."

NEUMÜNSTER LYZEUM, c. 1911, THE "SEMINARISTINNEN." FRIEDA RIEWERTS IS SEATED, FAR LEFT; HELENE PAHL-AESCHLIMANN IS STANDING, FAR RIGHT. HEDI RATJEN AND ELSE MEINERTS, THE GIRLS WHO SET OFF THE BOMBS IN LEHMANN'S GARDEN SHORTLY BEFORE HE LEFT FOR WICKERSDORF, ARE STANDING, SECOND AND FIFTH FROM THE LEFT.

FRIEDA RIEWERTS AND HELENE PAHL-AESCHLIMANN.

known and well-respected Lutheran minister in the town.[51] By the beginning of
1910 Martha knew of the complicated mutual attraction between her husband
and his student—even though Lehmann and Frieda had not yet confided the full
depth of their passion to one another. Martha had met Frieda by this time, since
Lehmann had twice invited the four girls to his house. The girls themselves were
all charmed by their teacher, admired his wife (who was a delightful and
vivacious hostess), and enjoyed playing with little Berthold. But as the passion
grew into mutually recognized love, and as the lovers gave way to their desire to
be together and took walks together over the meadows and along the dykes
around Neumünster, Martha understandably began to become alarmed and
showed her apprehension and jealousy through resentment and spite. At first
Lehmann and Frieda were themselves convinced of the innocence of their
Platonic love—sex seemed to play no role at all. Frieda quite openly told her
parents of her walks with her English teacher and was amazed when they
instantly forbade her to accept any more such invitations. But the power of their
love was too great, and the couple continued their trysts in furtive secrecy.

Lehmann was all too aware that his whole livelihood and teaching career were
at stake, and he occasionally made half-hearted attempts to free himself from the
passion which now ruled him. At the beginning of October 1910 he and Martha
moved into Neumünster and took an apartment at Marienstraße 41—just round
the corner from the school. Then, on 4 October, he took a trip to Italy (made
possible by a loan of 400 Mk from a friend of his aunt Doris) and began to breathe
a little easier as he left Neumünster behind: "O meine Trübheit fällt ab mit der
Sonne."[52] On his way south he fell in with the Expressionist poet Armin T.
Wegner, whose first book of poems had appeared the previous year, and they
decided to continue their journey together. The two young men made a stop in
Bolzano, where they saw Weber's *Freischütz,* shared lodgings, and then
continued on to Verona. Here Lehmann was able to write in his diary "Die
Ekstase Italiens hat mich erfaßt."[53] After two days in Verona, they proceeded to
Venice. By this time Lehmann felt that Wegner had developed " ... ich will nicht
sagen unsympatische, aber doch mir jetzt unerträgliche Seiten seines Wesens,"[54]
and so they parted company. Venice proved to be the highlight of Lehmann's
Italian journey. Not only was there San Marco, "ein blühendes Steinwunder,"[55]
but also San Michele, the Academia delle belle arti (to which Lehmann repeatedly
returned), the delicious mixture of styles from the Byzantine and the Greek to the
Italian, the innumerable palazzi, but also the street singers, the gondolieri and
even, anticipatory of Thomas Mann, an ominous " ... Erscheinung eines
häßlichen Mannes ... er war ganz kahl am Kopf, hatte fast kein Kinn und spielte
bettelnd seinen Leierkasten."[56] Above all there was the experience of the
"unendlich melodischen, geliebten Sprache"[57] and the ultimate realization that
" ... es vollendet sich auch so ein Stück meiner Erziehung, glorios und
unbewußt."[58] After a week in Venice, Lehmann took the train to Milan, where he

WILHELM LEHMANN, 1908. PRESENTED TO FRIEDA RIEWERTS AND INSCRIBED: "ICH SCHWANKE, OB ICH DIR DIES GEBEN SOLL. MAGST DU ES NICHT, SO VERNICHTE ES. ICH WAR TOTAL GEHETZT UND GESTÖRT ALS ICH ES OSTERN, UM DIE ZEIT WO ICH KANDIDAT AM KIELER GYMNASIUM WAR, AUS IRGEND EINER GRILLE (ICH GLAUBE, UM MICH AN MIR SELBST ZU BERUHIGEN) MAL MACHEN LIEß.

FRIEDA RIEWERTS (1889-1975), c. 1908.

stopped just long enough to take a long, admiring look at the Gothic cathedral and its splendid stained glass, before travelling back to Neumünster.

This pleasant interlude did nothing to improve matters with Martha and served to underline the very real place Frieda had assumed in Lehmann's emotional life. The diary he kept during his trip was dedicated to "Mildred Lawson," and he occasionally expresses a wish that they should both learn Italian together. Frieda Riewerts's letters to Lehmann following his trip are full of references to Lehmann's desire that they should both learn Italian. It therefore seems likely that Mildred Lawson is simply a cover-name for Frieda, especially since Lehmann had once experienced Martha's wrath when she read a passage in his diary relating to Frieda. At all events, once Wilhelm Lehmann returned from Italy there was an increase in the number of letters that couple secretly exchanged.[59] By March 1911 they were planning to go to Berlin for the Easter break and to meet there in the anonymity of the large city—and suddenly the affair becomes reminiscent of Lehmann's relationship with Martha five years earlier. Meanwhile they were doing their best to avoid using the intimate Du even in private, "aus Vorsicht und Ängstlichkeit"[60] lest they unwittingly drop into the familiar in public. Their concern was fully justified, for Frieda had difficulty explaining the situation to her parents when they one day intercepted a postcard to her from Lehmann in which he had naturally but carelessly used the intimate form of address. It proved impossible for Frieda to go to Berlin at Easter, so that no meeting took place. By Whitsun, as plans were hatched for a meeting in Lübeck, there was talk of a possible divorce, and Frieda somewhat nervously began to hope for a future in their relationship. By this time the other girls began to notice how her eyes would light up whenever Lehmann appeared. But still the couple did their very best to hide their love from the outside world. Although both Lehmann and Frieda were able to spend Whitsun in Lübeck, there proved to be no chance to meet, and so they looked forward to the summer holidays and a possible rendez-vous at Wyk auf Föhr. In order to communicate quickly, they relied on a complex system of signals involving hands in pockets, handkerchiefs displayed in a certain fashion, and like subterfuges.

By July 1911 there was a crisis in the Lehmann household. Martha was by now fully aware of what was going on, and there was a show-down. Lehmann insisted on a degree of independence, blamed their marital difficulties on Martha's absolute dependence on him, and, with his nerves at breaking-point, went to Schönberg to rest and think. By now the Heimanns were aware of the situation, and Gertrud, knowing only too well how difficult it was for Martha, had in May exhorted Lehmann to make a decision and act on it.[61] As usual, however, he found himself incapable of such a definite course of action. Then, shortly after his return to Neumünster from Schönberg in mid-July, Martha fell ill. How would Martha manage without him? And what about Berthold? Berthold had been mentioned continually by Martha in her imploring letters to Lehmann during his sojourn at Schönberg, and now he began to think of a future where he would be separated from his beloved son. By October 1911, just after Frieda had sent Lehmann a lock of her hair and timorously called him her "Verlobter," there was suddenly a break in his relationship with Frieda. Faced with Lehmann's prevarication, she categorically stated that she was not willing to share him with Martha; he, for his part, felt unable to leave his son and wife without care and support. In addition there were religious differences. Lehmann's ties with established religion had never been strong, and he was now a definite free-thinker. Frieda, on the other hand, was unable to overlook the very deep bond with the Christian religion which she had inherited through both her strictly Lutheran father and almost pietistic mother. The plans to meet in Berlin were suddenly scrapped. But then, just as suddenly, they both set off for Berlin and met there as initially planned. The crisis was over, and a gradual move towards a definite separation from Martha was initiated.

The developments in his marriage and his increasingly more powerful emotional and, by now, sexual ties to Frieda made Lehmann all too aware of his precarious professional situation. In view of the fact that a colleague had just been dismissed from the Neumünster Lyzeum for criticising the Kaiser, Lehmann was justifiably convinced he would lose his position and never gain another in the public school system if a scandal broke. The cost of a divorce, the child- and wife-support payments which would certainly be levied on him, and a new marriage all meant that he would need a secure position in the next few years. Wickersdorf seemed to be the answer for a number of reasons. It was, of course, far removed from Neumünster where everybody knew everybody and where a scandal would be the inevitable result of what was likely to be a difficult divorce. Then the progressive spirits of the "Freie Schulgemeinde" would probably be more likely to accept a divorced man as a teacher than would the staid fuddy-duddies of provincial and conservative Schleswig-Holstein. Furthermore, there might well be an opportunity for Frieda to teach at Wickersdorf and thus supplement their income. Finally, at least this was how Lehmann saw it, life in the communal boarding-school would be cheaper than elsewhere. Heimann was still urging Lehmann to commit himself wholly to Wickersdorf, and Lehmann did now make a formal application for a position there. At the same time he applied to the state authorities for an early release from his contract, and, by February 1912, it was all settled: Lehmann was to begin teaching at Wickersdorf in April 1912.

Martha had in the meantime moved out of their apartment in the Marienstraße, taking Berthold with her. And so Agathe moved in for the remaining few weeks in Neumünster to keep house for her helpless son. She had known about the marital problems for some time and was fortunately very understanding of the situation, which she assessed in a (for her) unusually balanced and rational way. Although she had grown to like Martha (as had the Heimanns), this did not prevent her from realizing that the couple were pathologically unable to live together successfully. While living in Neumünster she got to know Frieda and accepted her in a friendly if not warm fashion, calling her by the familiar Du. She seemed to be resigned to the probability of divorce and re-marriage, and was, perhaps, able to accept the situation philosophically, having herself been through a similar ordeal some two decades earlier.

As Lehmann's thoughts began to center on divorce and re-marriage, he was faced with the problem of finding a lawyer. Frieda, far more gifted in practical matters than her lover, had long been encouraging him to sound out the possibilities of divorce through a lawyer acquaintance of hers, one Willy Voss. This Lehmann did in March 1912 and was pleased to hear that the legal problems were not insurmountable. Heimann meanwhile had recommended Martin Beradt (1881-1949), a lawyer and a man of letters, and a habitué of the "Donnerstags-Gesellschaft,"[62] a group of like-minded spirits who met on Thursdays in Steinerts Weinstube on the corner of the Kurfürstendamm and the Joachimsthalerstraße.

While these thoughts were preoccupying him, Lehmann was again threatened by his worsening financial situation. His earnings from his teaching were swallowed up as fast as he received them, as were those from Trebitsch and other sources. Old Herr Dreis, of course, was no longer supporting the couple— although he did not, as yet, suspect that his son-in-law was aiming for a divorce. To meet the most pressing of bills, Lehmann had sold the piano at the end of 1911. He now cast around for someone willing to buy his library from him and asked Heimann if he knew of anyone. Heimann advised against this rather extreme move, as did Agathe, and the latter even went so far as to persuade Martha that Lehmann should not be expected to part with his books under any circumstances. With the preoccupations of a possible divorce and new marriage, his precarious financial position, and the anticipation of a new life in Wickersdorf, Lehmann somehow managed to get through the final few weeks in Neumünster. It had been a harrowing time. His marriage had fallen apart irrevocably; his financial situation had worsened—he had been unable to repay the loan he had received for his Italian journey, and was now, with his Shaw revision work finished, borrowing money from Trebitsch to pay bills and more pressing debts. Worst of all, his literary work had come to a standstill. But there were compensations. He was in love again and experiencing what he described as "Mädchenliebe"—something he had not known in his relationship with Martha. He had managed to adapt his teaching methods to his own particular strengths and was now enjoying his teaching. He had branched out into the new area of lyrical prose and with Cardenio und Celinde, had completed his first such work to be published. And he saw in Wickersdorf the chance to escape the stuffy Philistinism of his colleagues in the state schools and settle into a more congenial atmosphere. Before he left, however, there was an event which seemed symbolically both to characterize the stormy years since his Staatsexamen and signify their end. On the evening of 26 March, he and Agathe were suddenly startled by two loud explosions in the garden in front of their house. Lehmann rushed outside and, as a likely explanation began to dawn on him, he was joined by the local policeman who had been attracted by the detonations. As he suspected, and as was later confirmed by Frieda, two of the girls who had objected to the amount of time spent reading Shakespeare in German during English lessons, had with the help of their friends set off two "regelrechte Dynamithbomben,"[63] no doubt intended to help him on his way to Wickersdorf.

6
Wickersdorf (1912-1917). The "Erzähler, in dem sich ein großer Dichter ankündigt."

IN THE YEARS 1904-1906 the father of the German "Landerziehungsheim," Hermann Lietz, fell out with the prickly and temperamental Gustav Wyneken. The latter, together with a number of fellow teachers from Haubinda (principally Paul Geheeb, August Halm, Fritz Hafner, Rudolf Aeschlimann, and Martin Luserke), broke away from Lietz; on 1 September 1906, they founded their own "Freie Schulgemeinde Wickersdorf."[1] The decision to locate their new school in a deserted and isolated country estate in the tiny village of Wickersdorf some eight miles southwest of Saalfeld was motivated both by its relative cheapness and its immediate availability, for Wyneken and his cohorts were assured of a goodly number of pupils from Haubinda, provided they could open their school quickly. Thus it came about that the new Freie Schulgemeinde was situated in the most beautiful but almost inaccessible rural surroundings some 1,800 feet up in the Thüringer Wald.[2]

After leaving Neumünster, Wilhelm Lehmann spent a few days with his brother Walter, who by now was pastor at the parish church of Hamberge just outside Lübeck. After the ever-increasing pressures of the past few months, he was badly in need of a rest, but the few days in Hamberge were hardly sufficient for his needs. Not only was the time too short, but Lehmann did not like his new sister-in-law, being of the opinion that his brother, in choosing the simple Emmy as his bride, had married below him. There had, in any case, been a gradual cooling in the relationship of the two brothers over the past few years. Emmy was probably merely a visible pretext on Lehmann's part which he used to explain a subconscious retraction of his old love and respect for his brother. The drifting apart began when Wilhelm became jealous of Walter's success in getting S. Fischer to accept his novella *Das abendrote Haus*. But then, ironically, it was probably intensified by Walter's abandonment of his barely started literary career for more scholarly theological writing[3] just as Wilhelm Lehmann was himself beginning to change from scholarship to fiction. All this notwithstanding, the few days in Hamberge were a respite and, on 11 April, a somewhat calmer Lehmann took the train to Berlin, where he was once again a guest at the Heimanns and where he began to plan for the new life ahead of him.

The most immediate problem which lay ahead was the divorce, and so Lehmann, a child of provinciality, sought to avoid a scandal by choosing the anonymous metropolis as the setting for this next dramatic step. Lehmann now took up Heimann's suggestion and went to see Martin Beradt, who, in the event, turned out to be the best lawyer he could have wished for. At Heimann's urging, Beradt, a co-founder in 1909 of the "Schutzverband Deutscher Schriftsteller," willingly took on the case for a minimal fee. It was decided that Lehmann should be the defendant, and, to Lehmann's great relief, Martha was persuaded to cooperate to a remarkable extent: "Ich bin zu allem bereit," she wrote, "wenn ich das Kind behalte."[4] The likely loss of Berthold was a matter of great concern to Lehmann, of course, but he was encouraged by his mother in the belief that Martha, being almost incapable of managing her own life let alone hers *and* Berthold's, would eventually relinquish him to his father—especially since he would soon be of school age and would be able to receive free schooling at Wickersdorf. Agathe, while cheering up Lehmann with this notion and hope, was nonetheless careful to suggest that Lehmann should remain single, and this proviso was of no small concern to her neurotic son. So while Beradt efficiently went about the business of arranging the divorce, Lehmann found himself worrying not only about the legal matters but also about the advisability of a new marriage to Frieda Riewerts. In addition there were ominous rumblings of a breaking scandal back in Neumünster, where Frieda was now practice-teaching. By now, as Frieda reported, Neumünster was aware of the separation of Lehmann and Martha (the household effects had been addressed to two different destinations) while Lehmann, as rumor had it, had spent no less than two weeks in Berlin with one of his girl pupils.[5] The news, just before the actual divorce hearing, that a senior teacher at his old school had just been summarily dismissed for expressing anti-monarchy sentiments[6] served only to increase his apprehension. Frieda, on the other hand, seemed unperturbed about it all and almost relished the excitement. When the news of the Lehmanns' broken marriage and of Wilhelm's presumed guilt penetrated to the vicarage, old Frau Riewerts reacted with unexpected understanding and sympathy for Wilhelm Lehmann. Frieda took this as a good omen, for she knew that her desire to marry a divorced man would meet with more objections from her zealously pious mother than from her father, who was blessed with a streak of liberal eccentricity. But then on 5 August 1912, Frau Riewerts died, still ignorant of her daughter's situation.

Soon after this a preliminary divorce hearing, which Lehmann was not obliged

WILHELM LEHMANN WITH MORITZ HEIMANN IN WICKERSDORF, c. 1913. NOTE
THE SANDALS WHICH WERE DE RIGUEUR IN WICKERSDORF.

WICKERSDORF c. 1906. BACK: MARTIN LUSERKE, THIRD FROM LEFT; PAUL
GEHEEB, BEARDED, STANDING SECOND FROM THE RIGHT. FRONT: GUSTAV
WYNEKEN, THIRD FROM LEFT, AUGUST HALM, FOURTH FROM THE RIGHT;
RUDOLF AESCHLIMANN SIXTH FROM THE RIGHT.

to attend, was fixed for 1 October. The result of this hearing was rather disturbing, for the case was said to be "schwach." The reason was clear: Beradt had initially been inclined to stress the physical violence which Martha had apparently suffered at the hands of her husband, but he had been persuaded by Lehmann and Gertrud Heimann to soften his line lest such revelations harm his client in his professional life. In the light of this hint from the court, the physical attacks were now brought into the foreground again for the actual hearing on 25 October, and Lehmann found himself in the painfully embarrassing position of admitting, indeed of even exaggerating the "Tätlichkeiten" meted out to Martha. The hearing proved to be rather brief, and the six-year marriage to Martha was duly dissolved. The trauma for Lehmann was considerable, as both the account in his later novel *Der Bilderstürmer*[7] and the letters written to his mother show.[8] Martha, as was inevitable, was awarded custody of Berthold, while Lehmann "mußte die Frau unterstützen, soweit es in seinen Kräften stand."[9] Between Christmas and the New Year Lehmann and Frieda met secretly in Hamburg, spending the night in the Savoy Hotel. They now began to discuss marriage in more definite terms, but when the Lehmann family heard that Wilhelm was indeed thinking of remarrying, both Walter and Agathe began to voice their skepticism and opposition. Walter felt that Lehmann would be better off unmarried; a wife, he thought, would only distract him from his creative work. This argument was, of course, likely to strike home with Wilhelm, for his marriage to Martha had certainly limited his creative output severely. Walter, however, did not know Frieda Riewerts well enough at this time to realize that this would not prove to be the case. Agathe's arguments against remarriage continued to center, for the most part, on Berthold, until news of the engagement was made official just after Easter 1913. That Lehmann was not relishing the thought of announcing his desire to marry Frieda is clear from the extraordinary tone of the first sentence of his sixteen-page letter, in which he, at the age of 31, actually felt it necessary to ask his mother's permission:

> Meine liebe, teure Mutter!
> Der Brief, den ich dir jetzt, Sonntag Nachmittag in meiner Stube sitzend, den Geschäften für eine Weile entronnen, schreibe, ist schon lange mir in der Seele überbrütet worden—enthält er nun doch nichts Geringeres als an dich, meine einzige und beste Mutter, die Bitte mir mit freudigem und wohlwollendem Herzen die Erlaubnis zu geben, nun doch noch wieder heiraten zu dürfen.[10]
> ....

Aware that he was on shaky ground, Lehmann felt obliged to justify his desire to marry by explaining how much more ready for marriage he was now as compared to some ten years earlier:

> ...Und meine sauer erkämpfte Überzeugung ist vor allem die, daß ich mich jetzt tauglich und berufen fühle eine Ehe zu führen. Vor 10 Jahren konnte ich das nicht, hätte es auch mit jemand anders als Martha nicht können, denn ich war ohne

Selbstbeherrschung und ohne Weisheit und Wissen. Nun, wo ich das *Wissen* um eine Ehe habe, will ich es fruchtbar machen und Frieda zum Weibe haben, ihret - und meinetwegen, nicht aus Trotz, nicht aus Schwäche, nicht aus Verblendung, sondern aus dem Willen und aus der Sehnsucht, das moralische Problem der Ehe—und das ist sie natürlich—lösen zu wollen und in der blühenden Hoffnung, es auch mit dieser Frieda Riewerts lösen zu können.... Was mich—damit ich ganz aufrichtig zu dir bin, der einzigen teuren Mutter, von der ich ganz genau weiß, daß sie zuerst bloß an das Glück, eine Jugend, an eine freie, leichte, beschwingte Existenz, ihres Sohnes denkt—damals im Herbst letzten Jahres dir meine Not und meinen Entschluß, nicht die neue Ehe einzugehen, mitteilen ließ, das war natürlich das Problem, Ideal und Wirklichkeit, d.h. künstlerisches Schaffen und praktische Existenz in Einklang zu bringen. Ich leide daran, wie jeder künstlerisch empfindende Mensch: seine Lösung ist stets eine Aufgabe, kann nur von 2 Menschen, die das beide wissen, angestrebt werden, und ist dann das beste Gedicht, das einem gelingen kann.... Ich weiß, daß in deinen Gedanken—und wie sollte das auch nicht der Fall sein?—eine Ehe meinerseits ein Synonym ist für Elend, kleinliche Schinderei, gebrochene Flügel, gequältes Hinausverlangen, unbezahlte Rechnungen, stets durch äußere Not gehemmtes Fliegenwollen....[11]

His anticipation of Agathe's objections did not help, however, and he duly received a stinging riposte just before his birthday:

Lübeck, d. 30 April 1913
Mein lieber Willy.

Ich bin aufs tiefste verletzt....—Ich empfinde diese *rasche* neue Eheschließung als etwas unsagbar Unanständiges und Unschönes. Und Berthis Schicksal—die heilige Hauptsache—schwebt in der Luft. Und du machst dich anheischig, du Ärmster, für 3 Haushaltungen zu sorgen? Und die großen Schulden, die Tausende an v. Höegh?

....

Mein lieber armer Sohn, du gehst wie ein Wahnsinniger mit deinem schönen Leben um. Ich vermag den raschen Wandelungen deines Herzens, den Wirrungen deines Lebens nicht mehr zu folgen. So mußt du dann ohne mich gehen; wir beiden wollen Abschied nehmen von einander. Ich will dem 4. Mai nicht gram sein um seine Gabe an mich; bist du doch durch 20 Jahre meine Freude und mein Stolz, meine starke Hoffnung gewesen. Ich werde mein kleines Hungerdasein noch eine Weile fristen, dann magst du kommen und mir ein Blümlein aufs Grab pflanzen.

Du wirst mich durch *nichts* mehr stören und quälen; ich will und muß Ruhe haben.

Gott sei mit dir und schenke dir Erfüllung auf allen Wegen! In tiefstem Schmerz, aber unabänderlichem Willen

zum letzten Mal

deine blutende Mutter.

Ich gehe vor Pfingsten auf einige Zeit meiner Gesundheit wegen fort.

Added on a slip of paper and included in the letter in the conviction that her argument would be strengthened thereby were the words: "Grete Hauptmann hat 11 Jahre warten müssen, ehe sie rechtmäßige Frau wurde." Once again Lehmann's remarkable and vulnerable sensitivity in the face of the demands and expectations of his martyred mother led to an unnecessary and unpleasant confrontation between them. It was almost as if Lehmann, in writing such a letter in the first place, was asking for the response which came, predictably and almost obligingly, from Agathe. Lehmann poured his heart out to Frieda, to the Heimanns, and to Walter, and spent the next several months trying to repair the fresh damage in his relationship with his mother.

Meanwhile Frieda had broken the news to her father, the Probst, who knew absolutely nothing of what had been going on for the past three years. But what had seemed on paper to be the more difficult task turned out to be remarkably straightforward in actuality. Frieda had carefully planned to have an ally on hand in the form of her brother Friedrich, who knew all about the love affair and who had played host to Frieda and Lehmann the previous summer. The Probst, unpredictable to the last, simply asked his daughter whether Lehmann was a "reiner und feiner Mensch,"[12] asked for time to think it over, and gave his permission through a telegram a few days later.

After five months of busy preparation the couple was married on 2 October 1913 in Heide by her brother-in-law Ludwig Schlee. Despite their earlier opposition, both Walter Lehmann and Agathe attended—the former being, for the second time, one of the witnesses. Friedrich Riewerts was the other. Lehmann, still not particularly at ease in large gatherings, spent a good part of the reception on the floor playing with Ludwig Schlee's infant children Ernst and Lisbeth.[13] It was not only that he felt more relaxed with children and enjoyed their company; he was also clearly possessed of some powerful charm which drew children to him and fascinated them. It had been in evidence ten years earlier when he played with the younger Twining children in England, leaving his contemporaries to their more sophisticated pursuits. It was still in evidence 40 years later when, a famous poet and the current recipient of the Kunstpreis des Landes Schleswig-Holstein (1952), he left the Mayor of Kiel standing at the reception held in his honor and played with the Mayor's little children instead.

Although Lehmann himself felt that he had changed and matured so much that he could be optimistic about his new marriage, the facts were somewhat different. He was probably no better equipped for marriage now than he had ever been—Walter Lehmann had summed him up accurately in this regard. But his optimism was nonetheless not at all misplaced. He had found in Frieda Riewerts a woman whose greatest desire was to possess Wilhelm Lehmann and ease his way through life to the great benefit of his art. His marriage to Martha had failed as much as anything else because he did not have the qualities necessary to do what he had idealistically, but foolishly, vowed to do at the outset: namely to protect her and deliver her from an inimical world. His marriage to Frieda, in which he was to be relieved of so many of the burdens of life, was to endure till his death.

Whatever Lehmann's worries about how his colleagues might react to his separation, divorce, and remarriage, they proved to be groundless in Wickersdorf. He was careful to keep Martin Luserke, the director of the school, well informed as to all developments, and he regularly spoke to his colleagues about his situation. He met understanding and sympathy wherever he turned. His colleagues were, to be sure, a remarkable group. Gustav Wyneken, it is true, was no longer officially at Wickersdorf. Having once founded the school with Paul Geheeb, he quickly proceeded to oust this worthy—who was in any case too complacent and lethargic by now. But Wyneken, despite his undoubted charisma, then proceeded to antagonize so many people in the school and in the local education authority at Meiningen that there was no question of his remaining as its director. Martin Luserke (1881-1968), only a year older than Lehmann, was in 1910 made director. It was he who was mainly responsible for building up a devoted staff and creating a congenial atmosphere. He himself was a writer who combined artistic and pedagogical interests by putting all his energy into plays for school performance. Shortly after Lehmann arrived in Wickersdorf, Luserke finished a dramatic adaption of the Grimm fairytale "Der Meisterdieb" and was preparing to produce it with a cast of Wickersdorf pupils.[14] Apart from the theatre, music and art both played a major part in the school's activities. Wyneken's brother-in-law August Halm was largely responsible for the extraordinary emphasis placed on music in the Freien Schulgemeinden, and although he was not at this time actually teaching at Wickersdorf, his presence there was a real force, and teachers like the Schuberts, Käthe Conrad, Bernhard Uffrecht, and Luserke, too, all contributed greatly to the musical life in the school. The very first day Lehmann spent there saw a performance of Bruckner's Fifth Symphony arranged for piano duet. Bruckner, together with Bach, as Lehmann reported to his mother, was "Morgen- und Abendlob"[15] in Wickersdorf. Lehmann soon found himself singing in the choir—it was the first time he had devoted himself to singing since his England stay a decade earlier—and in general he heard and made more music than at any time prior to his move to Wickersdorf. Art was in the capable hands of Fritz Hafner, a superlative teacher and considerable artist whose landscapes Lehmann likened to those of Caspar David Friedrich.[16] The Lehmanns were presented with one of Hafner's Wickersdorf landscapes by the staff as a wedding gift, and other Hafner paintings and illustrations periodically brightened the life of the Lehmann household. In addition to Luserke and Hafner, there was, above all, Siegfried Krebs (1882-1914), a writer of Lehmann's age who was just achieving his first literary successes with the S. Fischer Verlag. Krebs was on good terms with both Moritz Heimann and Oskar Loerke, whose work Lehmann now got to know through Krebs and who was soon to become a close friend. In 1912 Krebs and Hafner cooperated on a Christmas present for Berthold—Krebs writing a fairytale which Hafner illustrated. How Berthold reacted is not known, but Lehmann himself was highly delighted.[17] Lehmann then, for the first time since his Berlin year, was among people who were open, receptive, stimulating, and creative, people with whom he could converse and discuss ideas.

Wickersdorf, however, did not lay stress only on spiritual, intellectual, and artistic pursuits. The development of physical attributes was equally important, and Lehmann saw here a chance of improving his physical health. He accordingly participated in cross-country running and morning gymnastics, swam, and took cold baths. Partly at Frieda's urging and partly because of practical necessity he finally learned how to ride a bicycle. Whenever the staff and pupils went on forays into the woods and fields to fetch timber, firewood, manure for the school garden, or to pick fruit, berries or nuts, Lehmann did his best to help. It was not easy for him. He was not possessed of any great practical ability, as we have seen; and he was, above all, a great loner. But the atmosphere was conducive to cooperation—it was, after all, a *Schulgemeinde*—and Lehmann found himself doing things he never dreamed possible. Although the physical activity and his desire for better health made for an improvement over his mood of the past few years, his journal still attests to many periods of depression and melancholy. Although such entries often are more indicative of his capacity for self-pity than of his actual state of mind, it should not be forgotten that Lehmann's financial situation at this time was worse than ever, and that he was working feverishly day and night to try to repay his debts and restore a degree of financial stability to his life in readiness for Frieda.

The accent on "Gemeinschaft" and "Kameradschaft" meant that each teacher was more or less expected to use any special ability in the arts, in sport or in handicrafts to the benefit of all. Wickersdorf instituted a number of intimate and public forums in which such talents were displayed. There were, for example, the "Lehrerabende" when teachers would talk about their own personal interests and pursuits—Hafner, for example, talked about Japanese art, which had for two decades been enjoying ever-increasing popularity among German intellectuals,[18] and which was of particular interest to Lehmann at this time, since he was about to begin work on the Anglo-American writer Lafcadio Hearn (1850-1904), who had played a large role in fostering Japanese literature and art in America, England, and, indirectly, in Germany. Then there was the "Abendsprache," in which, before the whole school (including the non-teaching staff), a teacher would read or talk about something of a literary or cultural nature. The house favorites had from the outset been Spitteler and George—mainly due to the influence of Wyncken. Lehmann now began to broaden the scope a little, reading fairytales, the Romantic poets, and his own translations from the English. It soon became but a short step to reading from his own new works, although he tended to do this in smaller forums. Thus began a lifelong addiction to reading aloud, whether in the family, among friends, at school, or at congresses and on the radio. In this way Lehmann was both practising what he later on so often preached— namely, that poetry should be read aloud—and fulfilling a need for recognition. His ability to read well and capture his audience has often been alluded to. Helene

Aeschlimann, for example, who taught at Wickersdorf from 1915 on, spoke of the way Lehmann would read Märchen, "mit denen er alle bezauberte."[19]

It was known that Lehmann was an aspiring writer, and he was given each afternoon free as far as was possible to enable him to follow his true calling. The trend away from comparative linguistics which began even in Voorde and continued throughout his Neumünster years progressed. In Wickersdorf he wrote only two essays which were even remotely concerned with linguistic topics: "Sprachpsychologisches," which was published in the *Germanisch-Romanische Monatshefte* in 1912, is less interesting than his unpublished "Liegt die Wahrheit in den Dingen oder in uns?" which Lehmann unsuccessfully attempted to get published in various journals and newspapers in 1912-1913. Both essays stem from Lehmann's preoccupation with Rozwadowski. "Liegt die Wahrheit. . . ." is, however, remarkable in that a distillation of all that Lehmann built out of his Rozwadowski study is coupled, almost incongruously, with his scientific reading and his current thoughts arising out of his reading of Thomas Carlyle. The true historian, like the scientist, or like mythic man, conceives truth subjectively and bestows meaning on the object by intense identification with it. This essay accordingly marks yet another step towards Lehmann's ultimate poetics, both in theory and in practice.

These two essays proved to be the last purely scholarly works that Lehmann produced. From now on, instead of attempting to be a scholar in a non-scholarly environment, Lehmann turned his pen towards projects in which he felt he could earn money—he was, after all, in dire financial straits: not only were all his debts to Heimann and to Heimann's generous friends outstanding; there were considerable debts stemming from his Italian journey, and also money owed to the von Höegh family, relatives of Martha's who had loaned the couple considerable sums in 1908-09. On top of all this came a demand from Martha's father that Lehmann repay some 600 Mk he had given them in 1910 with no expectation of repayment.[20] In an endeavor to earn extra money and get out of debt for good and all, Lehmann set about the preparation of two school texts for the publishers Velhagen & Klasing and Carl Winter. The first, which he had begun while still in Neumünster, was an annotated edition of some writings of Thomas Carlyle. The edition brought him 400 Mk and was also to provide him with some material for a later novel. The other volume reflected Lehmann's interests and tastes to a greater degree and consisted of two tales by the Scottish writer George MacDonald (1824-1905). The edition, which earned Lehmann some 200 Mk, contained the tales *The Golden Key* and *Crosspurposes,* an introduction and vocabulary, and six color illustrations by Paul Scheurich. An attempt to produce a reader devoted to the polar explorer Shackleton failed for the want of a publisher—despite Heimann's help. Heimann was, however, able to secure for him a commission from Rütten & Loenig to write a biographical introduction to an edition of Lafcadio Hearn's letters. Lehmann completed this project, sent his lengthy and detailed introduction off in August 1913, and received 350 Mk in payment. The edition was never published, however, probably falling victim to World War I.

In addition to these projects, which involved a considerable amount of work for the already over-taxed Lehmann, he prepared a number of translations from the English. He had been periodically translating poems and passages from his beloved English for at least the past decade. During his last two years at Neumünster, when he taught older pupils, Lehmann had used translation exercises as a teaching device and had, as we have seen, often had his four senior girls translate the Grimm fairytales into English and back again. He had also read W.B. Yeats with them, and Frieda had translated a few passages of the Irish writer. Lehmann now sent off a number of his own translations together with some by Frieda to various literary journals. His own translation of H.G. Wells's "Socialism and the Middle Classes" appeared in the *Neue Rundschau* in January 1913, and was followed in March by "Socialism and the Family," which was dashed off at such speed that Samuel Saenger had to send it back with a sharp letter demanding more careful work. The fee for these two pieces went to pay the court costs for his recent divorce hearing (99.50 Mk). An earlier translation of a poem by Meredith ("Dirge in the Woods") and one of the poem "C.L.M." by the British poet John Masefield (1878-1967), who was just now making a name for himself, were turned down by Richard Dehmel. Lehmann's enthusiasm for Masefield's work led him to write a short essay on the poet (which appeared in the *Kritische Tribüne* in October 1912 and brought him 35 Mk). He also wrote to Masefield and was heartened by a friendly response and copies of *The Everlasting Mercy* and *The Widow in the Bye Street*. In 1912 Jakob Hegner's *Neue Blätter* printed translations of two short pieces from Yeats's *The Celtic Twilight*.[21] The translator's name was not appended, but it is likely that these translations were done by Frieda Riewerts. Certainly she was responsible for the translation of a short passage by the Scottish writer, traveller, politician, and sometime anarchist R.B. Cunninghame Graham (1852-1936). This piece dealt with the rise of Britain during the reign of Queen Victoria and appeared in Albert Helms's *Die Zeitschrift* in 1913.[22] In the same year this journal also printed Lehmann's translation of two Irish anecdotes by W.B. Yeats.[23]

Now, as ever, Lehmann was fascinated by things Irish. It was now, for instance, that he wrote his brief essays on Ireland which appeared in the *Neue Rundschau* and *Der neue Merkur,*[24] and it was now that he corresponded briefly with Charles Bewley (1888-1969), a brilliant and fascinating Irishman, who, like Oscar Wilde before him, had been awarded the coveted Newdigate Prize for English Verse while at Oxford University, only to forsake literature entirely for the law and politics.[25] Lehmann used Bewley's article on the "Irish National Theatre"[26] when writing his "Irisches" note for the *Neue Rundschau*. He soon afterwards wrote to compliment Bewley, the "begabten irischen Schriftsteller,"[27] on his poems.[28] Another Irish writer whose work Lehmann came across at this time was James Stephens (1882-1950), like Joyce and Virginia Woolf an exact contemporary of his. Lehmann's respect for Stephens's poetic gift knew no bounds, and he assiduously read and re-read whatever he could lay hands on while in Wickersdorf. And it was now that he made a move to bring out two editions of Irish folktales for German readers. The first was a new edition of the *Irische Märchen* which Karl von Killinger (a cousin of Ludwig Uhland, incidentally) had included in his six-volume collection *Erin* (1849). After managing to arouse the interest of the Hyperion Verlag in Berlin for the venture, Lehmann was saddened to see the whole affair come to nought with the advent of World War I. The other edition was a German version of a number of tales (translated by Frieda Riewerts) from Lady Gregory's *Kiltartan Wonder Book* (1910). He applied to her for permission to publish them, but dropped the project as being too time-consuming when she insisted that any publication should be of the whole book and should include her sister's original illustrations.

What Lehmann had really been doing over the past few years—at some remove both geographically and chronologically to be sure—was to participate both as a philologist and as an emergent poet in the Irish Renaissance, which, in all its varied emphases, was essentially a drive for the revival and preservation of all which was deemed quintessentially Irish—the Gaelic language, folklore, sagas, religious elements, the mystical, closeness to nature, the supernatural. Lehmann knew the work of those true fathers of the revival –Standish O'Grady (1846-1928) and Douglas Hyde (1860-1949), the founder of the Gaelic League. Those early works by Yeats which did so much to popularize Irish folklore, *Fairy and Folktales of the Irish Peasantry* (1888) and, of course, *The Celtic Twilight*, had long been part of his reading, as had Yeats's poems. The stages through which Lehmann passed in his literary development were almost identical to those in Yeats's own career. Both owed a great debt to Romanticism and Neo-Platonic traditions; both experienced a loss of religion which they replaced by a mythology; both were enthralled by the mystery and magic of the natural; both venerated Blake, were set in the same mystical tradition, and were descended therefore (directly or indirectly) from Jakob Böhme; both came under the influence of Imagism, and both sought a Unity of Being through a Unity of Culture.

The same combination of realism and fantasy which marks the work of Yeats also pervades the work of James Stephens. Lehmann acquired and read *The Crock of Gold* in 1913 and *The Demi-Gods* (which he inscribed "Dieses liebe Buch bittet, zart behandelt zu werden") in 1914. He was impressed by Stephens's "Essay in Cubes" contained in the April (1914) issue of *The English Review,* and he eagerly devoured anything remotely Irish which he found in this journal, in the celebrated *Athenaeum, Everyman* (he subscribed to both), *The Irish Book Lover, The Mask* and, in particular, *The New Age*—to all of which he had access during his Wickersdorf years.

The fact is that Lehmann from 1912 on had more contact with English literature than with German. Most of this contact came through the journals mentioned above. He therefore found himself, despite the financial difficulties which plagued him now as ever, ordering dozens of English books just because they had been reviewed in such a way as to make them sound appealing to him. Some were works by now forgotten authors, but they impressed Lehmann at the time: Frederick Niven's *A Wilderness of Monkeys* was one; George MacDonald's *Ranald Bannerman* another; while Leonard Merrick's *The Position of Peggy Harper,* "woran ich ja die Romantechnik lernen will"[29] was a third. Other books, such as the works by Stephens and Masefield mentioned above, and works by Hilaire Belloc, Padraic Colum, Ralph Hodgson, and Walter de la Mare, were of greater quality. The years following 1910 were, however, of vital importance in the literary and cultural development of Europe, and it was precisely this development, viewed primarily through British eyes, which fascinated Lehmann and undoubtedly began to exert some degree of influence on him. For the moment, however, his main aim was to do precisely what Heimann had exhorted him to do in 1909: write a novel—or at least a larger prose work—and the appearance of *Cardenio und Celinde* in August 1912 gave him some much needed confidence. *Cardenio und Celinde* was, as we have seen, closely autobiographical. Vivid though Lehmann's imagination was when it came to description or individual images, it just did not stretch beyond his own personal experiences. Given the power and importance of the two major events in his life between 1910 and 1914—his separation and divorce from Martha, and his love for and marriage to Frieda—it is hardly surprising that they should figure prominently in the works he now began to write.

It is significant that Lehmann's truly creative writing began immediately after his marriage to Frieda Riewerts. Scarcely back from their honeymoon on Sylt, Lehmann left the practicalities of life entirely to his new wife and began to write a tale he initially called *Der goldene Tod,* but which ultimately appeared under the title *Maleen.* The work was finished by February 1914 and accepted for publication—apparently by Franz Blei for *Die weißen Blätter.*[30] For some reason, probably the war, it never appeared in this journal and was first printed in 1918 in the *Neue Rundschau,* earning Lehmann 400 Mk. The tale concerns one Jelden Galbraith, modelled closely on Lehmann himself, and his unhappy marriage to Maleen, an older woman with a striking head of hair (= Martha).[31] The tale is patently autobiographical, deals with the circumstances of Lehmann's marriage to Martha and traces their life together in Gnissau (= Eldena), where their first child dies, in Siebenbürgen (= Malente), where Galbraith prepares for his examination, in Driesen (= Kiel), where he finds his first state teaching position, and in Grabow (= Neumünster) where he falls in love with Jorinde Holder (= Frieda Riewerts). The marriage disintegrates, Jelden and Maleen separate, and Maleen—here Lehmann departs from biographical fact—kills herself. Jelden, despite this liberation, is still oppressed by surroundings in which he can find no peace of mind—nature, it seems, excludes him: "Irgendwo gedieh eine Freiheit. Es galt, sie zu finden."[32] The tale introduces the basic theme of

Lehmann's work from this point on: the quest of a person, alienated by our divided civilization, for a unified existence as an integral part of a "heile Welt." There are many stylistic elements which will become typical of his fiction: the introduction of fairytale names and episodes, dreamlike visions, extremely graphic metaphors. But these elements are not well integrated for the most part. It is possible that some of the work's structural weaknesses stem from the revision which Lehmann undertook late in 1915 before submitting it to Samuel Fischer, but it is more likely that *Maleen,* being the first work of any length by Lehmann, suffered on account of his inexperience.

Lachnits Versuchungen was the original title of Lehmann's next work, which he began in early 1914, finishing the first draft by June of the same year, and which was to appear under the title *Der bedrängte Seraph* in 1915.[33] Like *Maleen,* the work is strongly autobiographical and covers much of the same ground as the earlier work. Where it differs from *Maleen,* however, is in the amount of fictional invention and in the more clearly central problem of Lachnit Bittersüß's (= Lehmann—the name effectively illustrates how Lehmann saw himself at this time) existential quest for integration into the cosmos. At the end Lachnit finds what he is seeking in Joneleit Kemter (a peasant girl, but nonetheless modelled on Frieda[34]), but only after a struggle during which it is not quite clear whether Lachnit will surrender to her or to the claim of the earth. Ultimately, he realizes that love for Joneleit is simply one manifestation of his love for existence:

> Lachnit saß, und die Nachtschatten schürten und lockerten ihn; sie bauten sein Gesicht ab und trugen wieder dazu, bis er unter das Gesetz trat und ein Sohn der Erde wurde. *Da gab er sich hin,* und er wurde leicht wie der Fruchtflügel des Ahorns, wenn er im Herbste in die Luft schmilzt. Der Mond trat zögernd hervor; er hatte lange gewartet. Nun beschien er das Feld und die Wiese vor der Dornhecke, die sich fröhlich in seinen Schein drängte, und beschien auch Lachnits verändertes Gesicht. Und die Nacht lief in den Morgen, an dem er Joneleit als Braut an der Hand hielt. (SW I, p. 45-46)

Despite the deeper philosophical implications of this struggle, the surface meaning conveys a very real worry of the author just prior to his marriage to Frieda. Could Lehmann, whose bond with nature was the most important aspect of his life—it was really this that made Walter Lehmann feel that "Ehelosigkeit" was the best state for his brother—surrender to Frieda? Or would Frieda not destroy the root of this bond by making demands on his being? By the end of *Der bedrängte Seraph,* the question appeared to have been resolved. In fact, Lehmann continued his love affair with nature to the exclusion of his wife till the end of his days, and the problem crops up in later works too.

Der bedrängte Seraph is more self-assured than *Maleen:* it "besitzt in der Metapherfügung eine größere Sicherheit."[35] Lehmann's inventions are more felicitous than in *Maleen*—Maleen's suicide, for example, was badly motivated and had a disturbing effect by virtue of its arbitrary intrusion.[36] But it is perhaps in the greater clarity of the central message and in the confidence with which this is conveyed that *Der bedrängte Seraph* scores and points most promisingly towards the future.

With *Der goldene Tod* (= *Maleen*) and *Lachnits Versuchungen* (= *Der bedrängte Seraph*) now complete in their first drafts, Lehmann and Frieda left Wickersdorf in the summer holidays of 1914 and journeyed to Neumünster, where they spent a few days with her father and received visits from most of Frieda's brothers and sisters. They then set off north on their bicycles, visiting more relatives in Heide and Husum on the way, for a two-week stay on the west coast of Denmark. Suddenly their leisurely rambles among the dunes of Blaavand and Varde were interrupted by the news of Austro-Hungary's declaration of war against Serbia and of German mobilization and her declaration of war against Russia, and they found themselves pedaling as fast as they could for Germany. When they reached Neumünster, they stopped for a while and Lehmann immediately wrote to his mother to assure her of their safety. His comments on the dramatic happenings of the last few days bear witness to his helpless naiveté in political matters and his veneration of England. But they also show that he did not share in the general public enthusiasm and nationalistic fervor running rampant at this time:

> ...Hoffentlich klärt sich die trübe Situation wieder auf: die Szenen an den Bahnhöfen etc. gehen einem stark an die Nieren. Wir wollen aber allem mit Gefaßtheit entgegensehen. Das Ganze erscheint mir vorläufig als ein ungeheures Unfaßbares. Vielleicht hilft England. Seit wann existiert dieser "Panslawismus"?[37]

Upon their return to Wickersdorf they found that some of their colleagues, including Krebs and Luserke, had already joined up and were fighting on the western front. The school had applied for an exemption from war service for others, including Lehmann, on the grounds that they were vital to the running of the school, and this dispensation was granted. Wickersdorf was initially gripped by the enthusiastic jingoism which pervaded the whole of Germany and, for that matter, France, Britain, and Russia, too. On the surface, perhaps, Lehmann occasionally appeared to be infected by the same enthusiasm. At the beginning of November, for example, he wrote to Agathe Lehmann: "Wie herrlich ist alles, was der deutsche Soldat tut, nicht? Wie lebt man, welch fabelhafte Zeit!"[38] But these words are ironic, for national pride and admiration for military matters did not come naturally to him now, any more than they did when he was a child living near the barracks in Wandsbek (see SW II, p. 396),[39] and the private thoughts committed to his journal reveal a different picture:

> Es ist Krieg, furchtbarer Krieg Deutschlands gegen Frankreich, Rußland und England....Am vorvorigen Freitag bin ich...weit zurückgestellt worden—eine entsetzliche Last fiel mir vom Herzen....Trotz der Siegesnachrichten ist der Krieg ein unvorstellbar Beängstigendes.[40]

The news that Luserke had been taken prisoner and that Krebs had been killed dampened everyone's spirits, and Lehmann, who had been asked by Krebs to be his literary executor in the event of his death, withdrew into himself and began to suffer each new catastrophe in the battlefield as if he himself were the victim.

Lachnits Versuchungen had been complete in a first draft before their bicycle trip to Denmark. While among the dunes of Blaavand, Lehmann had hit upon his later title: *Der bedrängte Seraph*. As the war raged, Frieda set about typing up a fair copy of this tale so that Lehmann could send it out to the publishers. Preoccupied with the fate of Luserke, the death of Krebs, and now the death of his former schoolmate Kriegsmann (reported to him by his mother), Lehmann cast about for a new theme to work on and, on 4 October 1914, was able to write in his journal: "Plan zu 'Virgil Rothmond' gefaßt." He wrote fairly quickly in view of the demands school life made upon the diminished staff in this time of war and material want, and had by the middle of December 1914 more or less finished the first draft of what had now been given the title *Der Feigling* and what was ultimately to appear as *Michael Lippstock*. In the next two months he revised his new work considerably, and he was thus able to take the finished revision with him at the end of February when he went to Berlin to see Heimann. Since Lehmann had the Friday off from teaching, he was able to leave Wickersdorf on the afternoon of 25 February, a Thursday. He accordingly went, upon arrival in Berlin, straight to "Steinerts Weinstube" on the corner of the Kurfürstendamm and the Joachimsthalerstraße, where he knew he would find Heimann together with his friends of the *Donnerstags-Gesellschaft*. The *Donnerstags-Gesellschaft* (see p. 120 above) comprised mainly artists, but people like Walter Rathenau and Martin Buber gathered there, too. It was, as Lehmann himself put it, "... eine beschwingte, zwangfrei zusammengestimmte Zunftgemeinschaft aus allen Künsten"[41] and on this occasion brought him face to face with two people who, as we shall later see, played a significant role in the development of his artistic genius: Oskar Loerke, and the artist E.R. Weiß. Lehmann spent the next three days in Berlin and finally laid before Heimann the finished manuscripts of both the *Bedrängten Seraph* (which had just been accepted by Efraim Frisch for *Der neue Merkur*) and *Die Farbenkugel*, as *Der Feigling* had temporarily been renamed. Further, he read extracts from both works. Heimann praised both works lavishly and told Loerke, whom they met in the S. Fischer Verlag, that Lehmann was to be compared with a Hermann Stehr, and that *Die Farbenkugel* was "fabelhaft schön." He did feel, however, that the final pages were a little "zuviel,"[42] by which he probably meant that they were somewhat extreme in the intensity and extravagance of their imagery. At all events Lehmann effected a few changes, submitted the work to S. Fischer and found it accepted for the July issued of the *Neue Rundschau*. *Die Farbenkugel* (= *Michael Lippstock*) once more underlines how dependent on his immediate biography Lehmann was when writing his stories. The Probst, Friedrich and Frieda Riewerts, and Walter Lehmann all found themselves rather accurately portrayed in the work, while Lippstock's frame of mind in face of the war was Lehmann's own. None of the directly biographical details helps towards an understanding of the work, however; on the other hand, the evolution of the title and the meaning of Krebs's death for Lehmann do provide a clue. *Michael Lippstock* as a title did not really stem from Lehmann. It was suggested to him by the publisher, and he went along with the suggestion. *Der Feigling* proved to be a misnomer once Lehmann had his hero go willingly to his death. The other two titles, *Virgil Rothmond* and *Die Farbenkugel* in particular, both stemmed from his friendship with Siegfried Krebs and their joint interest in Philipp Otto Runge. Krebs had written a doctoral dissertation on Runge and Tieck, and had published it in 1909. Lehmann was also very interested in the Romantic painter and collector of the two tales *Machandelboom* and *Von dem Fischer un syner Fru* (see p. 41 above), and he possessed the 1840 first edition of Runge's *Hinterlassene Schriften*. Many times they had discussed Runge together. And now that his friend was dead and Lehmann was faced with disposing of Krebs's library and sorting out his manuscripts, many of the thoughts they had exchanged welled up in Lehmann's mind once more and found their way in distilled form into *Michael Lippstock.*

The theme Lehmann had introduced in *Maleen* and *Der bedrängte Seraph* (namely of a person lost in our modern alienating civilization seeking reintegration into the "heile Welt" of nature) continued to obsess him in *Michael Lippstock.* The role of love in this quest is again central, but the artistic means Lehmann directs towards his end mark a distinct progression, and a new dimension to a possible resolution of the problem is introduced. Michael Lippstock's (= Lehmann's) attempts to achieve an *unio mystica* center on a fervent scrutiny of nature in an endeavor to extract meaning from what is seen. But the threat from an alien environment makes Lippstock seek to impose his own ordering visions on the senseless void which so often afflicts him. Through his love for Johanna Rothmond (= Frieda) he achieves momentary union with a harmonious universe. The outbreak of World War I threatens to destroy everything until Michael gradually begins to see death as a release into an eternal fusion with the cosmos. Lehmann had always been preoccupied with the notion of death. Even as a child he had obstinately kept his little garden plot in the shape of a coffin (see p. 13 above). Later his preoccupation with death manifested itself as a somewhat adolescent flirtation with suicide as a possible release from a pronounced and narcissistic *ennui*. The war and now the death of a good friend led him to see death as an ultimate answer to the eternally nagging existential question which dogged him.

But apart from love and death as possible means to a sublime *unio mystica* (a popular theme in German literature since Wagner, of course), Lehmann used, although in rather oblique form, art as a means to salvation. Although Michael Lippstock is not clearly designated an artist, he nonetheless continually affirms art throughout the work. He does so not only through his constant and conscious

FRIEDA LEHMANN, c. 1913, AT THE TIME OF HER MARRIAGE AND THE
PROTOTYPE OF LEHMANN'S EARLY FICTIONAL HEROINES.

THE VICARAGE IN NEUMÜNSTER. ON THE REVERSE FRIEDA HAS WRITTEN:
"PASTORAT (UNSER HAUS) NEUMÜNSTER. GARTENSEITE. X MEIN WOHN, - O
MEIN SCHLAFZIMMER." THIS IS THE MODEL FOR THE HOUSE IN *MICHAEL
LIPPSTOCK*.

flights of imagination, his image-making, but most clearly in his altercation concerning art and religion with his brother-in-law Nathanael and with Anna Bibe on the subject of words and "das Letzte." "Das Letzte" is the ultimate truth of existence and cannot be captured in art except by means of "das Vorletzte."[43] Michael's concern is accordingly not with the great abstraction of the universe, but with the phenomena which visibly comprise it. This notion might well have come straight from Lehmann's much revered Jakob Böhme. But it might equally well have stemmed from Philipp Otto Runge who, as Krebs pointed out and documented so clearly, appropriated the Silesian cobbler's philosophy and used it as a background to his work in his final, mystical phase 1803-1810. The main works which Runge produced during this period were his "Zeiten" (in all their various versions) and the theoretical tract *Die Farbenkugel*.[44] In his "Zeiten" Runge expounds his idea that the time cycle of the day shows the progression from birth to death, which for Runge meant "die Wiedervereinigung der Liebenden, die Aufhebung der Grenzen Zwischen Ich und Du, Körper und Seele."[45] Resting in God or in the Primal Being points forward to new beginning, to regeneration, to "Morgen," however, and thus the essential cycle of existence is portrayed in an organic and natural form. The sun (or divine light, the essence of Primal Being) plays a central role in this cycle and is also an equally important part of Runge's theory of colors. In *Die Farbenkugel* Runge expounds his view that there are two basic principles: Light (= white or good) and dark (= black or evil). Since we cannot look upon light (the sun) directly because it is too bright for human eyes, and since we *should* not look upon evil, God has provided for three primary colors to reflect the principle of light: namely blue, red, and yellow. Blue represents the Father, is the color of the heavens and holds us in awe; red is the great mediator between heaven and earth (the color of the sun when we are able to look upon it at dawn or dusk), and yellow (= Fire) is the consoling force, the source of light in the night; it is the moon, the reflection of the sun at night. The "Farbenkugel" which Runge constructed from these first principles is much more complex, of course. But since, as Krebs put it, it is "ein Symbol der ganzen Welt mit allen ihren Gesetzen und selbst allen sittlichen Verhältnissen,"[46] it could be readily taken over by Lehmann and used, together with the message behind the "Zeiten," as a sustaining frame in *Michael Lippstock*. Michael's quest passes repeatedly through the stages of the day towards gradual peace in the evening and at night. The moon (in reality, as well as represented by Johanna *Roth-mond*) is a welcome reflection of that supreme blinding truth of the midday sun which so often disturbs Michael. The sun (light) is "das Letzte" in Lehmann's terms and must therefore be appreciated and portrayed through a mediator—the moon, Johanna, "das Vorletzte." The color red constantly appears as a mediating aid: Johanna's red mouth, Ammerdahn's red hair, the red petunia. Michael's final cosmic union is death, which comes to him in the late evening and night. When Johanna hears of his death, it is in the morning, and she immediately gives birth to a son. Thus Michael finds continuance in the world of individuation, of Kassner's *Individualität,* finds universal oneness in the "heile Welt," in Kassner's world of *Identität.*

Michael Lippstock marks a progression over Lehmann's previous two works in that the basic theme is more intricately worked over and the accompanying imagery is of necessity more striking. The intrusion of art in the service of art adds a further means beyond the fairytale motifs to Lehmann's avowed end: the re-attainment of an ordered, unified cosmos. The complex of intricate and extravagant imagery reflects the confusion of Michael in mustering the array of varied motifs at his disposal. To unite them structurally, Lehmann was often obliged to bury them deep. The work is therefore a curious mixture of obtrusive and outrageous images and almost hermetic underlying philosophies. This is its great weakness. Had Lehmann ever resolved the problem while keeping on the same path, it would have been an artistic *tour de force.* As it is, *Michael Lippstock* stands as the most lyrical of Lehmann's fictional works and, since the gap between its lyricism and the prose narrative form is so great, it points rather insistently towards the necessity of the lyric genre for Lehmann's message and as an outlet for his peculiar literary gift. For the moment, however, Lehmann remained bent on carrying out the program Heimann had set him: to write a novel.

Much of what Lehmann described in *Michael Lippstock* concerning the war (the medical examinations, training, requisitions for food) was known to him only through hearsay—former pupils and teachers returning on leave as well as parents and relatives of pupils were often visitors at Wickersdorf and gave vivid accounts of their adventures. Throughout the next few years he was to experience all that went into his novella and much more besides. After the first shock of the war had passed and Lehmann had found himself deferred indefinitely, he had relaxed considerably—after all, the war was not going to last very long anyway. But then, despite the early successes, people began to speak of a longer fray, and by mid-May 1915, when the Italian crisis was looming large, Lehmann was becoming alarmed lest the war claim him as a combatant, too. His alarm proved fully justified, for he was called for a medical examination in Saalfeld on 20 May:

> Am 20. Mai ging ich in tiefumnebelter 4 Uhr Morgenfrühe hinunter; rechts saß, wie ein Preisbulle, der Major, Brust voll Ehrenzeichen, höhnisch und elegant abfertigend, links der Stabarzt. Ich hatte mich auf eine gründliche Untersuchung gefaßt gemacht, zumal die Gendarmen Entkleidung diesmal befohlen: eine Farce aber war's, kaum war ich entkleidet ins Zimmer getreten, als der Major rief 'Infanterie' und ich zurückkam, ohne neue Notiz auf dem Paß.—So stand ich, in Not.... [47]

He accordingly decided to apply once again for a deferment, sent in his application, and heard that "...das Gesuch sei genehmigt worden. O wie erleichtert!" [48] The relief was temporary. By March 1916 Lehmann had been found "kriegsverwendungsfähig" and had filed yet another application for deferment: "...jede Minute kann die Entscheidung eintreffen....ich bin seit lang-langer Zeit nicht mehr lebendig, lebe in einer Qual, fühle mich wie ein zusammengedrückter Knäuel wie eine zusammengepreßte Lunge, die nicht mehr kann und siechend einen Tag müde nach dem anderen über die Berge klimmend halb nur noch sieht....[49]

His low spirits were not simply due to his anxiety regarding the war. For some months now, ironically at precisely the time his domestic life was calmer than it had ever been and when he was flushed with his first literary successes and proud of his standing as a teacher,[50] the tension within the school administration had increased to an uncomfortable degree, and Lehmann was being drawn inexorably into the resulting conflict.

Even after Wyneken had been ousted from the school leadership in 1910 he was still able, in his capacity as a member of the board of trustees, to take a rather active part in school affairs. As long as Luserke was holding the reins, however, Wyneken's interference had been kept within reasonable bounds, so much so, in fact, that he began to make plans in 1913 to break away (once again!) with some of his disciples and found a new school. This move was scotched by the outbreak of the war. Once Luserke departed for the western front and almost immediate captivity, Wyneken, who had been kept abreast of events at the school through his sister Lisbeth, began actively to usurp the leadership and assert his will to an ever-increasing degree. Lehmann, like so many others initially impressed by this charismatic (and gifted) figure, had as early as July 1912 seen him for what he was,[51] and as Wyneken began to spread his view that the intellect must rule supreme and that emotion had no place in school life, Lehmann began to take a positively antagonistic stance.[52] It began harmlessly enough in the early days as Lehmann introduced his readings of fairytales, Romantic "Kunstmärchen" and poems. The contrast between what Lehmann so successfully offered and the grotesquely solemn celebrations of the ponderous and pompous Spitteler and Stefan George who had become cult figures under Wyneken, was immediately apparent. Since the Wyneken brigade, especially Lisbeth, was capable of forceful statements to the effect that Goethe was inferior to George,[53] a difference of opinion gradually developed into a breach so wide that the Lehmanns would not accept invitations to social gatherings if Lisbeth Wyneken was present.[54] By 1916, the antagonism was such that the two factions took to sitting at different tables in the communal dining-room.[55] The actual cause of this particular skirmish was, as so often the case, not of tremendous import: the question had simply arisen as to whether the dormitories should be administered by Jaap Kool, who looked after business matters, or whether they belonged in the field of teaching. This area was in the somewhat weak hands of Bernhard Hell at this time. He, along with Lehmann, Rudolf Aeschlimann, and a few others, was of the opinion that it should be financially administered by Kool, but that the pedagogical province should be attended to by himself and his colleagues.

Bernhard Uffrecht, a socialist and the later founder of the Freie Schul- und Werkgemeinde Letzlingen, and Wyneken's sister Lisbeth disagreed. They felt that the administration of the dormitories should be wholly a matter for themselves and attacked both Kool and Hell and the latter's more vociferous allies.

Behind this breach, however, indeed behind all the many conflicts at Wickersdorf, lurked the cantankerous figure of Gustav Wyneken. At this point he was quite happy to let his sister and Uffrecht be his voice and push a little for Uffrecht to replace Hell. But the moment Uffrecht did indeed take over in the summer of 1916, he turned against him and even managed to oust him from the leadership. Wyneken was, in fact, such a contentious person that all relationships with him were doomed to split asunder. Although both Hans Dieter Schäfer and Burley Channer speak about Magerhold, the representation of Wyneken in *Der Bilderstürmer,* as being "ins Dämonische gesteigert"[56] a quick perusal of the periodical *Die Freie Schulgemeinde* through the years 1912-1920 (the years Lehmann was connected with Wickersdorf) or of *Der Vortrupp* for the year 1917 reveals a Wyneken either actively engaged in contention or the subject of controversy.[57] The vehemence with which he attacks and defends what are really very minor points suggests that he was, in reality, as demonic as his fictional counterpart. Whatever his controversies with others, or even with Lehmann over school matters, there is no doubt that the true source of the rift between Wyneken and Lehmann lay in their opposing outlooks: Wyneken's subordination of everything to the "objektive Geist" he described in his book *Schule und Jugendkultur* (1913) and Lehmann's subjective affirmation of existence through concrete imagery. A year after the climactic events of 1916 (by which time Wyneken was pressing his fighting spirit in service of his fatherland), Lehmann rather soberly recorded in his diary: "Als ich die letzten Aufzeichnungen (vom vorigen März) eben wieder durchlas, wunderte ich mich über den Umfang, den die Wynekensache da in meinem Leben einnimmt."[58] The fact was, however, that these altercations played such havoc with Lehmann's nerves that he became irritable, began smoking heavily again, and found himself vomiting from time to time.

Faced with the gnawing fear of imminent call-up and growing tension among his colleagues, Lehmann found solace where and how he could: namely in the woods and uplands surrounding Wickersdorf. After his early attempts at communal gymnastics, jogging, and skiing, Lehmann soon dropped back into his old habit of taking long walks alone. He observed the weather, the changes in flora and soon grew to know just where he would find deer, foxes, weasels, salamanders, and snakes. His acquaintanceships with these various animals rapidly grew into intimate friendships—at least on Lehmann's side:

Fand heute an derselben Stelle (hat gegrabenes Loch unter einer jungen kleinen Fichte) wieder meine Freundin, die Kreuzotter (ich ließ sie in jenes Loch

VISIT OF CARL SPITTELER IN WICKERSDORF, c. 1910. SEATED NEXT TO SPITTELER
IS HELENE VOIGT-DIEDERICHS; OPPOSITE HER IS HER HUSBAND EUGEN
DIEDERICHS, THE PUBLISHER. FAR LEFT, RUDOLF AESCHLIMANN, FAR RIGHT IS
ADOLF KÖSTER.

GUSTAV WYNEKEN (1875-1964), c. 1910. LEHMANN MODELLED MAGERHOLD IN
DER BILDERSTÜRMER ON WYNEKEN.

WILHELM LEHMANN, c. 1914.

WILHELM LEHMANN IN WICKERSDORF, c. 1915.

entschlüpfen) und zwar gehäutet. Ihre Haut, an die Tanne abgestreift, habe ich gefunden und hier. Sie sah hübsch frisch, bleich braun aus.[59]

Despite the terseness of such journal entries, there is a wealth of detail in them. This passage attests not only to the careful way that Lehmann, with painter's eye, observed the natural scene, but also to the zeal with which he scientifically assessed the environment and life habits of the creatures he observed. His room was filled with an assortment of snake skins, the broken shells of birds' eggs, the contents of the waste balls regurgitated by owls and such like. The previous winter Lehmann had seen a fox in the woods where he regularly tramped:

Heute Nachmittag aber, als ich durch den Schnee nach der Rodelbahn in den Meuraweg ging, sah ich bald—unversehends—von links nach den Eichengebüsch-hängen hinauf einen—*Fuchs* laufen; schien schwereres dunkelschwarzbraunes Tier zu sein, schnaufte auf dem Boden. Ich suchte nach seinen Spuren, er ist ganz vom Rohrbach (wo ich Näheres verlor) heraufgekommen, immer gradaus, Spuren schön sichtbar. An kleiner Tanne nahe Rodelbahnlichtung fand ich seinen Harn, den ich, da vereist, in Taschentuch nahm, köstlicher herb-süßer Geruch; dann ging ich die Spur nochmal zurück.—Nachher verschwand noch in den Eichenbüschen wieder ein wildes Kaninchen oder so.—Wunderschöne weiße ruhevolle Schneelandschaft.—Schrieb weiter (langsam) am "Feigling."[60]

The proportion of natural description compared to the briefest mention of his creative work amply demonstrates just how important these solitary excursions into nature were for Lehmann.

But, although they compensated in great measure for the growing unpleasantness of intercourse with a number of his colleagues, these excursions were not sufficient to hold Lehmann permanently in a Wickersdorf devoid of Luserke and Krebs and with only Aeschlimann as a real friend to redress the balance of a belligerent Lisbeth Wyneken, her brother (whenever in Wickersdorf), and Bernhard Uffrecht. He accordingly began to look around for other positions, the directorship of the new Wandsbek Lyceum, for example.[61] This position appealed to him for a number of reasons: it was in Wandsbek, replete as it was with all the happy memories of his childhood in the Pächterhof, it was a state school (Wickersdorf had been in and out of financial trouble since Lehmann had joined the staff in 1912), and the director's position, although involving a great amount of work, would be both well-paid and secure against any call to arms. Lehmann's application was unsuccessful, however, as was his application in March 1917 for a similar position in Lübeck.

Despite his periodic low spirits in face of the continuing war and the atmosphere in the staff common-room, Lehmann was considerably buoyed up by his first literary successes: "Ich bin froh, zwei Erfolge im Kriegsjahr," he wrote in October 1915, referring to *Der bedrängte Seraph* and *Michael Lippstock*.[62] The moment he was finished with *Michael Lippstock,* he started on a new project. Throughout June 1915 he worked steadily on what soon received the title *Der*

Bilderstürmer, and in the long summer vacation he was able to devote himself entirely to the novel. By the end of July, by which time he and Frieda had gone to Neumünster, he was able to write the last line sitting in the peaceful seclusion of the garden house at the vicarage. After a restful August in their beloved Schleswig-Holstein, the Lehmanns returned to Wickersdorf, and Lehmann set himself to the revision of his novel and to making a fair copy of it. Frieda saw to it that he had the peace he needed. She not only did her own stint of teaching, but also took on many of the chores her husband should have been looking after—the *Kameradschaft,* for example.[63] One afternoon at the end of October, with the first winter snow gently falling (the snow-geese had passed early that year, Lehmann had recorded), Frieda returned from teaching to find her husband looking pale and wretched, and clutching a sheaf of printed pages in his hands. He describes the scene in his essay "Gedenkwort für Moritz Heimann":

> Einige Tage nach dem Erscheinen [of *Michael Lippstock*] fand mich meine Frau nach der Vormittagsarbeit erblaßt und elend. Ich hielt in der Hand die aus der Rundschau gelösten Blätter, wie sie von oben bis unten, von Anfang bis zu Ende, der Maler E.R. Weiß mit handgeschriebenen, zornigen Glossen versehen hatte. Heimann hatte sie mir kommentarlos geschickt.[64]

At a remove of almost fifty years, Lehmann's memory fails him just a little, for he received these marginalia some two months after the publication and, what is more important, Heimann did not by any means send them "kommentarlos." Lehmann records the event in his diary in slightly different detail: "Ich habe schweren Bruch erlitten. Am vorvorigen Sonntag schrieb mir Heimann, meine literarischen Aussichten wären nichts, dazu den gedruckten "M.L." mit bissig detruierenden Anmerkungen."[65] Weiß's bitterly sarcastic comments were exceedingly painful, but could have eventually been shrugged off as the immoderate reaction of someone who knew no better. With Heimann's criticism,[66] however, it was a different matter. Heimann had warned Lehmann throughout the writing of *Michael Lippstock* that his florid imagery would offend the average reader. Here was the proof of it, plus a further warning from Heimann that Lehmann's future as a writer was doomed as long as he persisted in this highly idiosyncratic style of writing. Lehmann, always ready to accept advice from his friend uncompromisingly, settled down to his revision of *Der Bilderstürmer* with a pen of moderation: "Gestern machte ich Kap. 10 'Der Bilderstürmer' fertig. Ende 9 ist schon nach dem Eindruck von Heimanns Brief remodelliert worden."[67] Henceforth Lehmann's fiction was to become ever more conservative.[68]

Lehmann's connections with the *Donnerstags-Gesellschaft* brought him into contact not only with E.R. Weiß, but also with Oskar Loerke. The same week that Heimann sent the Weiß comments, Loerke wrote to Lehmann[69] and said: "Ihre Novelle ist mir tief hin und tief her geklungen, wie ich es wollte."[70] The acquaintance, which began in February 1915, soon blossomed into a friendship,

OSKAR LOERKE (1884-1941), c. 1915.

so that whenever Lehmann went to Berlin he was at least as desirous of seeing Loerke as he was Heimann. In fact, the relationship may be said to have begun earlier, for Loerke had been a friend of Siegfried Krebs, and Lehmann had often heard his Wickersdorf friend praise Loerke. When Krebs was killed and Lehmann set about dispersing Krebs's library, he took a number of books not wanted by the family into his own collection. One of these was Loerke's volume of poems *Wanderschaft* (1911), which he read with great interest in January 1915, sharing his enthusiasm and gain with the rest of Wickersdorf in an "Abendsprache" containing "Gedichte von Rückert und Loerke, der mir, seit ich den Band Wanderschaft bei Krebs entdeckte, eine Revelation ist."[71] At the same time, Lehmann was reading the Irish poet James Stephens: "Loerke gegenüber und James Stephens gegenüber verzweifle ich an meiner—o—Kunst."[72] Lehmann and Loerke were able to meet only when Lehmann travelled to Berlin, as he did, for instance, in the Christmas break of 1915. The following Christmas vacation Lehmann and Frieda spent over a week in Berlin and, on Monday 8 January 1917, Lehmann read the first six chapters of his new novel *Die Entwurzelten* (later to be published as *Die Schmetterlingspuppe*). Loerke was, as Lehmann recorded in his diary, "entrückt, sagte u.a. 'Ich bin überhaupt der Meinung, daß Sie bald den Platz bekommen müssen, der Ihnen gebührt.'"[73] The following day Lehmann read a few more pages, and Loerke again responded positively: "Herrlich.... Da haben Sie etwas Schönes fertiggekriegt."[74] Lehmann was, needless to say, delighted with the response and always submitted whatever he wrote to his new friend from this point on.

The mutual attraction of the two poets is not difficult to understand. The volume *Wanderschaft* is full of closely observed nature vignettes such as Lehmann loved and was later to use successfully in his own poetry. The poem "Im Vorübergehen" in *Wanderschaft,* for example, begins:

> Des Drahtzauns rostige Waben
> Umziehn des Laubfalls Husch.
> Man sieht Maulwürfe graben
> Im leeren Schneebeerbusch.

and points rather clearly to Lehmann's later poetic style. Not surprisingly Lehmann marked this poem with the one word "Schön" in his copy. The similarities between the two writers later led many critics to label Lehmann a disciple of Loerke—an assertion Lehmann challenged in his short essay "Warum ich nicht wie Oskar Loerke schreibe."[75] In this essay Lehmann approvingly quotes a letter from Reinhard Tgahrt, in which Tgahrt distinguishes subtly between the two poets, finding in essence that Loerke calls upon pathos to a greater extent than Lehmann and celebrates existence in broader terms, whereas Lehmann tends to be attracted (perhaps even distracted) to a greater degree by details and specifics.

Loerke's praise for *Michael Lippstock* to some extent counteracted Weiß's attack and Heimann's more tactful criticism so that Lehmann did not altogether lose heart. He was thus able to get on with his revision of *Der Bilderstürmer,* which he sent off to Fischer towards the end of 1915 who, by March 1916, agreed to print it both as a serial in the *Neue Rundschau*[76] and as a book. Lehmann received 1,000 MK for *Der Bilderstürmer,* and Fischer, who was well disposed to his new author, asked whether he did not have another short story for the *Neue Rundschau.* Lehmann obliged by quickly revising *Maleen* and sending it off. It came out in 1918 in the May issue.

Der Bilderstürmer, Lehmann's first real novel and first work to appear as a book, deals primarily with Lehmann's Wickersdorf experiences, but cannot avoid reference to the divorce. It also depicts Lehmann's love for Frieda. Wyneken is portrayed unsympathetically but accurately in Magerhold, Luserke in Gilbert Mannhardt, and Rudolf Aeschlimann in Raffael Rinroth. The description of the buildings and lay-out of the Piesemang estate is an accurate depiction of Wickersdorf, while life at the school is rather well and fully portrayed in the novel.

The novel starts, in a sense, where *Michael Lippstock* left off. "Der Tag kreischte mit den Farben eines Kakadus" is the very first sentence, and there is an abundance of similar imagery in the next few chapters. The argument "das

Letzte" versus "das Vorletzte," which was introduced in *Michael Lippstock,* is also an important part of the story—although it is dealt with on a slightly different plane. The conflict in *Der Bilderstürmer* is less within one single character, however, than between two main characters with their adherents and their ideas: namely Beatus Leube (= Lehmann) and Magerhold.[77] These two characters represent two opposing outlooks on the world: Leube's is essentially subjective and imaginative, Magerhold's is objective and intellectual. Leube will attempt to find ultimate truth via concrete images and specific phenomena (= "das Vorletzte"), Magerhold storms straight to the absolute goal (= "das Letzte"). In addition there is the sexual aspect. As in *Michael Lippstock,* sexual union is, as a form of creativity, also a means to an *unio mystica.* After an unsuccessful marriage to Agathe,[78] Leube finds with Friederike Wesendonck the compatibility which enables him to see meaning in life. Magerhold repudiates sexual love—except when he loses control and plunges into a relationship which is as tragic as it is brutally exploitive. Where *Der Bilderstürmer* differs radically from *Michael Lippstock* is in the function of death. In the latter work Lippstock had willfully chosen death and had escaped from an overly antagonistic human realm into a synthesis with nature. In *Der Bilderstürmer,* Hollebüttel provides an acceptable human realm and suggests that life on earth can be meaningful. Leube can therefore affirm life—at least a life with Friederike. Magerhold, through his Icarian flights directly to the Absolute, to "das Letzte," and his repudiation of his natural surroundings, succumbs to a sun-stroke and dies. In view of Runge's theories dealt with above, the fact that it is the supreme power of the sun (which can be experienced only indirectly through a mediator) which kills Magerhold is significant.[79] Had he been blessed with Lippstock's or Leube's image-making capabilities, with the gift of imagination or poetry, he could have avoided this fate, but he was not. But whatever Magerhold represents, whatever his inimical position with regard to nature, a final reconciliation does take place:

> Der Himmel, der Blutzeuge alles Geschehens, verbarg, seiner Macht froh, die Erinnerung an seinen Feind in seinem tiefsten Schoß, und der Widerstreit träumte sich zur Ruhe eines neuen, heiligen Anfangs.
> (SW I, p. 128)

How often was this message of a new beginning in nature to be repeated over the next few decades!

Der Bilderstürmer marks a further step in Lehmann's literary progress. Biographical elements, although still forming the essential background, are of lesser importance—indeed they can be misleading.[80] By working out his conflict through two characters rather than within one main personage, Lehmann moved away from pure lyricism and took a step towards the fictional mode. In a sense, however, it is a retrograde step in that he follows the pattern of the nineteenth century novel rather than continuing his experiments with the subjective, lyrical, and psychological possibilities occupying such writers as

Virginia Woolf, Marcel Proust, and Robert Musil. Perhaps the Weiß-shock forced him a little in this direction. It probably pushed him to a degree of moderation in his imagery—at all events the imagery, although still exceedingly rich, is more controlled than in *Michael Lippstock* and therefore more generally acceptable.[81] Partly for this reason, the novel, as Channer has demonstrated rather well, has a tight and well-wrought *lyrical* and not narrative structure.

The contemporary reviews of *Der Bilderstürmer* should have been gratifying to Lehmann, since they were at best very enthusiastic and at worst guardedly positive. His only reaction to the reviews, however, came in a letter to Heimann in which he quotes part of Arthur Brausewetter's review in the *Berliner Börsenzeitung*[82] in such a way as to suggest that he found the reviewer lacking in insight.[83] In the same letter, however, he alludes to Alfred Döblin's reaction: "Dagegen lobte Alfred Döblin in einem schönen Briefe den Bdst. sehr, mir zur allergrößten Freude."[84] Döblin's enthusiasm was matched by other illustrious writers and critics such as Oskar Loerke, Oscar Bie and the young Kurt Pinthus. Loerke spoke of an "Erzähler, in dem sich ein großer Dichter ankündigt" and asserted that the book had been welcomed "enthusiastisch."[85] Bie, well acquainted with Lehmann's work by now, stressed the young poet's lyrical gifts and spoke of the figures in the novel as "Träger der Visionen und Sprecher der Lyrik, Wesen für die Beziehungen zur Natur."[86] Kurt Pinthus spoke of "eine neue Ausdrucksmöglichkeit zur Darstellung äußerer und innerer Ereignisse" and was of the opinion that Lehmann was and must remain "eine einmalige Erscheinung." He pointed to the author's love of the concrete as opposed to the abstract and to his predilection for anthropomorphization within the realm of nature, and he enthusiastically welcomed this singular new talent to the literary scene.[87] The one guarded review came from Otto Schabbel. He appreciated the undoubted lyrical gifts of the young author but also threw in an objection: "Noch ist mancher Schwulst und manche Geschrobenheit des Ausdrucks zu beklagen."[88] Schabbel thus seized upon the very same weakness that Weiß had so intemperately attacked in his *Michael Lippstock* marginalia, but nonetheless he remained generally enthusiastic. The only other review to raise any objections to Lehmann's style stemmed from the pen of Friedrich Düsel. He felt that Lehmann "wird zum Sklaven seiner ungezügelten, unerzogenen Einbildungs-kraft" and that it would be "jammerschade, wenn sich Lehmann aus diesem Rausche nicht erholte, um Menschliches menschlich zu gestalten!"[89]

Der Bilderstürmer and the three shorter works of fiction, had all been produced since his marriage to Frieda during a period of what seems to have been domestic stability. But to imagine that all problems in Lehmann's domestic life ceased with his marriage to Frieda would be wrong. The marriage itself was certainly successful in a way that Lehmann's first marriage had never been. Frieda's expertise in practical matters was an enormous boon to Lehmann and, although his financial problems certainly did not disappear overnight, Lehmann hardly mentions them in his diary or even in his letters after their marriage, except to note occasionally that they have just paid his mother's rent, or sent her 100 Mk. Once Berthold came to Wickersdorf, his support of Martha diminished and became very irregular. But this is perfectly understandable when one considers that Wickersdorf had been obliged to cut salaries drastically once the war began. The better-off staff received nothing whatever; Lehmann, whose need was appreciated by the administration and his colleagues, received 100 Mk per month. The improvement in his financial situation was undoubtedly due to Frieda, whose love for the man she had won manifested itself primarily in easing his way through a problematic existence. For his part, Lehmann was fully aware of the love and help which Frieda so freely gave, but he was also aware of what he himself was not always able to give:

> Ich habe in diesen Tagen die Erfahrung gemacht, wie deutlich ich es empfinde, daß ich mein Weib sehr sehr lieb habe. Es nimmt zu leicht bei mir, wegen nervöser Labilität, sinnliche Formen an und es ist gut, daß sich die Aufspeicherung stets so entladen kann, aber es ist wie ein Tuch, das Gefühl für sie, in das ich mein Gesicht hüllen kann. Wer hängt denn mit aktiver Neigung an mir außer ihr? ... Und weil ich sie doch so sehr lieb habe, habe ich mir vorgenommen, all diese Tage, ihr mehr zu sein, mehr mit ihr zu *gehen* vor allen Dingen. Es ist eben garnicht an dem, daß ich etwas versäume d.h. "meine Arbeit", wenn ich mich ihr entziehe. Sondern es ist bloße schlechte Angewohnheit, Nervosität: dies Wort muß leider viel bei mir decken.[90]

He goes on to list a considerable number of things he had done to demonstrate his love for Frieda. The impression left, however, is that this was all a response to his guilty conscience: his penchant for going his own lonesome way (which had led Walter to question the wisdom of remarriage) did not leave him—now or ever.

His relationship to his mother once the marriage had taken place was marked by a rare and lasting peace. The one continuing problem which overrode all others concerned Berthold and Martha. He saw Berthold at first rather seldom when a meeting could be arranged in Lübeck at his mother's or in Hamberge through Walter and Emmy. But in the summer vacation in 1915, he and Frieda were allowed to have Berthold with them in Wickersdorf for three weeks. What he saw of Berthold's development did not please him, and he wrote a long letter to Agathe describing his impressions and telling the reader as much about his approving attitude to Wickersdorf as about his son's development:

> Bei dem guten Gesamteindruck Bertholds fiel mir betrüblich und schmerzlich vieles auf, was früher anders war: seine kindliche Echtheit ist durch die Atmosphäre, in der er ja leben muß, so ins Konventionelle, Matte, Schwächliche verwischt worden, daß es mich oft von Grund aus betrübte. Rührend war sein leidenschaftliches Bestreben, hier in den Gang des schönen, herben Wickersdorfer Lebens hineinzukommen: ich machte natürlich an ihm noch einmal die Probe auf das ganze Wickersdorfer System, und es hat glänzend bestanden. Diese scharfe Einteilung des Tages, die unerbittliche Strenge der Forderungen des Tages: sie wirkte herrlich auf das Kind. Es ist ja das

Bezeichnende, daß er sich sehnt nach einer festen Hand, nach einer strengen, hellen Autorität: erst dann fühlt ein Kind naturgemäß sich glücklich. Dort ist er der haltlosen Schnoddrigkeit des Johannes Dreis und des alten Dreis dazu der Schwäche seiner Mutter ausgeliefert: ich wüßte keine Atmosphäre, die ein werdendes Kind ungünstiger beeinflußt....

... er schreibt reizend, liest elegant: aber viel wichtiger ist mir der Stil seines Lebens. Er stolpert so dahin, sieht nichts, hat das Präcise und entzückend Exacte seines Sprechens, seines Verhaltens fast ganz verloren. Alles ist altklug, conventionell an ihm, er macht den Eindruck, als führe ihn seine Mutter auf allen möglichen Verwandtenbesuchen herum, da sitzt er dann und hört das—halb mitleidige, halb klatschhafte—Geschwätz der Erwachsenen und das sind die Eindrücke, die in seine, meines lieben Jungen Seele, der ich so ganz anderes bestimmt habe, einströmen. Kein Wunder, daß er so wird! Mit 10 warmen Kleidungsstücken ist der Arme noch immer behangen (ich liefere pünktlich und angemessen das Geld, aber das Zeug sitzt ihm nicht, nichts ist einfach und genau gearbeitet), es ist ordentlich tragisch anzusehen wie er sich Morgens und Abends mit dem Zeug herumquälen muß: wie soll er da Schnelligkeit und Adrettheit lernen. O welch ein Gegensatz zu der Erziehung hier! wo jeder, vom Kleinsten bis zum Größten, in seine praktischen 3 Sachen schlüpft, auf den Glockenschlag sich einstellt und alles funktionieren muß.[91]

For all his concern about Berthold as long as he was in Martha's care, Lehmann was to do very little for his son's development when he did eventually have the chance.

Martha's handling of financial matters was also of great concern to him—although, since his account and Martha's account of their financial arrangements differ so radically, it is impossible to say where the blame for the contention lay. It is at all events clear from Martha's letters between 1914 and 1918 that her moods and opinions oscillated wildly. She changes from the "Du" form of address to the "Sie" form and then back again on numerous occasions. Sometimes the second person is dropped altogether and she alludes to her former husband in the third person as "Bertholds Vater." She moved in and out of her stepfather's house in Kiel several times and, in April 1916, moved with Berthold to Munich to stay with her half-brother Johannes Dreis, now studying at the university there. Her reasons for the moves were always the same: she moved in with her stepfather whenever it proved financially necessary (old Herr Dreis could always use a housekeeper now that his wife was dead), and she moved out because he was maltreating her. In August, asserting that Johannes Dreis was abusing her, she suddenly elected to move to Jena. Lehmann's hopes that she might now allow Berthold to attend Wickersdorf were fulfilled, and on 14 September the eight-year-old Berthold could write to his Grandmother Lehmann: "Jetzt binn [sic] ich hier Wickersdorfer Sextaner" and describe his first experiences of Wickersdorf life to her. On the back of the same letter, Lehmann alluded but briefly to his relief at Berthold's arrival and easy adaption to his new life. Instead he described the problems arising from Martha's new living situation. She was most upset at her treatment at the hands of her half-brother who, she was convinced, was about to report her to the police as "gemeingefährlich" if she did not immediately return to him in Munich; and then her stepfather was accusing her of having stolen "Bettfedern" from him. For his part Lehmann trusted neither her stepfather nor her half-brother, but was nevertheless of the opinion that Martha was ill: "Uns muß Martha als eine arme Kranke gelten, hilflos und sinnlos."[92] Certainly she seemed to be suffering from some kind of persecution complex, for no matter which way she turned, someone or something seemed to threaten her. Jena seemed, at first, to offer a refuge from Johannes and her stepfather. But, in January 1917, any peace which might have existed in her new surroundings was completely shattered when she came across the recently published *Bilderstürmer* in *Die neue Rundschau* in which she, as Agathe, is rather unsympathetically portrayed. Deeply hurt, she sent off a sad and disappointed letter which was in deep contrast to her earlier enthusiastic response to *Michael Lippstock:*

> Ich erwarte keine freundlichen Briefe und keine Freundschaft mehr von Bertholds Vater nachdem ich seine letzte Dichtung gelesen. So schreibt mein Freund nicht. Aller gute Geist ist wohl aus Bertholds Vater gewichen.[93]

Perhaps due to Heimann's good offices (he, like most people not closely connected with her, remained on friendly terms with Martha) and perhaps due in part to her former husband's friendship with Eugen Diederichs, Martha had secured employment in one of this publisher's offices. By March, however, she was obliged to give up this position because of the embarrassment caused her on two accounts. Johannes Dreis had apparently come into her office one day and behaved so arrogantly that her position among her colleagues became untenable—precisely what Johannes said and did is unclear: and the book-keeper had come across *Der Bilderstürmer* and had begun reading out passages pertaining to the hapless Martha to his amused colleagues.[94] Wherever Martha interacted closely with other people, the inevitable result seemed to be strife, and Martha felt persecuted.

By now it was becoming increasingly clear that, although Lehmann's treatment of Martha during the marriage and after was often shabby, she was a person of such contrasts that life in close proximity with her was exceedingly difficult. Most people who met her and spent no more than a few hours with her were charmed: the Heimanns, Helene Aeschlimann, Agathe Lehmann even. Martha was clearly a woman of great beauty, vivacity and charm. But there was an obverse side to her character which made life with her in the same household well nigh impossible: namely her disorganization and impracticality in domestic and financial matters.[95] Stories concerning her irrational behavior while directing the Lehmann household are legion: she would prepare a great quantity of fruit for jam only to find that she had no sugar and that it was Sunday, or she would take Lehmann's salary at the beginning of the month and buy new furniture only to be obliged to sell it all a fortnight later when she had no money for food. She was also very possessive and could react bitterly if she felt that others were treating her unfairly, and such was often the case with her young husband and her child—both of whom she was obliged to relinquish precisely because of her impractical nature. Certainly the combination of Martha and Lehmann was doomed no matter how great their mutual love. The legacy of their disastrous marriage remained with them for the remainder of their lives and became apparent through periodic requests for extra money, recriminations when payments were missed, or through difficulties in Lehmann's relationship with Berthold. The memory of a once potent love seemed to remain, however, for it is said that Lehmann (with typical scant regard for Frieda's feelings) kept a photograph of his first wife on his private writing desk many years after the divorce.

7
The War (1917-1918). "Es ist schwer zu leben...."

IT WAS DURING Berthold's first few months at Wickersdorf in late 1916 that Lehmann forged ahead with his next novel, *Die Entwurzelten,* which was published by S. Fischer under the title *Die Schmetterlingspuppe* in 1918. *Maleen* and *Der bedrängte Seraph* had portrayed the confusion of an alienated young man not yet fully aware of the cosmic magnitude of his problem. *Michael Lippstock* had continued this theme, but had suggested that death could be the reconciliation so longingly sought, eclipsing even love as a means to an *unio mystica. Der Bilderstürmer* had described the conflict of two opposing world views, the objective and the subjective, *Geist* and *Natur,* and had portrayed the conflict by means of two main figures rather than within one single character. *Die Schmetterlingspuppe* combines all these themes and emphases and shows the conflict both in the inter-personal relationships, within the one central character, Loeski (= Lehmann), and within the poetic imagery of the work.

The novel is still haunted by purely autobiographical events, although these are subordinated and well-integrated into the fictional frame of the fable. Loeski, a teacher tortured by the necessity of living with insensitive and unimaginative fellows, of living in a world seemingly made pointless through the ravages of a typhus epidemic,[1] can nevertheless be brought to realize that this absurd world can and does have meaning as long as he allows himself to merge into the realm of plants and animals all throbbing with life and waiting to absorb him. Death, far from being a negation of life, is simply a form of life. Walking through the woods and fields, Loeski realizes this and is restored to some semblance of peace:

Die Seuche war möglichenfalls vorbei. Sie war auch nur eine Form des Lebens, sie war auf den fauligen Blättern der Ahornbäume, die die Dorfstraße in Queiß einsäumten, in den Bach gestiegen und dann in die Häuser. Loeski atmete erleichtert auf. Ein Hund hatte seine Wunde mit breiter, wohliger Zunge geleckt; diese große, süße Wunde hatte er nach langer Zeit wieder deutlich gespürt; sie war offen und

hochrot; Gewißheiten und Freuden flatterten wie Vögel über ihrem Spalt. Wer an den Rand dieser Wunde trat, wurde schwindelnd des Daseins gewahr. Sie hielt den Irrglauben von ihm fern, sie war sein einziger Hort. Die Epidemie, das Wissen um das Sterben in Queiß und den vielen Dörfern hatten ihn zu lange verschlossen gegen den Biß des Lebens, dessen Zähne knirschten, daß es ihn von der Tiefe zur Höhe wirbelte, wo er sich hielt mit Lerchenleichtigkeit, fliegend und singend zugleich, eins nicht ohne das andre, eben wie die Lerche. Alles andre war nicht.
(SW I, p. 175)

Thus far, Lehmann seems to have arrived at the point where *Michael Lippstock* left off. But Loeski's life at the "Rosenkreuzerschule"[2] is so unsatisfying that when his wife, Christine, leaves him, he immediately terminates his connections with the school. Loeski, who seeks a sense of oneness in a vital natural world and wishes to see "das Dasein unverfälscht und quellend" (SW I, p. 182), cannot reconcile himself to life at a school where, as its leader Christoph Rosenkreuz (= Wyneken) says: "wir halten uns an die Überschwenglichkeit der großen Begriffe und sorgen dafür, daß das Leben zu den Ideen emporsteigt." (SW I, p. 182)

Whereas in almost all his previous works Lehmann had described an escape from a marriage which was stultifying and the subsequent beginning of a new relationship which seemed meaningful, in *Die Schmetterlingspuppe* he varies the pattern somewhat. In Christine, Loeski has a wife who is all he could wish for. She is part of the unified cosmos he so ardently yearns for:

Ihre kräftigen Beine waren beim Laufen zu sehen. Und Stanislaus freute sich. Er war mit einem Schlage aus seinem erregten Brüten herausgerissen. Wenn er die kräftigen und doch zierlichen Beine seines Weibes sah, dann sah er auch gleich die Glieder des Zitronenfalters, der heute zwischen seinen Büchern ausgeschlüpft war, und auch gleich die Kolbengelenke der Grashüpfer, und dann das Ganze, in welchem die Füße aller drei standen.
(SW I, p. 188)

She knows the names of the stars and says "statt 'rechts' und 'links' 'südlich' und 'nördlich'" (SW I, p. 190). But the relationship is nonetheless not quite right. Loeski is too wrapped up in himself or, at best, in self and nature, to contribute much to his relationship with his wife.

Having severed all connections with the "Rosenkreuzerschule," Loeski travels to Ireland. What this country meant for Lehmann has already been dealt with (see above p. 000 and p. 000). It is in this country that elemental nature seems to flourish almost magically, mythically; here that Loeski seems able to lose himself ecstatically and merge with the mythos that is everywhere so obvious. His first encounters are auspicious: a vision of Christine, gypsies, the fair, and the cattle market where he comes across Tabor—a man gifted in his way with animals, especially when helping them during pregnancy and birth. In these new surroundings Loeski meets other Germans who, like him, have pulled up roots and settled here.³ These other uprooted people are Theodor Comichau, an urbane and musical merchant much given to irony, and Ariadne Kellner, who is Comichau's lover.⁴ Lehmann is attracted not only to Tabor (who seems to embody that balanced existence within nature as part of it), but also to Comichau and Ariadne. He admires Comichau's urbanity—especially in the early days—and he is fascinated by Ariadne's beauty. During the Irish chapters, Loeski tries to bring his three new acquaintances together, hoping that they can all enjoy a Tabor-like existence in this mythical land. But he fails. Tabor is too completely part of nature to do more than just tolerate Loeski. Comichau and Ariadne despise Loeski's outlook and see Dubran only as a primitive and dirty rural community. After he is overcome one day by the heat and the elemental sensuality of nature, Loeski falls upon Ariadne in a wild outburst of sexuality. Ariadne flees. She and Comichau are then found to have committed suicide (this double suicide is not, to my mind, adequately motivated), and Loeski, having failed in Ireland, returns to Germany. His Irish experience simply underlined his feeling of alienation; furthermore, in succumbing to his sexual urges so wantonly, he broke not only a bond of trust with Christine, but also a deepening union with nature. Back in Germany he attempts to find a peaceful and harmonious existence within nature by working on a farm, but here, too, the essential union he seeks eludes him: his relationship with farm animals, unlike Tabor's, is through art—he sketches the beasts, but only the individual parts of them; he captures the beauty of their structure, but not the essence of their being in its functionality. Around him are the farm-workers and farm-girls tumbling carelessly and wantonly in the hay. In despair, Loeski throws himself from a hayloft in emulation of an owl and finds death.

The message of *Die Schmetterlingspuppe* is more somber than that of *Der Bilderstürmer* in that there is no way to an integrated life in an ideal community. In the earlier novel Friederike had found her way to a meaningful existence in Hollebüttel, and Leube had been close to a similar relationship with the community, if only through his love for her. Loeski is never absorbed into the Irish community he so admires. Neither does he achieve any relationship at all akin to Leube's with Friederike. The message of the *Schmetterlingspuppe* is more somber than that of *Michael Lippstock,* too: Loeski kills himself in despair at not being able to achieve the position in life he desires, whereas Lippstock willingly goes to his death with the positive aim of being absorbed back into the cosmos. Loeski is unable to find any meaningful human relationship—even in Ireland, where Tabor provides such a good role-model, and even in a marriage with someone who is, like Johanna and Friederike in the other works, a support and a helping link to a harmonious existence in a unified world of man and nature.

The appearance of *Die Schmetterlingspuppe* in July 1918 (with, ironically, a cover design by the Fischer Verlag artist E.R. Weiß!) meant that Lehmann had now produced two novels to appear in book form in the space of just over one year. The critics were thus able to draw comparisons and comment on the author's development. Loerke[5] and Pinthus[6] continued to be enthusiastic, and both stressed not only the uniqueness of Lehmann's creative talent, but also the lyrical quality of the work. A measure of the impact caused, albeit among the few, by Lehmann's emergence onto the literary scene, can be seen from the fact that Pinthus's review was one of two of the work to appear in the same issue of the same journal (*Zeitschrift für Bücherfreunde*—the other review was by Friedrich Sebrecht). Furthermore, the Austrian critic Adalbert Muhr was sufficiently attracted to this emergent writer to sketch a short appreciation of him in the Viennese periodical *Der Merker*.[7] Both Muhr and Pinthus raised and dismissed the question which preoccupied Schabbel and Düsel in their reviews of *Der Bilderstürmer*. Pinthus begins his review as follows:

> Nach dem Erstlingsbuch 'Der Bilderstürmer' zeigt dieser zweite Roman, daß der erste kein einmaliges Experiment war, sondern daß hier eine ungeheuerliche Begabung, furchtbar in sich selbst verstrickt, sich krampft und windet, schreit und strahlt und aus ihrer Not eine Tugend macht, indem sie aus der Dumpfheit von Wollust und Leid nach dem Ausdruck durch das Wort ringt.

Coming from someone who did not know Lehmann, this is a remarkably accurate summary of both the writer and the man. Muhr expresses the same view in rather similar terms:

> Manches mag noch eingeschoben, übertrieben, unklar, überladen, abstrus erscheinen, als wuchernder Bildüberfluß. Dies scheint mir indes keine Affektation zu sein, sondern etwas Mitgewachsenes, Unverhinderbares. Eine strotzende und strömende Elementarität breitet sich aus, einer neuen Vermittlungs-, Gestaltungs-möglichkeit Ankündigung und Verheißung.

Other favorable reactions to *Die Schmetterlingspuppe* came from his old friend from his Berlin days, Hermann Stehr, and from Alfred Döblin, who was fast becoming a new friend. Döblin's comments are as accurate as they are sympathetic, and they reveal both a deep understanding of and an affinity for Lehmann's work:

> Ihr neuer Roman,—den ich vom Verlag eben noch erhalten habe,—ist außerordentlich schön. Es ist garnicht nötig, das näher zu beschreiben und zu begründen. Man muß ihn langsam, Silbe um Silbe, lesen, um von dem ganzen, öfter ganz bezaubernden Bilde nichts zu verlieren. Das Buch ist ein bedeutender Fortschritt über die mir bekannten beiden anderen. Es ist reicher, gedankenvoller, innerlich geweiteter; es ist mit einer—finde ich wenigstens,—großen Ruhe und Objektivität, mit Sophrosyne geschrieben. Ich habe jetzt noch mehr als früher die Ähnlichleit des Ganzen mit Böcklin empfunden: die Stumpfheit der Charakteristik, die naturangeähnlten Menschentypen, die nicht individuell verbleiben,—die reigenhafte Verbindung der Menschentypen, Tiertypen, Pflanzentypen. Es ist ein schönes süßes und feierliches Buch, zu dem ich Ihnen Glück wünsche, wie ich mir selbst Glück wünschte, als ich es selbst langsam seitenweise pro Tag zu mir nahm.

Ich habe kritisch nichts auszusetzen; es ist durchaus Ihr bestes Buch. Ich schreibe Ihnen nächstens einige stilistische Bemerkungen,—gelegentliche Unausgeglichenheiten, Banalitäten,—es ist nichts von Belang.—[8]

Hermann Stehr compared *Die Schmetterlingspuppe* with *Der Bilderstürmer* and also marked an improvement. But in praising the work, he also touched upon the issue of Lehmann's extravagant imagery:

> Ihr Buch ist gegen das vorherige ein Fortschritt mit weitem Abstand. Die Partien, in denen Sie den zerstörerischen Reichtum der Bilder und die Exzentrizität des Temperamentes zu den inneren Bedingungen des Werkes und den einzelnen Gestalten und Situationen zu bändigen vermögen, sind gegen das frühere Werk in erheblicher Zahl gewachsen.[9]

The fact was that Lehmann was unable to avoid this issue, and he began to be plagued with self-doubt to an ever-increasing degree. Despite the claim on him by the war—the novel was revised and went through proofs while Lehmann was particularly apprehensive about being sent to the front—Lehmann was very much concerned with this matter, the more so since Heimann had once again raised it when he read the manuscript before the work went to press. Heimann's was still the word which mattered, and it alone was sufficient to set Lehmann thinking about matters of style. At the time of the publication of *Der Bilderstürmer* and when Lehmann was working on *Die Schmetterlingspuppe,* Heimann had warned him about trying to produce too much too quickly, and his criticism had taken effect:

> Ich spüre die Grundwahrheit deiner Ratschläge: die eilig gebratenen Hammelkoteletts müssen aufhören, der Schinken muß geschnitten und in den Rauch gehängt werden mit all den Esentien, die einem lebennährenden Schinken zukommen. Habe Dank, du hast Recht![10]

But it was not easy to change his style or working methods so that, when *Die Schmetterlingspuppe* was at the proof stage one year later in March 1918, Lehmann was still concerned about the quality of his work:

> Mit dem Heutigen sende ich den Rest der Korrektur meines Buches "Die Schmetterlingspuppe" an Fischer ab. Ich glaube nicht, daß es etwas bedeutet. Mir scheint, daß Deine Mahnung damals "Hüte dich vor dem Spezialistentum" zu Recht besteht. Ja, das "Buch" scheint mir verzweifelt nahezustehen den Marzipanaden eines Keyserlink [sic]. In guten Momenten hoffe ich auf Möglichkeiten, das nächste Buch besser, bedeutsam, reiner und richtiger zu erschaffen: ohne Requisitenpoesie, ohne dies beständige Schielen nach der Mutter Erde....[11]

Despite Lehmann's own skepticism, however, and despite Heimann's reservations, it should not be overlooked that Lehmann had produced no less than two exceedingly dense novels and three lengthy stories in less than four years—and all this while attending to other duties and coping with the anxieties of a very difficult period. This is remarkable fecundity and demonstrates that he had certainly overcome many of the problems which had kept him from creative writing earlier, even if he had not yet found his true métier as a lyric poet. There is no doubt that *Die Schmetterlingspuppe* marks an improvement over all his previous works. It is his first piece of fiction in which the purely lyrical is accompanied by a discernible thread of inter-personal action, and it is the most clearly structured and well-rounded book so far. The rather gloomy tone may be ascribed to two factors: the war and Lehmann's ever-increasing sense of foreboding, and the realization that he was not able to shed sufficient of his introverted self-centeredness to lead the loving married life he had hoped for and desired when justifying to himself his wish to marry Frieda. Human love no longer seemed to be a way for him to reach that mythical unity he so earnestly longed for, and the world was so full of destruction that any relationship of man to nature seemed doomed to fail.

How Frieda reacted or felt as she typed up *Die Schmetterlingspuppe* and saw what was in effect her marriage split asunder in her husband's latest book is not known. But her preoccupations during the generation and birth of the novel in late 1916-early 1917 were closer to day-to-day reality and were of a more practical nature. Hardly, it seemed, had she and her husband welcomed Berthold into the family of Wickersdorf (Berthold lived in a dormitory with the other children and not with the Lehmanns), when Frieda became pregnant. It was not an easy pregnancy. The couple was constantly obliged to seek medical advice, which, however, was usually relatively reassuring, and Frieda suffered considerable discomfort. She did not give up teaching and continued to take on a good deal of the burden which by rights should have been her husband's. Adding to the discomfort and to the kidney trouble which was a constant source of nagging pain, was the cold of a hard winter in which fuel was so scarce (due to the war) that only a few rooms could be heated. Every so often Frieda was obliged to take to her bed, and her husband would teach her classes for her. As the pregnancy progressed, Frieda's condition seemed to worsen, and both, but Frieda in particular, began to get more and more depressed. Once again Lehmann demonstrated a peculiar lack of common-sense as he tried to help. Convinced that the local doctor was incompetent, he wrote to a specialist in Rudolstadt a considerable way away, giving the symptoms, and was then surprised to get an answer saying that no advice was given by mail. Meanwhile he began to make arrangements for Frieda to go to Heide in Holstein so that her sister Lina could be on hand for the birth. The Heimanns both warned against this long and uncomfortable journey, and Lehmann, at a loss, finally decided to write to Julius Levin, that man-of-letters, physician, and violin-maker extraordinaire, whom he had met through the *Donnerstags-Gesellschaft,* and who was Oskar Loerke's usual partner in piano and violin sonatas. Levin confirmed the local doctor's appraisal and insisted that for Frieda to travel up to Schleswig-Holstein was "purer Wahnsinn."[12] The plan to go to Heide was immediately dropped. Instead Lehmann took Frieda to Saalfeld on 16 May and checked in at the *Frauenklinik* there. They were none too soon, for although the child was not expected until mid-June, a son, whom they initially intended to call Wilhelm Konrad Lehmann, was born on 22 May nearly one month premature. Labor was short and the birth relatively easy, but there was "dafür allgemeiner nervöser Zusammenbruch"[13] so that Frieda refused to see her husband. In fact, Frieda was not only severely weakened but also feverish, and it was several days before she was out of danger and began to recover. The child, who soon received the given name Pelle (after the hero of Martin Andersen Nexø's novel *Pelle Erobreren*—a naming not without a certain ironic twist as events turned out) thrived, and two weeks later they were both back in Wickersdorf.

While these developments in the family were taking place, the war continued unabated, and the enormous casualties meant that it was really only a matter of time before Lehmann himself was forced into a soldier's uniform. Throughout 1916 (when Wyneken was called up) the period of each deferment dwindled to a mere three months, each one of which threatened to be the last. Still his luck seemed to be holding out, until, in March 1917, he was told there would be no further deferments. On 28 May 1917, the Saalfeld "Meldeamt" sent him a scrap of paper with the one sentence: "Sie haben den Beginn der Sommerferien nach hier zu melden." On 15 July, Lehmann found himself in Saalfeld in a reserve infantry regiment, where he was subjected to the trials and humiliations which go towards the making of a soldier: haircut, uniform issue, basic training, and the loss of freedom and individuality. For some fortunate souls, such rigors seem harmless enough, and they come through unscathed. Wilhelm Lehmann did not belong in this category. From the beginning it was torture, as the one sentence he sent Heimann on 4 August shows:

Aus einem gequälten, greulichen Lebenslauf voll Hetze, Hast, wahnsinnigem Tempo, beständigem Putzen, Waschen, Reinigen, Exerzieren
Grüße
Lehmann

Physically, he was at a low ebb to begin with, and all exercises and training came doubly hard to him. By 25 September he was so exhausted that even an unsympathetic military doctor assigned him to a "Tag Bettruhe... wegen völliger Erschöpfung."[14] Never able to adjust to officious personalities, he ran foul of every Napoleon with corporal's stripes that he came upon—and there were many of them. His uniform did not fit him, his gasmask was the wrong size, no suitable helmet could be found for him, the mechanics of his rifle escaped him, and the realization that he was learning how to kill his fellow human beings struck him hard when they came to bayonet-training. All that could be said on the positive side was that he was not fighting at the front and that he was, first in Saalfeld, then after his transfer to Rudolstadt in November 1917, fairly near to Frieda, Berthold, and Pelle. But active service at the front seemed to be drawing closer, although he still had hopes that one of two plans to serve without actually

BERTHOLD LEHMANN, WICKERSDORF, c. 1916.

c. 1922. STANDING, LEFT TO RIGHT FRIEDA LEHMANN, WILHELM LEHMANN,
LITA LEHMANN-MARSCHALK, MAX MARSCHALK, EMMY LEHMANN, WALTER
LEHMANN. SITTING: THIRD FROM LEFT, DORIS LEHMANN, FOURTH FROM LEFT,
PELLE LEHMANN.

WILHELM LEHMANN WITH HIS WICKERSDORF COLLEAGUE WILLY BEZNER,
RUDOLSTADT, 1918

fighting might succeed. In 1916 Heimann had given Lehmann's name to a certain Prof. Dr. Hönn, who was arranging for some German counter-measures against the French "Haßpropaganda" and was looking for some collaborators. In September 1916 Lehmann had been summoned to Berlin to discuss the matter with Hönn and a Legationsrat von Hahn. He put forward his idea of writing a novel centered on life in Wickersdorf which would put the German forward as a peace-loving and cultured human being incapable of the atrocities of which the French were accusing the Germans. This plan had met with a promising reception, but Lehmann had heard nothing more in the meantime. Lehmann had therefore also inquired about the chances of being assigned to a signals regiment to do wireless work—his knowledge of French and English being his trump card here (or so he hoped). The various people he applied to were all unable to help, however, so when, in September 1917, it really seemed as if he would soon be sent to the front, he made another attempt to obtain a furlough working with Hönn against the French propaganda. At first it seemed he would be unsuccessful, but by January 1918 he had learned that Hönn had at least applied for a three-month leave period for Lehmann to engage in this important propaganda work.[15] His hopes were not high because he had just been assigned to a "Rekrutendepot"—the last station prior to the dreaded journey to the front—and expected to be sent westwards any day. But on 12 January Lehmann wrote to Heimann and told him how the unexpected happened:

> Seit einer Woche fix und fertig eingekleidet fürs Feld—da kommt am Tage bevor der Abtransport endgültig festgesetzt, Nachricht aus Berlin, daß Prof. Hönn bzw. Legationsrat von Hahn einen 6 wöchentlichen Urlaub zur Herstellung der bewußten Schrift für mich beim Ers.- Batt. beantragt hat. Ob es genehmigt wird, weiß ich noch nicht—jedenfalls aber bin ich vom Transport, der heute Mittag 2:58 abgegangen ist, noch zurückgestellt worden bin [sic]. Das ist eine ungeheure Erleichterung für meine Frau und mich.

The leave was granted, and Lehmann found himself trying to carry out the project which had sounded so easy a few months earlier—after all, was it not simply *Der Bilderstürmer* made more accessible? With its positive side brought to the fore? The book, to be written for a potential Norwegian audience, was to be one of a series entitled "Der Kampf der Deutschen," put out "zur Aufklärung des neutralen Auslands." Lehmann settled down to family life in Wickersdorf again and began to write what was initially called *Jakob Zwengsahn und seine Freunde* but which soon became known as *Das fröhliche Tal*. It was not easy:

> Mit der Arbeit, deretwegen ich die 6 Wochen frei bekommen habe, geht es sehr schlecht, um nicht zu sagen: garnicht. Die 6 Bände, die das A.A. [i.e. Auswärtige Amt] mir geschickt hat (o diese Papier Gabriele-Reuter, ganz grauenhaft!) scheinen mir recht belanglos.[16]

What emerged from Lehmann's reluctant pen was a watered-down hodge-podge of ideas and events which bore striking resemblance to the content of not only

Der Bilderstürmer, but also that of *Michael Lippstock.* After five chapters devoted to a description of life in a calm and harmonious school community, the "Fröhliche Tal" (= Wickersdorf) in which the history teacher Jakob Zwengsahn (= Lehmann) is a central figure, war breaks out. Wurmbrandt, the director of the school (= Luserke), immediately volunteers and is soon in captivity. After momentary hesitation, Zwengsahn also joins up. When he returns on leave, the big question occupying everyone's mind is "Wurmbrandt oder Hesser" (= Wyneken), who was now playing an active part in school affairs. Zwengsahn and Hesser engage in an earnest debate in which the old conflict "Geist und Natur" is central. Zwengsahn returns to the front and is killed while reconnoitering.

The work has none of the colorful and intricate imagery of Lehmann's other works. It also has no scenes of action or memorable characters likely to appeal to a broad readership. Lehmann's attempt to engage in dialogue for the first time fails in that the characters talk in a stilted language devoid of any natural tone. It is, in short, neither fish nor fowl, and the Foreign Office turned it down. There are occasionally passages which convey a Lehmannesque idea or attitude quite well, like the following description of the so ardently yearned for *unio mystica* of man in nature:

> Weltgesichtigkeit, das war das gleichmäßige, das maßvolle Schweben im Raum und in der Zeit, offen jedem Hauch, wie der Vogelkörper von den ungeknechteten Lüften umspielt.[17]

If obliged to sum up Lehmann's poetic philosophy and his heroes' quests in one word, one might do worse than to choose the one word "Weltgesichtigkeit."

By 20 March, Lehmann's leave was over, and he was obliged to report back to his base in Rudolstadt. For a while everything seemed to hang in the air, and the monotony was relieved (and Lehmann's apprehension increased) by a course in "Granatwerfen" in the month of May: "Es blüht alles und ich bin im Granatwerferkursus, scheußliches Mordinstrument."[18] It now seemed as if there was nothing more he could do to avoid active service at the front and, in his dreadful anxiety, Lehmann's thoughts dwelled more and more on death. On 6 May, two days after his 34th birthday, he wrote to Heimann and asked him a favor: "Dies noch, wenn es so weit ist, dann bitte ich Dich dringend, verlier meine liebe tapfere Frau, obgleich Du sie ja noch nicht kennst, und meinen kleinen Pelle *nicht* aus dem Auge. Es ist schwer zu leben... ich habe so vieles versäumt." At about the same time, he wrote to a chemist acquaintance and asked for poison. He got it: "Die Dosis, die ich sende, würde für etwa 20 Mann reichen."[19]

Lehmann seemed surrounded by death. In April they had heard that another of Frieda's brothers had been killed—he left a wife and two small children. And his mother, who had recently been bothered by a recurrence of the growths for which she had undergone surgery the previous year, was now clearly dying. On 15 June he wrote to Heimann: "Mutters Ende steht bevor...," and wondered whether

Heimann could manage to rush a copy of *Die Schmetterlingspuppe*, now about to appear, to her. Two days later she was dead. Had she died at a time when her son, her eldest son, was less preoccupied with what he saw as his own rapidly approaching appointment with death, he might have reflected on her passing and what it meant for him. As it was, he was later to think back with guilty conscience upon this mother who had single-handedly brought him up (together with Walter and Lita) in the most adverse circumstances and with great sacrifice. Had he considered the privation entailed as she endeavored to provide a cultured home with books and music, the wherewithal to study (he himself was later to refuse his own son Berthold so much as a single penny towards his studies!), he might have forgiven her the pain she caused him and the mistakes (costly mistakes) she made as she applied those subtle and not so subtle pressures towards the one over-riding end: that he not grow up like his father.

But the Fatherland called. On 6 August, Lehmann found himself assigned to another regiment and was three days later en route for France. From 13-20 August he found himself taking part in the last fierce exchanges around Verdun, which had been in bitter contention since the beginning of 1916. Meanwhile the allied forces were advancing further to the north in a final offensive against the Hindenburg position, and Lehmann was sent from one hopeless situation to another as he joined the forces trying to stem the oncoming tide around Cambrai and St. Quentin. Losses on both sides were great, with the Germans losing three men for every allied soldier killed. Lehmann, having anticipated such horrors over the past three years in his fiction and diaries, found his nerves cracking and his physical reserves dwindling by the minute: "es war eine außerordentliche Anstrengung für mich; drei bis 4 mal beschloß ich abzuhauen, quälte mich aber durch bis z[um] Schluße."[20] His exhaustion was such that he dared not unpack his knapsack for fear he could not re-pack it in time to move on with his comrades when the time came. In the what seemed to him to be aimless marching back and forth, he was always at the rear, and his strength was flagging. On 3 September, having had his fill of active service, Lehmann quietly slipped away from his unit and set out for enemy territory. The situation at this time was so confused, with constant skirmishes involving the continual loss and regaining of ground, that the best scout might have been forgiven for not knowing precisely where the enemy was. The hapless Lehmann would, at the best of times, have experienced difficulty in finding his way across to the enemy. In the general confusion and in his drained state, it would have been a miracle had he made it unscathed to the allies. After four days and nights of wandering through fields and villages in the battle area,[21] he had finally had enough, and he gave himself up to a group of German soldiers from the "Ortskommandantur Flavion," who then sent him back behind the lines to a military jail in Namur, where he remained from 10-17 September. Upon arrival in Namur, Lehmann was questioned closely about his actions. He was searched, deprived of all personal belongings—including, to his grief, his "Talisman," a picture of a Chinese bronze horse—and treated with some contempt. Prisoners were provided with coffee ("schales Gebräu") and bread for breakfast, porridge (which Lehmann could not stomach) for lunch, and coffee and bread again in the evening.[22] From 4:30-5:00 in the afternoon there was minimal exercise. Each cell (there were three prisoners in Lehmann's cell) was provided with a little reading matter—the *Düsseldorfer Zeitung* and, incredibly, an article by Gundolf on Bergson torn out of the *Jahrbuch für die geistige Bewegung*,[23] which Lehmann read repeatedly. He worried a lot about Frieda and Pelle, longed for specific reading matter ("Hätt ich jetzt hier Jean Pauls Komet oder Dostojewski"), and wondered, not surprisingly, about his fate: "Wie wird man," he ends his abbreviated but detailed account, "sich gegen mich verhalten?"

Frieda Lehmann was informed that her husband was missing in a terse note sent on 9 September. On the same day his remaining belongings were also sent: "1 Rasierapparat, 1 Pinsel, 1 Nähzeug, Briefpapier, 1 Brille." On 11 September a somewhat unlettered comrade, one Johann Czabajski, sent a rather more reassuring note; in it he expressed his conviction that Lehmann was in captivity:

> Hochwohlgeborene Frau Dr. Lehmann
> Ich wollte Ihnen mit teilen daß ihr Mann Willi seit 2. September vermißt ist in der Kompanie. Das Paket mit der Weste habe wieder auf der Schreibstube abgegeben zum zurück schicken. Ihr Mann ist wohl in Gefangenschaft geraten. Wen sie solten von ihrem Mann eine nachricht bekommen so bitte teilen sie mir mit wo er sich befindet.

Beside herself with anxiety, Frieda wrote on 17 September asking for more information. The letter crossed with a note telling her that Lehmann was now back with his company:

> Die Kompanie teilt Ihnen hierdurch mit daß Ihr Mann, Landsturmmann Wilhelm Lehmann, heute bei der Kompanie eingetroffen ist.

What might have been somewhat reassuring news then became utter confusion when she received the following answer to her original letter of inquiry:

> In Beantwortung Ihres anliegenden Briefes teile ich Ihnen ergebenst mit, daß Ihr Herr Gemahl infolge Nervenzerrüttung, hervorgerufen durch die heftigen Kämpfe zu Anfang d. Mts. in der Nähe von Bapaume seinen Truppenteil am 8. Sept d. Jhs. unerlaubt verlassen hat und dann bis zum 14.9. im Etappengebiet und im Generalgouvernement Belgien umhergeirrt ist, bis er sich am Abend des 14. Sept. freiwillig einer Patrouille der hiesigen Ortskommandantur stellte. Er wurde zunächst von seinen Kameraden aufs beste bewirtet und verblieb bei der hiesigen Stelle zwei Tage. Alsdann erfolgte von hieraus seine Überführung nach Namur, wo er da [an] die dortige Ortskommandantur zum Weiteren übergeben wurde. Über seinen gegenwärtigen Aufenthalt kann ich Ihnen leider keine Auskunft geben; ich nehme an, daß er sich noch in Namur befindet. Eine diesbezügliche Anfrage Ihrerseits bei der Ortskommandantur in Namur würde Ihnen für sicher darüber Aufschluß geben. Zu irgend welcher Besorgnis liegt kein besonderer Anlaß vor. Es

sind dies Vorfälle, die jetzt des öfteren vorkommen und die—soviel mir bekannt ist—auch nachsichtig und entschuldigend beurteilt werden. Indem ich Sie bitte, sich wegen der Angelegenheit keinerlei unnötige Aufregungen machen zu wollen, zeichne ich mit vorzüglicher Hochachtung....[24]

This interesting document reveals just how great the confusion was at that time, how many soldiers were cracking under the strain, and the naiveté of this particular writer who seemed to believe that such cases were in general treated with sympathy and understanding.

Lehmann had, in fact, been accused of cowardice and desertion while in custody in Namur, and had the German lines not needed every available man and no unnecessary distractions through courtmartials and the like, he would certainly have been tried, found guilty, and probably shot. As it was, the trial was postponed, and Lehmann was sent back to his company—hence the brief note given above. It was not until May 1920 that the following letter informed Lehmann that the proceedings against him were being dropped:

zur Mitteilung, daß das gegen Sie beim Gericht der 22. Div. schwebende Verfahren wegen Feigheit und unerl. Entfernung gem Verordg. v. 7.12.18 bedingt niedergeschlagen ist—Es nimmt seinen Fortgang, wenn Sie innerhalb 2 Jahren seit dem 12.12.18, wegen eines seit diesem Tage begangenen Verbrechens oder vorsätzlichen Vergehens zu einer längeren als 3 monatigen Gefängnisstrafe verurteilt wurden.[25]

Hardly back with his comrades, Lehmann found himself fighting in the same defensive battle of Cambrai-St. Quentin with the retreating Hindenburg army. Once again, on 18 September 1918, he slipped away from his unit, and this time successfully gave himself up to some Canadian troops.

Notes

Chapter 1

1. "Biographische Notiz," which appeared in *Die literarische Welt* (15 January 1932); "Bildnis der Eltern und erste Kindheit," which first appeared in *Bewegliche Ordnung* (1947); *Mühe des Anfangs* (1952); and "Biographische Nachricht," appended to the Reclam *Gedichte* (1963).

2. *Mühe des Anfangs,* SW II, p. 387.

3. Ibid. He is quoting Schopenhauer.

4. See, in particular, Agathe Wichmann to Friedrich Lehmann, 18 December 1880, 13 January 1881, and 17 April 1881.

5. Agathe Wichmann to Friedrich Lehmann, 5 February 1881.

6. Agathe Wichmann to Friedrich Lehmann, 5 January 1881.

7. Agathe Wichmann to Friedrich Lehmann, 5 November 1880.

8. Agathe Wichmann to Friedrich Lehmann, 5 March 1881.

9. Friedrich Lehmann to Agathe Wichmann, 4 January 1881.

10. Friedrich Lehmann to Agathe Wichmann, 2 December 1880.

11. See below, p. 000.

12. Agathe Wichmann to Friedrich Lehmann, 19 October 1880.

13. Caroline Wichmann to Agathe Lehmann, 20 February 1882.

14. Christian Wichmann to Agathe Lehmann, 21 June 1882.

15. Caroline Wichmann to Agathe Lehmann, 21 October 1884.

16. Caroline Wichmann to Agathe Lehmann, 21 February 1884.

17. An accomplished linguist, Agathe had intended to learn Spanish in the year prior to moving to Venezuela, but had been frustrated in this endeavor through pressure of work.

18. Caroline Wichmann to Agathe Lehmann, 21 July 1884.

19. "Bildnis der Eltern," p. 181; *Mühe des Anfangs,* SW II, p. 387. This affliction marked only the beginning of a long history of eye trouble which finally reduced Lehmann to near blindness.

20. Throughout "Bildnis der Eltern" and *Mühe des Anfangs.*

21. The lion Lehmann thought he remembered may be seen as a symbol of that paternal Dionysian sensuality. It, like Friedrich, remained behind—from now on Agathe (and Apollo) was in the ascendancy.

22. Agathe Lehmann to Caroline Wichmann, 18 October 1886.

23. This booklet may be found at the Deutsches Literaturarchiv in Marbach am Neckar.

24. Friedrich Lehmann to Johanna Lehmann, 16 October 1887.

25. Agathe Lehmann to Caroline Wichmann, 2 December 1887.

26. Friedrich Lehmann to Johanna Lehmann, 26 October 1889.

27. Ibid.

28. This was an address given on the occasion of the 90 year jubilee of the Matthias Claudius Gymnasium in Wandsbek—Lehmann's old school. See *Matthias Claudius Gymnasium. Mitteilungsblatt, 1962-63,* Heft 2.

29. "Bildnis der Eltern," p. 186.

30. *Mühe des Anfangs,* SW II, p. 395.

31. Interview with Walter Erben, 27 June 1977.

32. Friedrich Lehmann to Doris Lehmann, 1 May 1891.

33. It might be argued that this practice was common in the nineteenth century. However, a glance at Friedrich's postcard is sufficient to show that ease of legibility was far from his mind.

34. Agathe Lehmann to Elisabeth Lehmann, 10 July 1891.

35. Pumplün & Lehmann to Agathe Lehmann, 16 November 1894. The text is as follows: "Um die im Jahre 1891 von Ihrem Manne verursachten Differenzen nun endlich mal geregelt zu kriegen, fordern wir Sie hierdurch bei Vermeidung sofortiger Klage auf, Sich darüber auszulassen, in welchen Raten und Zwischenräumen, wenn Sie gleich alles anschaffen können, die Beträge getilgt werden sollen. Wir bitten diesmal um Ihre *directa* Mittheilung und uns nicht wieder an andere Leute zu verweisen, resp. uns zuzusenden, es sei denn, daß diese die Sache mit uns ordnen."

36. Valeske Kock to Agathe Lehmann, 21 August 1891.

37. "Bildnis der Eltern," p. 182.

38. SW I, p. 529.

39. Friedrich Lehmann to Doris Lehmann, 24 July 1891.

40. Friedrich Lehmann to Doris Lehmann, 16 October 1891.

41. Friedrich Lehmann to Elisabeth Lehmann, 8 December 1891.

42. *Mühe des Anfangs,* SW II, p. 398.

43. Ibid., p. 391.

44. "Bildnis der Eltern," p. 183.

45. *Mühe des Anfangs,* SW II, p. 399.

46. Ibid. See also *Weingott,* SW I, p. 267.

47. *Mühe des Anfangs,* SW II, pp. 394-395.

48. Ibid., p. 399.

49. Ibid.

50. Ibid., p. 407.

51. Ibid., p. 400.

52. See Hans Dieter Schäfer, *Wilhelm Lehmann. Studien zu seinem Leben und Werk* (Bonn: H. Bouvier, 1969), p. 3.

53. *Mühe des Anfangs,* SW II, p. 400.

54. Ibid., p. 403.

55. Ibid., pp. 403-404.

56. See letter quoted above, p. 000.

57. Indeed, there were no true uncles. Both Friedrich and Agathe had only sisters, so the two boys, who so desperately needed male guidance and counsel, were surrounded by aunts only.

58. *Mühe des Anfangs,* SW II, p. 402.
59. Ibid.
60. See below, p. 000.
61. Lehmann particularly remembered how Lachmann declaimed "und nähmst du Flügel der Morgenröte, so entgehst du dieser Sorte nicht"—see *Mühe des Anfangs,* SW II, p. 405. Just how applicable these words were to Lehmann's own situation so soon after his schooldays is not difficult to imagine.

Chapter 2

1. SW II, p. 409.
2. See p. 000 above.
3. Soon after Lehmann heard Thila Plaichinger, she departed for Berlin. Strangely, Lehmann seems never to have heard her during his year in this city; indeed, he seems to have gradually lost interest in opera upon leaving Strasbourg.
4. *Mühe des Anfangs,* SW II, p. 412.
5. Henry Adams, *The Education of Henry Adams. An Autobiography* (Boston: Houghton Mifflin Co., 1961), p. 77.
6. F. Sefton Delmer was the father of Dennis Sefton Delmer, better known to many Germans through his journalistic work both before and after World War II, and for his anti-Nazi propaganda work during it.
7. *Mühe des Anfangs,* SW II, p. 413.
8. Ibid., p. 412.
9. Diary, 23 November 1901.
10. Diary, 10 January 1902.
11. Diary, 21 February 1902.
12. Once, at the Charlottenburg Opera, their hilarity at the pathetic scenery of the Wolves' Ravine in Weber's *Freischütz* was such that some indignant members of the audience threatened to have them thrown out. See *Mühe des Anfangs,* SW II, p. 413.
13. Diary, 23 February 1902.
14. Diary, 1 July 1902.
15. Diary, 27 September 1901.
16. Diary, 19 November 1901.
17. Diary, 2 April 1902.
18. Diary, 15 November 1901.
19. Diary, 19 November 1901.
20. Ibid.
21. Ibid.
22. Diary, 3 November 1901.
23. Diary, 8 November 1901 and 19 November 1901.
24. SW III, p. 174.
25. Diary, 15 November 1901.
26. Diary, 23 September 1901.
27. Diary, 24 November 1901.
28. Diary, 15 November 1901.
29. Diary, 27 September 1901.

30. Diary, 25 September 1901.

31. Diary, 19 November 1901.

32. Diary, 23 November 1901.

33. Diary, 27 September 1901.

34. Diary, 28 October 1901.

35. Diary, 15 November 1901.

36. Diary, 23 September 1901.

37. Diary, 19 November 1901.

38. Diary, 15 November 1901.

39. Diary, 3 November 1901.

40. Diary, 27 September 1901.

41. In his article "Er war kein Enkel Eichendorffs. Zum Eichendorffbild im unveröffentlichten Frühwerk Wilhelm Lehmanns," *Literatur in Wissenschaft und Unterricht* 6 (1973): 1-22, Günter E. Bauer attempts to disprove any relationship between Lehmann and the Romantic poet. However, any poet who combines those Romantic trappings of "sehnsuchtsvolle Ferne," "Waldhorn," and "ich spannte weit die Flügel" is surely too close to Eichendorff not to have been influenced by him in some way.

42. The advice was given to Jochen Jung, the author of *Mythos und Utopie. Darstellungen zur Poetologie und Dichtung Wilhelm Lehmanns.* (Tübingen: Max Niemeyer Verlag, 1975).

43. *Mühe des Anfangs,* SW II, p. 415.

44. The remarkable Marschalk family consisted of Max, the composer and music critic of "Tante Voss"—the *Vossiche Zeitung,* and his sisters: Gertrud, a considerable artist herself (as a fine bust of her husband proves), married to Moritz Heimann, Elisabeth, married to Emil Strauß, and Margarete, Hauptmann's third wife. Max Marschalk was later, after his divorce, to marry Lehmann's sister Lita. Lehmann was thus somewhat indirectly related to some of the major literary figures at the beginning of the century.

45. For information concerning Efraim Frisch and the *Neue Merkur,* see Guy Stern, *War, Weimar, and Literature. The Neue Merkur 1914-1925* (University Park: Pennsylvania State University Press, c. 1971), and *Konstellationen. Die besten Erzählungen aus dem "Neuen Merkur." 1914-1925* (Stuttgart: Deutsche Verlags-Anstalt, 1964), in which Lehmann's story *Der bedrängte Seraph* (1915) is included.

46. In his *Psychopathology of Everyday Life* (1901) Freud describes how leaving objects behind by accident often signifies the person's passionate but unconscious wish to return to the locus of a pleasant experience.

47. Diary, 19 December 1901.

48. Lehmann to Heimann, 19 December 1901.

49. See SW II, p. 258; see also *Vergessene und Verschollene: Moritz Heimann, eine Einführung in sein Werk und eine Auswahl* (Wiesbaden: F. Steiner Verlag, 1960), and Moritz Heimann: *Die Wahrheit liegt nicht in der Mitte* (Frankfurt: S. Fischer Verlag, 1966).

50. Lehmann to Heimann, 5 January 1902.

51. See SW III, p. 263.

52. Diary, 4 February 1902.

53. Ibid.

54. Diary, 7 February 1902.

55. Diary, 11 February 1902.

56. Diary 12, February 1902.

57. Ibid.

58. Diary, 20 February 1902.

59. SW III, p. 105.

60. SW III, p. 334.

61. Diary, 20 February 1902.

62. Diary, 19 February 1902.

63. Ibid.

64. Ibid.

65. Diary, 4 February 1902.

66. Diary, 10 January 1902.

67. Diary, 7 February 1902.

68. Diary, 10 January 1902.

69. Diary, 19 February 1902.

70. Diary, 8 March 1902.

71. Diary, 19 March 1902.

72. Diary, 21 March 1902.

73. Diary, 13 April 1902.

74. Ibid.

75. Diary, 19 May 1902.

76. See *Mühe des Anfangs,* SW II, p. 427.

77. Ibid.

78. Diary, 18 June 1902.

79. See *Mühe des Anfangs,* SW II, p. 428.

80. Diary, 6 July 1902.

81. Ibid.

82. Diary, 31 July 1902.

Chapter 3

1. For this information concerning Lehmann's stay in Devon, I am greatly indebted to Mrs. Winifried Storr (née Twining), whose memory at a remove of almost 80 years is startlingly fresh, and to Dr. Daniel Twining, the son of Daniel Twining Senior. The Twining house, originally a farmhouse, still stands, and is now the Knowle Hotel.

2. *The Salcombe Times,* 30 August 1902.

3. SW II, p. 428.

4. Lehmann to Heimann, 8 October 1902.

5. Lehmann to Rothenstein, 3 February 1903.

6. *Mühe des Anfangs,* SW II, p. 429.

7. Ferdinand Holthausen (1860-1956) produced, among many other works, an *Etymologisches Wörterbuch der englischen Sprache* (1917) and an *Altenglisches etymologisches Wörterbuch* (1932-34).

8. Lehmann to Heimann, dated April 1903.

9. See *Studien,* p. 12. The version of the poem is the one given by Schäfer, who took it

from the manuscript of the poems Lehmann sent to the *Neue Rundschau* in 1907. It differs slightly from the version found in *Mühe des Anfangs* (SW II, p. 437). As Lehmann (and Schäfer) points out, the Lungenblume and not the Leberblume was actually meant.

    10. Lehmann to Gertrud Heimann, undated, c. July 1903.

    11. SW II, p. 431.

    12. Lehmann to Moritz Heimann, 11 July 1903.

    13. See *Mühe des Anfangs,* SW II, p. 431. See also *Maleen,* SW I, p. 131.

    14. Lehmann to Gertrud Heimann, 18 July 1903.

    15. Lehmann to Gertrud Heimann, undated, c. July 1903.

    16. Lehmann to Gertrud Heimann, 12 September 1903.

    17. Ibid.

    18. Lehmann to Heimann, 3 December 1903.

    19. Lehmann to Gertrud Heimann, 10 December 1903.

    20. Lehmann to Gertrud Heimann, 20 February 1904.

    21. *Der Wanderer und sein Schatten,* No. 322.

    22. Diary, 10 June 1905. See also Lehmann's late poem "Sperber aus Stein," SZ, p. 26.

    23. Diary, 6 February 1903.

    24. Ibid.

    25. See SW III, p. 402.

    26. Diary, 20 March 1903.

    27. Lehmann to Heimann, undated, c. October 1904.

    28. Heimann to Lehmann, 3 May 1904.

    29. Lehmann to Heimann, undated.

    30. Lehmann to Gertrud Heimann, undated, c. April 1905.

    31. Agathe Lehmann to Wilhelm Lehmann, 18 October 1905.

    32. Lehmann to Heimann, undated, c. October 1905.

    33. For a thorough appraisal of Lehmann's philological investigations and publications, see Uwe Pörksen's article "Beziehungen Wilhelm Lehmanns zur Literatur des Mittelalters und zur Philologie der Jahrhundertwende," in *Mittelalter-Rezeption. Gesammelte Vorträge des Salzburger Symposions "Die Rezeption mittelalterlicher Dichter und ihrer Werke in Literatur, bildender Kunst und Musik des 19. und 20. Jahrhunderts,"* eds. Jürgen Kühnel, Hans-Dieter Mück, Ulrich Müller (Göppingen: Kümmerle Verlag, 1979), pp. 380-417.

    34. Adolf Köster (1883-1930) was a man of many parts. He started out as a student of theology but rapidly changed to philosophy and literature. By the end of 1906 he had produced a book on Pascal and soon thereafter became Professor of literary theory in Munich. Between 1908 and 1918 he regularly contributed short stories to journals such as *Simplizissimus, Die Rheinlande,* and *März.* After World War I, during which he was a detached and unchauvinistic war-correspondent for *Vorwärts,* he entered politics as a Social Democrat and served both as Minister for the Interior and then as Foreign Secretary (at 37 the youngest ever). At the end of his short life he was in the diplomatic corps—his undoubted talent for diplomacy possibly saw its hardest test in l'affaire Lehmann. For further information on Adolf Köster, see Kurt Doß, *Reichsminister Adolf Köster, 1883-1930,* (Düsseldorf: Droste Verlag, c. 1978).

    35. Köster to Lehmann, undated, c. 21 January 1906.

    36. Ibid.

    37. Lehmann to Gertrud Heimann, 14 January 1906.

38. Walter Lehmann to Wilhelm Lehmann, undated. See also *Mühe des Anfangs,* SW II, p. 442.

39. Lehmann to Heimann, 27 January 1906.

Chapter 4

1. *Mühe des Anfangs,* SW II, p. 445.
2. Ibid.
3. Ibid., p. 447.
4. Ibid., p. 445.
5. Lehmann to Heimann, 8 March 1906.
6. For a realistic portrait of Pastor Behm—as well as a depiction of their life in Eldena— see *Maleen,* SW I, in particular p. 139. The line "The busy bee has not time for sorrow" appears in Blake's "The Marriage of Heaven and Hell." Lehmann seems to have particularly liked this work, for he appropriated other lines from it—see p. 000, p. 000, and p. 000 below.
7. SW II, p. 443.
8. Diary, 21 February 1907.
9. Diary, 6 December 1906.
10. Diary, 17 December 1906.
11. Diary, 29 December 1906.
12. SW III, p. 231.
13. SW III, p. 187. For a more detailed account of the meaning of Rozwadowski for Lehmann, see Pörksen, "Bezichungen," pp. 386-391.
14. SW II, p. 447.
15. *Die neue Rundschau* 25 (1914): 586.
16. For a complete list of Lehmann's linguistic publications, see Schäfer, *Studien,* pp. 270-271.
17. Lehmann to Heimann, 23 July 1906.
18. Lehmann to Heimann, undated.
19. See Schäfer, *Studien,* p. 20 and p. 134.
20. On 18 December he recorded his own misgivings at the number of cigarettes he was smoking: "Rauchte von 11 bis 1 Uhr 8 Cigaretten"—see Diary.
21. Diary, 30 November 1906.
22. Diary, 18 December 1906.
23. Hauptmann to Lehmann, 2 November 1906.
24. Köster to Lehmann, 14 December 1906.
25. Heimann to Lehmann, 21 November 1906.
26. Heimann to Lehmann, 24 December 1906.
27. See Diary, 21 December 1906.
28. See Diary, 30 December 1906.
29. See *Mühe des Anfangs,* SW II, p. 450.
30. See Diary, 3 February 1907.
31. Diary, 10 January 1907.
32. See *Mühe des Anfangs,* SW II, p. 451.
33. Ibid., p. 452.
34. Ibid.

Chapter 5

1. Diary, 16 February 1907.
2. Diary, 8 May 1907.
3. Ibid.
4. Diary, 20 October 1907.
5. See the strongly autobiographical petition Lehmann wrote in applying for exemption from military service on 8 June 1908, in which he includes many details of his financial state.
6. Heimann to Lehmann, 19 March 1907.
7. See the aforementioned petition.
8. Lehmann to Heimann, 12 September 1907.
9. Diary, 20 October 1907.
10. Diary, 25 October 1908.
11. Lehmann to Heimann, 6 October 1907.
12. Diary, 7 January 1908.
13. Wilhelm Lehmann to Martha Lehmann, undated—c. January 1908.
14. This, and the following quotations describing his ordeal are from Lehmann's Diary, 2 February 1908.
15. Heimann to Lehmann, 2 February 1908.
16. Diary, 6 March 1908.
17. Heimann to Lehmann, 29 March 1908.
18. The whole sorry episode regarding Lehmann's part in the Trebitsch Shaw translation is well described by Mendelssohn in his monumental book *S. Fischer und sein Verlag* (Frankfurt am Main: S. Fischer Verlag, 1970), pp. 419-420.
19. Heimann to Lehmann, 29 May 1908.
20. Heimann to Lehmann, 1 March 1910.
21. See Mendelssohn, *Fischer,* p. 420.
22. Lehmann to Heimann, 31 May 1908.
23. Lehmann to Heimann, 18 June 1908.
24. Lehmann to Heimann, 31 May 1908.
25. Lehmann to Heimann, 18 June 1908.
26. Lehmann to Heimann, 23 January 1909.
27. See Diary, 2 December 1908. Zeitler was a Leipzig bookdealer who was in the habit of putting out lavish catalogues.
28. Diary, 1 December 1908.
29. The two works Lehmann read at this time were *Confessions of a Young Man* (1888) and *Memoirs of My Dead Life.* The marginal notations in both works attest to the interest with which Lehmann read them.
30. Lehmann marked the following sentence from *Confessions:* "To read freely, extensively, has always been my ambition, and my utter inability to study has always been to me a subject of grave inquietude— study as contrasted with a general and haphazard gathering of ideas taken in flight."
31. See *Studien,* p. 22 and p. 272.
32. SW III, p. 187.
33. Lehmann had headed his dissertation with a quotation from Blake's *Book of Los:* "Truth has bounds, Error none."

34. Lehmann to Schäfer, 25 July 1965.

35. Diary, 19 July 1908.

36. See in particular the poem "Noch kann ich stehen bleiben..." which Schäfer reproduces in *Studien,* p. 22.

37. This passage is to be found on a loose sheet of paper inserted in Lehmann's diary for 1909.

38. This text, together with Heimann's critique of it, may be found in the *Neue Rundschau* 76 (1965): 650-652. See also Schäfer, *Studien,* pp. 23-24.

39. Heimann to Lehmann, 23 August 1909.

40. Ibid.

41. Heimann to Lehmann, 19 November 1908.

42. Lehmann to Heimann, 30 December 1908.

43. Lehmann to Heimann, 25 March 1909.

44. This circumstance is described in Lehmann's novella *Michael Lippstock,* which was to appear in the July (1915) issue of the *Neue Rundschau.*

45. Diary, 28 August 1909.

46. Diary, 30 August 1909.

47. Conversation with Frau Aeschlimann, 3 July 1977.

48. Diary, 30 August 1909.

49. *Studien,* p. 159.

50. See D.A. Scrase, "The Dialectic in W. Lehmann's Nature Imagery" (Ph.D. diss., Indiana University, 1972), pp. 96-105.

51. Virgil Rothmond in *Michael Lippstock* is modelled closely on Probst Riewerts.

52. Diary, 5 October 1910.

53. Diary, 6 October 1910.

54. Diary, 10 October 1910.

55. Diary, 8 October 1910.

56. Diary, 9 October 1910.

57. Diary, 6 October 1910.

58. Diary, 9 October 1910.

59. Usually letters were exchanged by the simple stratagem of inserting them in the exercise books as they were handed to and fro for correction.

60. Frieda Riewerts to Lehmann, 3 May 1911.

61. Gertrud Heimann to Lehmann, 5 May 1911.

62. For information concerning the "Donnerstags-Gesellschaft" see Schäfer, *Studien,* p. 33. See also the catalogue prepared by Tilman Krömer and Reinhard Tgahrt for "Oskar Loerke. Eine Gedächtnisausstellung zum 80. Geburtstag des Dichters" at the Schiller-Nationalmuseum in Marbach am Neckar, 1964, pp. 20-25, and Mendelssohn, *Fischer* pp. 405-406.

63. Frieda Riewerts to Lehmann, 26 March 1912 and 3 April 1912.

Chapter 6

1. For a detailed description of the events surrounding the foundation of Wickersdorf, see Heinrich Kupffer, *Gustav Wyneken* (Stuttgart: Ernst Klett Verlag, 1970), p. 47 et seq.

2. Heimann described the position of Wickersdorf as follows: "Wickersdorf ist ein

kleines und armes Dorf in Thüringen, das man von Saalfeld aus auf einem schönen Spaziergang von 1 1/2 Stunden, bergaufwärts erreicht. . . . "—see Heimann's brief report "Wickersdorfer Jahrbuch 1908," *Die neue Rundschau* 20 (1909): 1079. If one was fortunate, or planned well ahead, one was often able to travel by the donkey cart which was owned by Fräulein Cordes, the sister of the German Ambassador in Peking (whose ten children all attended Wickersdorf), and a lady who liked to maintain social contacts to the school.

3. This is the view of Hans-Windekilde Jannasch, who knew both brothers well—see *Spätlese. Begegnungen mit Zeitgenossen* (Göttingen: Vandenhoeck & Ruprecht, 1973), pp. 71-72.

4. Martha Lehmann to Wilhelm Lehmann, undated.

5. Frieda Riewerts to Wilhelm Lehmann, 10 June 1912.

6. Agathe Lehmann to Wilhelm Lehmann, 22 September 1912.

7. See SW I, pp. 52-53.

8. Wilhelm Lehmann to Agathe Lehmann, 25 October 1912 and 17 November 1912.

9. Wilhelm Lehmann to Agathe Lehmann, undated.

10. Wilhelm Lehmann to Agathe Lehmann, 20 April 1913.

11. Ibid.

12. Wilhelm Lehmann to Agathe Lehmann, 20 April 1913.

13. I am indebted to Lehmann's nephew Ernst Schlee for this information. Schlee is the well-known art historian and folklorist, who was director of the Schleswig-Holsteinische Landesmuseum in Schleswig and, like his uncle before him (1952) a recipient of the Kunstpreis des Landes Schleswig-Holstein (1979).

14. For an appraisal of Martin Luserke as a human being and pedagogue, see Hans-Windekilde Jannasch, *Spätlese,* p. 95 et seq.

15. Wilhelm Lehmann to Agathe Lehmann, 15 April 1912.

16. Wilhelm Lehmann to Agathe Lehmann, 26 April 1912.

17. See Diary, 23 December 1912.

18. See Ingrid Schuster, *China und Japan in der deutschen Literatur, 1980-1925* (Berne & Munich: Francke Verlag, 1977).

19. See Schäfer, *Studien,* p. 27. For more information concerning Lehmann's readings in Wickersdorf, see Jannasch, *Spätlese,* p. 64.

20. Around the beginning of 1913 there were two developments which eased Lehmann's financial situation considerably. In January he borrowed 600 Mk. for a year at minimal interest from his colleague Frau Dr. Alice Wachsmuth. And the remarkable Moritz Heimann, perhaps motivated by realistic insights as well as good-hearted generosity, told Lehmann to forget about all the money he owed them.

21. *Neue Blätter,* ed. Jakob Hegner, Heft 6 and Heft 12, 1912.

22. *Die Zeitschrift,* ed. Albert Helms, 3. Jg. Heft 18, 1913.

23. Ibid., Heft 13, 1913.

24. See above, p. 92.

25. Bewley made a name for himself as a patriotic defending counsel for IRA soldiers during the Troubles. In the late twenties he entered the diplomatic service of the Republic of Ireland, finding his way first of all to the Vatican and then, in 1933, to Nazi Germany, where he hob-nobbed with the Party dignitaries and got to know Hermann Goering particularly well. After the war he wrote a provocative defensive biography of Goering. Contact between Bewley and Lehmann ceased in 1920.

26. See *The Dublin Review* 152 (1913): 132-144.

27. Diary, 4 March 1913.

28. No letters from this pre-war period are extant. The four letters from Bewley to Lehmann which still survive date from 1920 and show Bewley's switch in interests from poetry to politics. He talks about the current troubled situation in Ireland with curfews, murders, random arrests, imprisonment without trial, and terrorist activities from all sides. At the same time Bewley promises to send Lehmann the *Nation* and the *New Age* and asks for *Jugend* in return.

29. Diary, 8 August 1912.

30. See Diary, 12 March 1915. See also Heinz Bruns, *Wilhelm Lehmann. Eine Chronik* (Kiel, Mühlau, 1962), p. 19.

31. The manuscript of *Maleen* shows that Lehmann first wrote the tale using the names Martha, Berthold, and Wilhelm. Martha developed via Marga to Maleen, Berthold to Bramante and Wilhelm via Jürgen to Jelden. The child Joachim appeared initially as Heinrich and then developed via Stapello to Reginer.

32. SW I, p. 169.

33. *Der neue Merkur* 2 (1915): 744-768.

34. "*Der bedrängte Seraph*," said Lehmann, "beschreibt die Begegnung mit meiner Frau." How Lehmann remembered this encounter is described in Guy Stern, "A Case for Oral Literary History: Conversations with or about Morgenstern, Lehmann, Reinacher and Thomas Mann," *The German Quarterly* 37 (1964): 495-496.

35. Schäfer, *Studien,* p. 30.

36. To what extent it was intended to be metaphorical or not is unclear. Immediately following Maleen's death Jelden is said to wake up, thus suggesting that it was all a dream. But Lehmann then describes just what it was that Jelden dreamed, and thus makes it clear that her suicide cannot be dismissed as his dream.

37. Wilhelm Lehmann to Agathe Lehmann, 3 August 1914.

38. Wilhelm Lehmann to Agathe Lehmann, 2 November 1914.

39. Dr. Johannes Voigt, who conducted Lehmann through London on his visit there in 1964, recounts that Lehmann, as they passed Buckingham Palace while the Changing of the Guard was taking place in all its splendor, did not slow down or so much as cast a glance in the direction of this military spectacle.

40. Diary, 14 September 1914.

41. See Wilhelm Lehmann, "Warum ich nicht wie Oskar Loerke schreibe," *Fünfzehn Autoren suchen sich selbst. Modell und Provokation,* ed. Uwe Schultz (Munich: List Verlag, 1967), p. 95.

42. Diary, 5 March 1915. See also *Michael Lippstock,* ed. David Scrase (Stuttgart: Akademischer Verlag Hans-Dieter Heinz, 1979), p. 58 et seq.

43. See Lehmann's poem "Das Vorletzte" (SW III, p. 608) which contains his philosophy in succinct poetic form.

44. Runge's *Farbenkugel* preceded Goethe's *Farbenlehre* (1810) by a mere two months. Goethe knew and respected Runge's work and sent him his own treatise the moment it came out so that Runge was able to read the *Farbenlehre* on his deathbed. In 1817 George Field published a theory of colors entitled *An Essay on the Analogy and Harmony of Colours.* Whether he was aware of Goethe's or Runge's work is unknown.

45. See the catalogue to the exhibition *Runge in seiner Zeit,* ed. Werner Hofmann (Munich: Prestel Verlag, 1977), p. 190.

46. See Siegfried Krebs, *Philipp Otto Runges Entwicklung unter dem Einflusse Ludwig Tiecks* (Heidelberg: Carl Winter Verlag, 1909), p. 84.

47. Diary, 30 May 1915.

48. Ibid.

49. Diary, 20 March 1916.

50. As a teacher Lehmann enjoyed considerable positive reinforcement. Not only did his pupils commend him (see Schäfer, *Studien,* p. 26), but on at least two occasions important visitors from the pedagogical field visited his classes and were effusive in their praise. In December 1912, Dr. Hermann Nohl, a pedagogue from Jena, pronounced Lehmann's English lesson "Ganz entzückend, entzückend! Diese Frische und Lust." (See Diary, 14 December 1912), and in 1915 Prof. Dr. E. Hausknecht thought Lehmann's teching was "famos" (see Diary, 27 March 1915). But the praise which undoubtedly meant most to Lehmann stemmed from Moritz Heimann who, since his son Fritz (who later became a painter and sculptor) was now a pupil at Wickersdorf, was sometimes a visitor here:

"Ich bin noch ganz voll von deiner Stunde. Merkwürdig, wie gleich Vollkommenes wirkt, einerlei ob es Kunstwerk oder eine Stunde ist. Lückenlos war die Stunde. Von der Bienenwabe haben die Mathematiker berechnet, daß sie die genialste Ausnutzung des Raumes darstelle. So war deine Stunde. Diese Lebendigkeit! lückenlos—und dabei alles scharmant und scharf." Ich war *so* glücklich, daß ein Heimann *das* von meinem Unterricht sagte. See Wilhelm Lehmann to Agathe Lehmann, 20 April 1913.

51. See Diary, 21 July 1912: "Wyneken ist mir doch nicht sympathisch mit seinen Bemerkungen über alles."

52. In December 1912 Lehmann gave Wyneken a copy of his essay "Liegt die Wahrheit in den Dingen oder in uns?" in the hope that he might publish it in his journal *Die Freie Schulgemeinde.* Almost immediately he saw the folly of this move: "Übrigens, was mir einfiel, Wyneken muß doch eigentlich meinen Aufsatz, der das Wahrheitssein als im Menschen wohnhaft verteidigt, seinem ganzen 'objektiven' Denken nach rundweg ablehnen!" And so it proved; see Diary, 16 December 1912 and 23 December 1912.

53. See Diary, 27 Janaury 1917.

54. See Diary, 3 April 1915.

55. See Diary, 25 February 1916.

56. See Schäfer, *Studien,* p. 27; see also Burley D. Channer, *Lyrical Structure in Two Novels of Wilhelm Lehmann: "Der Bilderstürmer" and "Weingott"* (Ph.D. diss., Ohio State University, 1971), p. 102.

57. Kupffer's book on Wyneken paints a similar picture.

58. Diary, 14 January 1917.

59. Diary, 12 June 1915.

60. Diary, 28 January 1915.

61. Diary, 24 November 1915.

62. Diary, 11 October 1915.

63. The boys and girls who were boarders at Wickersdorf (the vast majority) were divided into "Kameradschaften" in much the same way that British schoolchildren belong to "houses." These "Kameradschaften" were assigned a teacher as leader and were given

names such as the "Füchse," the "Gemsen," or the "Bären." The "Kameradschaften" engaged in extra-curricular group activities, such as games, hikes, handcrafts and were designed to foster close interaction between teachers and children.

64. See SW III, p. 265.

65. Diary, 27 October 1915.

66. Alas, the letter is lost. Its contents can only be guessed at from what Lehmann recorded in his diary and from the odd comment in various letters.

67. Diary, 27 October 1915.

68. See Schäfer, *Studien*, pp. 78-124.

69. Loerke's letter arrived on 25 October 1915, but the letter is not extant.

70. Diary, 27 October 1915.

71. Diary, 17 January 1915.

72. Ibid.

73. Diary, 14 January 1917.

74. Ibid.

75. *Fünfzehn Autoren*, ed. Schultz, pp. 95-103.

76. See *Die neue Rundschau* 22 (October-December 1916).

77. See Schäfer, *Studien*, p. 31.

78. It is significant that Lehmann should choose to clothe Martha with the name of his mother. Both relationships caused him much worry and pain. But the fact that he chose the name Agathe points also to a total lack of tact or feeling, which is only partly to be explained by motives of artistic integrity. Although there is no record of Agathe's reaction upon finding her name used for a character unsympathetically portrayed in her son's novel, it is hardly likely to have escaped her, and she was almost certainly offended. Lehmann was also rather insensitive to the hurt likely to be caused by his portrayal of the Luserke marriage in the novel. Although Heimann and Aeschlimann both warned him as the novel was going to print, it was too late to make any changes—see postcard from Wilhelm Lehmann to Moritz Heimann, 19 October 1916.

79. This interpretation of the sun's significance, based as it is on an assessment of Lehmann's readings at the time and on a close interpretation of *Michael Lippstock*, differs somewhat from both Schäfer's and Burley Channer's interpretations. Schäfer, viewing Lehmann's use of the sun image in his whole work and seeking to explain it in terms of the current literary historical developments, sees the sun too narrowly as a destructive force— although he is quick to allude to a "Hoffnung auf den Sinn der Erde" (*Studien*, p. 88). Channer sees the sun and summer in too narrowly a positive frame—Magerhold, the "enemy" is overcome by "nature's awesome force" (*Lyrical Structure*, pp. 122-124), i.e. the sun. There is, of course, truth in both views, neither of which is negated by my own reading.

80. In this respect, see Channer (*Lyrical Structure*, p. 119), where he quite rightly takes issue with Schäfer over an interpretation drawing on Wyneken's attitudes to adolescent sexuality. Although what Schäfer asserts (*Studien*, p. 27) is in itself accurate, it has no real bearing on Lehmann's novel.

81. There are no surviving manuscripts of *Der Bilderstürmer*, so that no close examination of the textual development is possible.

82. See Arthur Brausewetter's review in *Berliner Börsenzeitung*, 6 July 1917.

83. Lehmann to Heimann, 9 July 1917.

84. Döblin's letter to Lehmann is not extant.

85. See *Die neue Rundschau* 28 (1917): 1284.

86. See Oscar Bie, "Ein deutscher Dichter" in *Frankfurter Zeitung,* 13 July 1917.

87. See Kurt Pinthus's review in *Zeitschrift für Bücherfreunde* NF 9 (1917-18): col. 421-422.

88. See Otto Schabbel's review in *Das literarische Echo* 20 (1917-18): col. 1240-1241.

89. See Friedrich Düsel, "Literarische Rundschau," *Westermanns Monatshefte* 62 (1917): 254-255.

90. Diary, dated simply Charfreitag 1915.

91. Wilhelm Lehmann to Agathe Lehmann, 13 September 1915.

92. Wilhelm Lehmann to Agathe Lehmann, 14 September 1915.

93. Martha Lehmann to Wilhelm Lehmann, 20 January 1917.

94. See Martha Lehmann to Wilhelm Lehmann, 24 March 1917. To what extent, if any, Martha was exaggerating in her account is, of course, impossible to ascertain. But the episode is one further indication of her chronic inability to cope in a world which seemed to be set against her.

95. Ample proof of the problems in living with Martha is provided by Georg Dreis (her stepfather), Wilhelm Lehmann, and, as we have just seen, Johannes Dreis (her stepbrother). Significantly, Martha complained that all three struck her, but there is no way of ascertaining the truth of this accusation. Lehmann's admission of "Tätlichkeiten" during the divorce proceedings is not, to my mind, conclusive proof of physical violence, since it was made expressly to sway the judge's opinion.

Chapter 7

1. Germany (and Europe) was hit by typhus epidemic at the time Lehmann was working on his novel. It touched directly on Lehmann's life inasmuch as it claimed one victim in Wickersdorf itself and the lives of the wife and three children of Max Maurenbrecher, a theologian and politician loosely connected with Wickersdorf and the sometime editor of the liberal journal *Hilfe.*

2. The choice of this name for the school is interesting. Lehmann, engaged on his Irish novel and reading Yeats, may have been attracted to Rosicrucianism (or to the name, at least) through Yeats's connections with the cult, which are touched upon several times in *Ideas of Good and Evil,* part of Lehmann's reading while at Wickersdorf.

3. The name Lehmann had originally chosen for his novel, it will be remembered, was *Die Entwurzelten.* But the editorial office of the S. Fischer Verlag had effected the change just before publication.

4. These two characters are loosely based on Lehmann's "friend" (the relationship was fraught with ambivalence) Max Marschalk and Lehmann's sister Lita, who married Marschalk.

5. See Oskar Loerke, "Vielerlei Zungen" in *Die neue Rundschau* 29 (1918): 1238-1239.

6. See Kurt Pinthus's review in *Zeitschrift für Bücherfreunde* NF 10 (1918-19): col. 421-422.

7. See Adalbert Muhr, "Wilhelm Lehmann" in *Der Merker* 10 (1919): 661-662.

8. Döblin to Lehmann, 12 July 1918.

9. Stehr to Lehmann, 14 July 1918.

10. Lehmann to Heimann, 18 March 1917.

11. Lehmann to Heimann, 1 March 1918. Lehmann is referring to the predilection of Eduard Graf von Keyserling (1855-1918) for erotic adventures set in the Junker estates of his native Courland.

12. Diary, 16 May 1917.

13. Lehmann to Heimann, 22 May 1917.

14. Lehmann to Heimann, 25 September 1917.

15. Lehmann to Heimann, 2 January 1918.

16. Lehmann to Heimann, 1 March 1918.

17. The manuscript of *Das fröhliche Tal* is to be found in the Deutsches Literaturarchiv in Marbach am Neckar.

18. Lehmann to Heimann, 6 May 1918.

19. Ludwig Ketzer to Lehmann, 9 May 1918.

20. Diary, 26 August 1918.

21. A vivid and accurate account of Lehmann's wanderings is contained in *Der Überläufer,* SW I, pp. 604-610.

22. All this information is contained on two extremely narrow slips of paper which Lehmann managed to acquire and conceal from the authorities. They are in the Deutsches Literaturarchiv in Marbach am Neckar.

23. The article in question is by Ernst Gundolf (not Friedrich) and is entitled "Die Philosophie Henri Bergsons." It appeared in the *Jahrbuch für die geistige Bewegung* 3 (1912): 32-92.

24. "Ortskommandantur Flavion" to Frieda Lehmann, 21 September 1918.

25. "Kriegsgerichtsrat" in Kassel to Wilhelm Lehmann, 19 May 1920.

Index